Holding On to the Faith

*Confessional Traditions
in American Christianity*

Edited by
**Douglas A. Sweeney and
Charles Hambrick-Stowe**

University Press of America,® Inc.
Lanham · Boulder · New York · Toronto · Plymouth, UK

Copyright © 2008 by
University Press of America,® Inc.
4501 Forbes Boulevard
Suite 200
Lanham, Maryland 20706
UPA Acquisitions Department (301) 459-3366

Estover Road
Plymouth PL6 7PY
United Kingdom

Library of Congress Control Number: 2008929744
ISBN-13: 978-0-7618-4132-6 (paperback : alk. paper)
ISBN-10: 0-7618-4132-6 (paperback : alk. paper)
eISBN-13: 978-0-7618-4257-6
eISBN-10: 0-7618-4257-8

™
⊖ The paper used in this publication meets the minimum
requirements of American National Standard for Information
Sciences—Permanence of Paper for Printed Library Materials,
ANSI Z39.48—1984

In Memory of Peter D'Agostino

Contents

Preface

Christian movements and denominations that "hold on" to traditional confessional standards have often been described in the story of American Christianity with phrases like "countervailing," "alternative," or "immigrant faith." By implication, they must be understood apart from the main narrative, which generally centers on an evangelical Protestant denominationalism that is more fully in tune with, even as it helped to shape, American culture, democratic and utilitarian. In recent years, it has become evident that, however the story gets told in the light of religious pluralism in the twenty-first century, groups that maintain their rootedness in doctrinal, liturgical, and institutional tradition are an integral part of the narrative. The chapters that follow explore a number of these traditions in the context of their American experience. How is it, and what does it mean, that they have not only survived but continue to flourish?

This book has its origins in a conference on confessional traditions in American religious history sponsored by the Institute for the Study of American Evangelicals (ISAE) at Wheaton College, Wheaton, Illinois, in September, 2005; the book is published under the auspices of the Institute. The conference received funding from the Lilly Endowment, where Chris Coble is program director for religion and Craig Dykstra is senior vice president for religion. We owe the privilege of editing this book to our role as commentators for several of the papers presented at the conference. While most of the authors presented earlier versions of their chapters at the conference, "Rome in America: Transnational Allegiances and Adjustments" by the late Peter R. D'Agostino is from his similarly titled book. We are grateful to the University of North Carolina Press for granting permission to adapt and reprint material from the book's preface and introduction.

We express our appreciation to Edith Blumhofer, director of the ISAE, and to Larry Eskridge, associate director, for their invitation to participate in this project and for their support in the creation of the book. Certainly, this book would not have been completed without Larry's diligent work at every stage. We are grateful to three persons who transformed the manuscripts into book chapters: John Van Wyk, research assistant at Trinity Evangelical Divinity School, and ISAE graduate assistants Katie Main and Elizabeth Wanee. We also wish to thank our institutions, Trinity Evangelical Divinity School (Deerfield, Illinois) and Northern Seminary (Lombard, Illinois), for their encouragement of our scholarship.

Douglas A. Sweeney
Charles Hambrick-Stowe
February, 2008

Introduction:
Confessional Traditions in America

Charles Hambrick-Stowe
Northern Seminary

Traditional ways of living the Christian faith – shaped and guided by confessional norms transported from Europe, deeply rooted in history – exhibit remarkable staying power in American religious life. Rather than withering away, time-honored language, practices, and ecclesiologies have not only survived but have established a vital ongoing institutional presence in twenty-first century America. This book explores how historic churches with distinctive confessional identities have persisted, maintaining lively existences in an American culture otherwise characterized by its modernity, a culture in which even theological conservatives generally adopt the ethos of pragmatic, democratic, individualistic liberalism. If, as Mark Noll has observed, American Christianity is notable for "the absence of confessional conservatism" in the pre-modern European sense of that term, it becomes all the more important to learn how confessional groups have managed to make their witness in this more "populist environment. Reflecting, for example, on the Lutheran and Roman Catholic experiences in America, Noll writes that "the task would seem to require steering between the Scylla of assimilation without tradition and the Charybdis of tradition without assimilation." The chapters that follow explore ways that churches adhering to a range of confessional traditions have addressed this challenge in the Odyssey that is American religious history.[1]

"Confessional" here refers broadly to ways of being Christian and of understanding the Christian faith that seek to be faithful not only to the Bible but also to historical understandings of the gospel as expressed in particular theological traditions. These understandings may be voiced in early Church or Reformation-era doctrinal statements (such as the ecumenical creeds, writings of the Church Fathers, the *Augsburg Confession*, the *Canons of the Synod of Dort*, or the *Westminster Confession*), a liturgical tradition (as with the Anglican tradition's *Book of Common Prayer*), an authoritative ecclesiastical structure (notably in Roman Catholicism), or even a record of hymnody and public witness (as in the Anabaptist tradition). Most of the ecclesial bodies discussed here have existed alongside each other in America for three centuries, although the relative strength of their presence has varied in different periods and, outside of Alaska, Eastern Orthodoxy only began to appear at the end of the nineteenth century. Historical monographs most often describe and explain them separately, but this book invites us to an ongoing and open-ended examination of common themes among their responses to American-style modernity, experience-oriented evangelical revivalism, and the Bible-centered empiricism that have dominated American religious life.[2]

Religious groups whose identity is linked with a confessional tradition have typically imagined or presented themselves as *the* faithful Christian witness within their confessional tradition for that specific time and place. Further, in most of these cases tensions have surrounded their definitions of authenticity within these traditions, so that historic confessions have often become both the fields of battle and the weapons brandished in ecclesiastical civil wars. Several chapters in this book address such tensions and conflicts within larger confessional bodies such as the Lutheran, Presbyterian, and Episcopal churches in America. Susan McArver, for example, points out that Lutherans "by and large may have agreed that the *Augsburg Confession* was their defining document" but argued and divided over what it meant to "affirm the Confessions." She concludes that, with factors like ethnic origin and date of immigration added to tensions surrounding pietism, "American Lutheranism," and orthodox confessionalism, it is so "difficult to speak of a single Lutheran identity or Lutheran experience in this country" that we must think of multiple "Lutheran identities and experiences." While on the surface Lutherans differed over whether or not to accommodate to American culture, in her study of the Missouri Synod Lutherans Mary Todd suggests that, more deeply, it was "conflict over the interpretation, application and authority of their confessional statements that kept Lutherans from fully engaging their culture." Lutheran identities were forged in opposition to other Lutherans. It would appear that to be a true Lutheran in America is to be *this* kind of Lutheran and not *that* kind of Lutheran. Eastern Orthodox disunity stemmed from that tradition's fusion of ecclesial and national identities, but Frances Kostarelos's chapter describes "developments that are lifting barriers that historically militated against Orthodox unity and outreach" as the ethnic divisions carried over from the national churches of the Old World have diminished in significance over time in the United States.

In the day to day lives of believers, while some groups may occasionally have touted confessional standards as almost platonic forms, historic theological formulations have more often functioned dynamically in the flux of life within religious communities as they developed in the context of wider American society. Confessionalism in this way might be considered as a Christian *practice* or *performance*. Historic formulas read as they do, but they are not just words in a book of worship or hymnal. The noun "confession" has meaning because it is also a verb—confessions are actively confessed. Real people confess their living faith by means of time-honored words and ritual actions.[3] And confessions are employed in many ways in different places over time. These chapters are interested in what happens when groups of believers have given them behavioral expression in new contexts, prayed and preached their phrases with their own voices, held their precise words lightly or tightly, revised them, defended them, accused with them, taught and evangelized and comforted with them, and so on.

In the same vein that confessions can be considered as Christian practice, distinctive practices themselves perform a confessional function in some ecclesial traditions. For example, James C. Juhnke points out that, while Mennonites and other Anabaptists did produce a few theologically normative confessional statements, it was primarily their patterns of behavior that gave voice to their confession of faith. Neither is the Episcopal or Anglican tradition known for its formal doctrinal statements; it was not the *Thirty-Nine Articles* or ancient ecumenical creeds that gave the church definition so much as the *Book of Common Prayer* as the basis for a common liturgical life of the church. Within this common life, Robert Bruce Mullin describes a historic tension between two competing models of what the Episcopal Church should be in the United States—the *nobles oblige* vision (the Episcopal Church as the culturally premier religious body of the nation) versus the "apostolocist" vision (the Episcopal Church as faithful witness to the apostolic faith and order). Kathryn Greene-McCreight's description of conflict within the currently embattled Episcopal Church can be understood within this framework set forth by Mullin, although she identifies divergent understandings of the role of the Holy Spirit as a core theological issue. Thus, the *nobles oblige* culture-shaping faction of the church affirms a Spirit of God active in progressive or prophetic causes (e.g., equal rights for homosexuals in church and society), while those identified by Mullin as "apostolocist" would tend to understand the third Person of the Trinity in connection with God's revelation in Scripture and tradition. Shared love for the liturgical practices of the *Book of Common Prayer* may no longer be adequate to hold the American church together as an institution, but the larger concept of an Anglican communion or tradition remains as strong as ever. Whether or not the Episcopal Church survives in the twenty-first century as a loosely united ecclesial entity with these two visions intact, it is still its liturgical worship that gives the Anglican tradition its identity. In this, Episcopalians and other Anglicans stand apart from both the evangelical and theologically liberal versions of the American Christian mainstream, even if many of them could more generally be identified as either evangelical or progressive on such issues as biblical authority, human sexuality, and the person of Jesus Christ.

The religious groups discussed in this book have been part of American society for a very long time, and some of them—Episcopalians and Presbyterians, for example—have enjoyed the benefits of cultural privilege. Nevertheless, their distinctive confessional forms and practices have also run against the grain of the egalitarian, homogenizing impulse of the American cultural marketplace. In the nineteenth century this "democratization" of American Christianity took the form of popular evangelicalism classically described by Nathan Hatch.[4] Popular evangelicalism is characterized by its own kinds of democratic reductionism at the start of the twenty-first century. Today one almost assumes that, in order to flourish, churches must be intentionally nontraditional assemblies that avoid denominational identification and offer "culturally relevant" electronically enhanced worship with sermons strong on application of "biblical principles" to everyday American life. But down the street or across the highway from fellowships that adopt this paradigm, believers continue to gather in churches honoring Lutheran, Reformed, Anglican, Orthodox, Roman Catholic, or Anabaptist confessional identities that, in varieties of ways, emphasize ecclesial tradition along with contemporary cultural engagement. Roman Catholicism, though buffeted by controversy and perennially struggling with how to balance tradition and accommodation to American culture, has continued to gain as a proportion of the population—especially with a burgeoning Hispanic/Latino membership with traditions of their own. Meanwhile, following several decades of market-sensitive mega-church success, some "younger evangelicals" in smaller "emerging churches" are exploring ancient liturgical practices and early church spiritual theology or embracing the rigors of Reformed confessional faith and practice.[5] What do we make of this persistence of tradition—and, especially, traditional confessional identity—in American religious life? Confessional forms of church life and Christian practice may seem to go against the grain of popular Christianity, but they remain a remarkable and enduring feature of American culture.

If the presence of confessional Christianity might seem anomalous in the first decade of the twenty-first century, its resurgence or, with some traditions, first appearance in America a century ago was even more surprising. More than twenty years ago, Martin Marty used the phrase "the irony of it all" to describe the fact that, while the turn of the twentieth century is commonly thought of as the Progressive Era, this was also the period when "virtually every enduring and vital American religious conservatism" appeared. "A contradictory outcome of events mocked the promise and fitness of people who thought cosmopolitan habits were to prevail, that progress would dominate, that modernist rationality could serve as a universal interpreter." Among the many ironies of the twentieth century is the fact that, as the liberal Protestantism that had seemed so culturally ascendant steadily waned in numerical strength over the course of the century, new "outsider" religious groups as diverse as Pentecostalism and Eastern Orthodoxy (in all its ethnic varieties) grew during the same period from meager beginnings to positions of respect and even prominence. Conservative Protestants of various confessional traditions, along with other religious movements that arose in reaction to mainstream American culture's "modernity," could be described as "transmodern," according to Marty. "When they reached for historic models and impulses, they then projected these so that they could help others find means to move beyond the modern."[6] Whatever else one may conclude, it appears that a great many Americans seek and find spiritual meaning not in what is new or most reasonable or appealing according to contemporary standards but in things that are old, mysterious, and time-honored.

Marty's discussion of the ironic growth of confessional and conservative religious groups at the turn of the twentieth century was notable because the history of the Christian faith in the United States has often been told in ways that minimize the significance of classical doctrine and ecclesial traditions. The standard narrative favors themes such as individual religious experience, evangelical revivalism, accommodation to American (e.g., frontier, Southern, progressive, etc.) culture, biblical restorationism, practical innovation in the church's institutional development, and charismatic and entrepreneurial leadership. Religious choices that move against the mainstream have still generally fit neatly into this narrative. For example, a teenage Joseph Smith in 1820, echoing the frustration of countless young American seekers with the competing claims of the denominations, returned home after his first spiritual vision able to announce to his mother, "I have *learned for myself* that Presbyterianism is not true" (my italics).[7] Finding some spiritual truth *for myself* is assumed to be the American way of being religious. Holding to a historic confession as a normative expression of eternal Truth seems un-American for its violation of the right of private conscience and abdication of the responsibility to think for oneself. Pundits from the eighteenth century to the present have assumed that Old World church traditions, with arcane confessions and hoary polities, could never survive the exigencies of New World marketplace religion.

In the early Republic, rationalists like Thomas Jefferson and romantics like Ralph Waldo Emerson envisioned the withering away of evangelical Calvinism and Methodism, along with Old World ecclesiologies and liturgies, with the advance of modern American citizens along more enlightened spiritual paths. Even a Christian and historian of the stature of Philip Schaff shared something of this perspective. It was Schaff's pioneering scholarship—first as professor at the German Reformed seminary at Mercersburg, Pennsylvania and subsequently at Union Seminary in New York City—that essentially recovered for American Protestants the significance of early church history, patristic theology, and (in the title of one of his massive collections) *The Creeds of Christendom*. But Schaff described the United States as "emphatically a land of the future" and "the Phoenix grave not only of all European nationalities . . . but also of all European churches and sects, of Protestantism and Romanism." With his characteristic sense of historical development, Schaff imagined that free competition among "the present confessions and sects"—which he viewed as the sinful "dismemberment" of the Body of Christ—would not result in the vindication of any one version of traditional Christian orthodoxy. "Rather . . . out of the mutual conflict of all something wholly new will gradually arise." [8] This conviction motivated Schaff's leadership in the ecumenical Evangelical Alliance and his enthusiasm, at the end of his life, for the World's Parliament of Religions (1893). From both historical and contemporary perspectives, the persistence of confessional traditions as we are broadly considering them is remarkable and calls for the further exploration that the chapters in this book advance.

The success of the Roman Catholic Church in the United States has often been chalked up to the ingenuity of its leaders in steering between the Scylla of assimilation and Charybdis of tradition while managing to retain Catholicism's essential ecclesial character and devotion. Still, the commanding historiographic narrative, among Catholic historians as well as American historians generally, has been the development of a distinctively *American* Catholicism in the United States between the mid-nineteenth and the mid-twentieth centuries. The late Peter R. D'Agostino in his seminal monograph, *Rome in America*, has demonstrated the inadequacy of this storyline. A portion of D'Agostino's preface and the introductory chapter are republished in this book, as he brilliantly reveals the ongoing importance of old world loyalties despite American cultural hegemony. In fact, Roman Catholics of Irish, German, Polish, Italian, and other national origins, despite their cultural distinctives, all shared a commonality even more powerful than that of the experience of living in the United States. Catholic identity in America was shaped by a prevailing "transnational Catholic ideology" in support of the papal struggle to reestablish the Holy Father's temporal power after the loss of the Papal States in 1870 under the unification of Italy as a secular nation-state (the *Risorgimento*). "Liberal Italy" limited papal power purely to the spiritual realm, confining the five late-nineteenth and early-twentieth century popes to life within the Vatican. Finally, after the rise of Fascist Italy, Pius XI negotiated the Lateran Pacts with Mussolini to create the political entity of the State of the Vatican City with the pope as temporal ruler. As D'Agostino puts it, "Rome, not Jerusalem, Washington, Baltimore, or Dublin, was the center of the American Catholic world from 1848 to 1940," uniting Catholics and enabling Protestants to define them as dangerously different. D'Agostino describes Catholicism in the United States until World War II as particularly Roman in nature while in dialectical relationship with American Protestant modernity.[9]

Christopher Shannon, meanwhile, describes the vitality of American Catholicism specifically as the ability to make itself at home with "hierarchical authority in their faith and egalitarian democracy in their politics." Despite the vehement anti-Catholicism that united otherwise squabbling nineteenth-century American Protestants—and, ironically, undermined the authority of their own Protestant confessional traditions—the Catholic Church was able to become "the semi-established church" in their own communities with strong educational and social institutions and identification with Democratic party politics. At the national level, however, Tammany Hall political clout and the specter of Catholics' ultimate allegiance to the papacy fueled Protestant anxiety, almost inevitably scuttling Al Smith's bid for the presidency. This led to a strange inversion, starting with John F. Kennedy, as Catholic candidates for office felt compelled to become more Protestant than Protestants on separating church and state. By the end of the twentieth century "every major Catholic leader in the Democratic Party chose their party over their Church" when it came to issues like abortion, while evangelical Protestants took up the banner of faith in the political arena. Abandonment of the public nature of Christian faith poses a special problem for Catholics because their confession of faith is understood not as a matter of individual choice but as belonging to a hierarchical church that itself embodies their faith. Shannan describes the Catholic Church as a "confessional tradition" without a particular document that carries definitional authority. Rather, it is "the broader tradition of the Church," with bishops and the papacy as "authoritative interpreters of this tradition," that constitutes the Catholic Church's confessional and ecclesial identity. He concludes that "at a time when the word partisan has become a synonym for self-interest, the American Catholic political tradition at its best reminds us that it once meant loyalty—to party, friends, family, community, and church."

The question of a church's confessional identity has even arisen in unlikely places and in denominations not noted for doctrinal fastidiousness. The example of the United Church of Christ, a denomination in serious decline by the end of the twentieth century, could suggest, contrary to the notion that the dead weight of tradition impedes spiritual progress, the disastrous outcome of confessional amnesia. Despite being an amalgam of historically Reformed and Lutheran-Reformed Unionist traditions, the United Church of Christ surrendered the ideal of holding fast to classical theological roots during the second half of the twentieth century in favor of social activism and progressive-minded theological freedom. As a commonly used textbook for the training of United Church of Christ clergy put it, "while some denominations establish their identity by inspecting the walls for breaches and requiring those persons inside to conform to essential standards, the United Church of Christ characteristically has held the gates open wide and cultivated diversity." Yankee Congregationalists, one partner of the United Church of Christ merger, of course, had already largely abandoned the Calvinist legacy of their Puritan and Edwardsean forbears by the end of the nineteenth century. Fondness for Neo-orthodoxy among many Congregational and German Reformed clergy between the two world wars, and the prominence of Reinhold and H. Richard Niebuhr in the Evangelical Synod, provided a tacit theological foundation for the union that created the new denomination in 1957. But by the 1980s some United Church of Christ seminary professors, in a proclamation titled "A Most Difficult and Urgent Time," decried the "void in sustained disciplined [theological] reflection that can claim the assent of the church," calling for "reconsideration of the historic and confessional roots of our church." In fact, it was becoming increasingly difficult for the denomination to participate with theological integrity in some ecumenical conversations.[10]

In the arena of Lutheran-Reformed dialog, for example, the Lutheran bodies that were uniting as the Evangelical Lutheran Church in America in 1987 affirmed their relationship with the Presbyterian Church (USA) and the Reformed Church in America, but threatened to exclude the United Church of Christ from ongoing dialog because of its perceived non-creedal identity and ungrounded congregational polity. United Church of Christ theologian Gabriel Fackre of Andover-Newton Theological School put forth a creative and politically successful response in which he emphasized the confessional nature of the denomination's founding documents as "the texts of the church." If taken more seriously, these documents "would provide the theological vertebrae so sorely needed." The original Basis of Union by which church leaders negotiated the creation of the United Church of Christ, for example, affirmed the biblical faith "which the ancient Church expressed in the ecumenical creeds, to which our own spiritual fathers gave utterance in the evangelical confessions of the Reformation, and which we are in duty bound to express in the words of our time as God Himself gives us light." Meeting with Lutheran, Presbyterian, and Reformed Church in America dialog partners, Fackre described confessionalism in his tradition as a linking of historic doctrinal standards with "the way things are done, or more exactly, the way things are handed on, the traditioning process of a faith community . . . an ethos, an atmosphere, a set of assumptions out of which people live and to which they return at critical junctures of decision."

This line of argument saved a place for the denomination in the eventual 1997 Lutheran-Reformed "Formula of Agreement."[11]

Fackre's rationalization of "the confessional nature of the United Church of Christ" helps illuminate James Juhnke's chapter, "Mennonites and Democracy: Shaped by War and Rumors of War." Juhnke confesses that "compared with . . . other religious bodies with centrally defined and authoritatively enforced statements of faith, the Anabaptists and Mennonites barely met the definition of a 'confessional tradition.'" Indeed, as he points out, "Anabaptists were the *victims* of magisterial confessions." Not that there have been no formal theological statements in Mennonite history. Juhnke starts by referencing the *Martyr's Mirror*, physically the largest blockbuster published in colonial North America, which includes the *Apostles' Creed* and three Dutch Anabaptist statements of faith as a preface to the martyr stories. It would be productive to explore more deeply ways that this whole book functioned like the Westminster or Augsburg confessions. The martyr stories set forth in words the exemplary model of a life of faith, for, above all, Mennonites are believers that have specialized in voicing the Christian witness (again, the noun becomes the verb) by witnessing with their lives and thereby becoming witnesses (martyrs). In the New World, beginning in tolerant colonial Pennsylvania, it was always a good thing for Mennonite identity when, during wartime, persecution by "local patriots" who violently "tyrannized" and "terrorized" Mennonites raised its ugly head. Pacifist performance—getting a chance to actually turn the other cheek—was what gave the community confessional identity as martyrs witnessing to the same faith as those in their historic big book.

It helped the Mennonite cause enormously that, despite the nation's "quasi-pacifist" self-image, the United States has always been "relentlessly expansionist and prone to violence," with an "ideology and practice of militarism" based on "the myth of redemptive violence." To be Anabaptist was to make one's confession by finding ways to stand against this national culture. The confessional challenge came during peacetime, Juhnke explains, as the quintessential European outsiders "became comfortable insiders within a pluralistic Pennsylvania system" that became "the original hearth of the American invention of denominationalism." The crisis of Mennonite identity arose because, in the old saying, those who came to do good did well. The performance ideal of suffering was reduced to mere humility. The right to vote and the obligation to pay taxes in a regime that benefited them so marvelously led inevitably to a more ambiguous confessional performance. The pluralism that was so beneficial contained the temptations of assimilation, not only to material success, but to influences from the happier (and eventually happy-clappy) faith of Pietism, revivalism, and evangelicalism. During the "century of total war" just past, Mennonites further accommodated to American religious culture by completing the shift from sect to denomination. This included the building of organizations and institutions similar to those of more "churchly" groups. But Mennonites retained their confessional difference in a number of ways—focusing on service, relief and development work, social reform, conscientious objection to war, alternative service, draft-resistance, and other forms of witness for peace. The irony of doing well when you're trying to do good continued as the Mennonite two-year program of voluntary service, modeled on the Selective Service requirement, flourished as long as there was a draft, but languished when the draft was discontinued. Public engagement as faithful witness in the early twenty-first century, ironically, is a sign of disarray within the larger Mennonite family as red-state-minded and blue-state-minded Mennonites perform their confession in very different ways.

If Juhnke's chapter on the least explicitly confessional of the groups under consideration focuses on tensions with mainstream American culture, James H. Moorhead's describes the self-consciously confessional tradition that has known the least cultural disjunction with the American context. In the words of his title, "Presbyterian confessional identity and its dilemmas" have not included the ethnic-cultural and language differences experienced by German-speaking groups like the Mennonites. Nor, after their earliest days of preaching without the approval of Anglican civil authorities in some colonies, have Presbyterians ever suffered as religious outsiders. Moorhead's chapter retraces the not-unfamiliar terrain of Presbyterian history, but makes it a trip worth taking because of his straightforward two-fold thesis. Moorhead demonstrates the connection between confessionalism and the emergence of the denomination as the form church life would take in the United States while also showing the persistence in Presbyterianism of the Reformed confessional tradition's vision of a *corpus christianum*. The twist here is that, while the first part of the thesis has to do with the role of confessions in distinguishing groups of Christians from one another, the second has to do with the faith's culture-transforming vocation. This appears to be the Presbyterian version of the Episcopal tension between "apostolocist" and "nobles oblige" ecclesial understandings described by Mullin. According to Moorhead, "much of the story of Presbyterian confessionalism in America would be a narrative of the ways in which it tried to navigate between its wish to maintain the particularity of its creed, liturgy, and polity and its wish to somehow be at the center of their society as its shapers and representatives."

The Presbyterian tension goes back to England where, shortly after the *Westminster Confession* was adopted, it became obvious that the aspiration of establishing "a common order and polity uniting all of those who took the name of Christ in England, Ireland, or Scotland" would never be realized. Rather than uniting Christians, from that point on a confession would serve to "demarcate oneself from others who called themselves Christians." This phenomenon was further fostered in the religious pluralism of the Middle Colonies where Presbyterians first settled and gained adherents in significant numbers. In such a mixed multitude, this aspect of Reformed confessionalism fueled the subscription controversy and the question of what constituted the "essential and necessary articles" of the *Westminster Confession*. The Reformed impulse toward social transformation, rooted in the sovereignty of God over all of life, simultaneously emerged with the revivals of the Great Awakening that cut across denominational lines and, at least to some extent, fueled the American Revolution. In the new Republic, "the Presbyterian Church opted to keep its confessional purity by claiming its place as one voluntary society among others in a free society" but it also helped lead the charge for culture-formation by becoming "part of a broader Christian coalition shaping society into a *corpus christianum*." The tensions erupted again and again—most famously in the Old School-New School and fundamentalist-modernist controversies with their simultaneously confessional and social-cultural dimensions.

The United Presbyterian Church in the United States of America published a *Book of Confessions* in 1967 that included a contemporary statement of faith along with historic doctrinal standards. The effect of collecting documents from across many centuries of Christian history was, ironically, to diminish the sense of confessions as "timeless propositions" and to elevate the dynamic, developmental nature of doctrine. Moorhead does not mention it, but the creation of a thoroughly contemporary, ecumenically-oriented *Statement of Faith* by the newly-formed United Church of Christ just a few years previously in 1959 no doubt influenced the Presbyterians as they undertook their own project. The United Church of Christ *Statement of Faith* is filled with present-tense verbs (God "calls the worlds into being . . . bestows upon us the Holy Spirit . . . calls us into his church . . . promises to all who trust him . . .") and mid-twentieth-century language echoing Tillich, Bonhoeffer, and the Civil Rights Movement (God "seeks in holy love to save all people from aimlessness and sin," creates the church as a covenant including "people of all ages, tongues, and races," calls Christians to "accept the cost and joy of discipleship," and promises "courage in the struggle for justice and peace"). For progressive-minded protestants, questions about the authority and applicability of older confessions were becoming hard to address—and, to many of them by the 1960s and 1970s, increasingly irrelevant.

Although the theologically conservative Christian Reformed Church in the late-twentieth century had little else in common with the United Church of Christ and mainline Presbyterians, they did share a reverence for the *Heidelberg Catechism*. If this 1563 confessional document was embraced loosely by the United Church of Christ (as part of its German Reformed legacy, honored with a 400th anniversary edition in 1963) and by Presbyterians (in whose 1967 *Book of Confessions* it was reproduced),[12] the Christian Reformed Church held the 1563 *Heidelberg Catechism* tightly as "univocal, unchanging truth." But despite their different approaches to doctrinal standards, Gabriel Fackre's proposition that confessionalism is manifest in "the way things are done" also finds distinct echoes in Christian Reformed practice. In his chapter James Bratt describes Christian Reformed confessionalism, at least through the first half of the twentieth century, not only as adherence to a strict theological position but also in terms of corporate ethnic culture and individual personal behavior in the face of American modernism and evangelicalism.

Bratt also undertakes an analysis of the Mercersburg theology of John Williamson Nevin and Philip Schaff in the German Reformed Church of the mid-nineteenth century. Mercersburg theology was distinguished by its high Christology, ecclesiology, and liturgy and by its emphasis on catechesis, devotion to creeds and confessions, and critique of American evangelical individualism. But to understand the intra-denominational German Reformed confessional conflict along the lines Moorhead explores among the Presbyterians, we would also have to include an analysis of the arguments of the so-called Old Reformed (anti-Mercersburg) party among the Pennsylvania churches, the perspectives of the Ohio and Sheboygan classes, and the secession of the North Carolina classis from the Eastern Synod in 1853.

The clash between the North Carolina classis or association of churches and the Pennsylvania-based Synod of the German Reformed Church that led to the separation of the southern churches essentially concerned conflicting inter-pretations of confessional norms within the context of evangelical culture. It was not simply a case of Piedmont revivalism versus Mercersburg confessionalism. While southern cultural differences played a role, the issue of slavery did not drive the controversy. The North Carolina Classis withdrew because of "the heresies of Mercersburg" which they condemned for being "at variance with the truth as it is taught in the word of God and our [Heidelberg] catechism." They denounced "the theory of 'natural organic historical development' as unfolded by the Mercersburg 'sect' [as] destructive of many of the most precious doctrines of the protestant faith." Mercersburg's over-emphasis on the doctrine of the Incarnation to the neglect of the Cross led to its positing of an essential continuity of the Incarnation of Christ in the institution of the church and a "Romish" understanding of the church as "the depository and continuation of the Saviour's Theanthropic life." The Synod argued in vain that the classis, as subservient to the Synod, had no right to secede. After the conclusion of the nation's Civil War when the southern states were forced to rejoin the Union, the German Reformed Synod sent a heartfelt message of sympathy for the "sad and distressed condition" of the North Carolina churches, clearing the way for reunion. But, as an 1895 *Historical Sketch of the Classis of North Carolina* stated, the doctrinal battles were not over, for "the Classis went back to fight, to contend for the faith of our fathers."[13]

Meanwhile, German Reformed churches across Pennsylvania, Maryland, and Ohio split and continued to fight at annual meetings over the liturgical implications of their theological understandings. One remarkable effort at reconciling confessional catechesis with evangelical revivalism was issued at the prompting of the Maryland classis in a Synodical Pastoral Letter in 1846. Decrying the neglect of "Bible and Catechetical instruction, of covenant and Church relations, of family religion, of confirmation, of the sacraments," the letter exhorted, "we may confidently expect a season of constant and most blessed revival . . . if a becoming activity prevails amongst us, in regard to a proper, scriptural training of the baptized children of our Church." While a synthesis like this was more easily envisioned than achieved in practice, devotion to the *Heidelberg Catechism* nevertheless remained a bond of unity within the contentious German Reformed Church. In 1863 the weary church observed a truce in its prolonged war over theology and liturgy long enough to celebrate the *Heidelberg Catechism*'s three hundredth anniversary. A month before Lincoln dedicated the cemetery just up the road in Gettysburg, and while the monumental dome was under construction on the Capitol building in Washington, the Eastern Synod meeting at Carlisle dedicated a massive tome of essays entitled *Tercentenary Monument* on the *Heidelberg Catechism* and its influence in German Reformed tradition. The church finally resolved its internal differences by adopting the live-and-let-live compromise offered by a Peace Commission in 1879.[14]

Although Philip Schaff had long since moved on from Pennsylvania to a much broader stage, the reconciliation of the German Reformed Church exemplified Schaff's view that, as Bratt explains, "confessions were vital for defining the 'bonds of union' in a given church fellowship." The German Reformed Church by the start of the twentieth century was free to open itself to the kind of pan-protestant ecumenism envisioned by Schaff, "the great work of the future – the reunion of Christendom in the Creed of Christ." Lines within the German Reformed Church were thus drawn quite differently from those that separated the two Dutch Reformed bodies, the Christian Reformed Church and Reformed Church in America. Dividing lines among factions within the Christian Reformed Church were even more distinctive, with ongoing tensions among "confessionalist-pietists" and "Kuyperian enthusiasts and confessionally minimalist evangelicals." But the way the *Heidelberg Catechism* worked in the complex life of all these Reformed church traditions underscores Bratt's conclusion that "the preeminent virtue of the confessions is their incarnation of memory . . . provid[ing] a historical bed of answers . . . rais[ing] for believers a lasting measure above the allegiances and insistencies of the day."

In the early twenty-first century it may no longer be so much the case that rising generations of believers revere the confessional traditions explored in this book as the "incarnation of memory" and the "historical bed of answers" with which they have been familiar since childhood. American society, and the experience of individual Americans, is characterized by religious fluidity and pluralism, along with increasing numbers of young people growing up with no religious training whatsoever. Some who embrace the Catholicism of their Irish, Italian, Polish, or Mexican ancestry or the Antiochian or Greek Orthodox Church of their grandparents no doubt experience feelings of homecoming. But more and more it is a matter of believers seeking out or stumbling into a church with a liturgical tradition more deeply rooted than the most recent popular worship song, a spiritual theology and set of practices expressed in time-honored language, a way of living the Christian faith that stands in opposition to the limitations and failures of modernity. In any case, it would be foolish to imagine that confessional traditions such as the ones discussed in this book will define the center of American Christianity in the twenty-first century, for the popular traditions of evangelical revivalism and rationalistic biblicism remain deeply rooted in the culture – and the culture itself will no doubt continue to develop along secularist and religiously pluralistic lines. But it would be even more foolish to believe that confessional forms of Christianity rooted in the early Church and Reformation era have had their day. The purpose of this book is to spark further conversation on the persistent and ongoing role of such traditions in American religious life.

Notes

1. Mark A. Noll, *The Old Religion in a New World: The History of North American Christianity* (Grand Rapids: Eerdmans, 2002), 24-26, 252.

2. See E. Brooks Holifield, *Theology in America: Christian Thought from the Age of the Puritans to the Civil War* (New Haven: Yale University Press, 2003).

3. See Miroslav Volf and Dorothy C. Bass, eds., *Practicing Theology: Beliefs and Practices in Christian Life* (Grand Rapids: Eerdmans, 2002), esp. Miroslav Volf, "Theology for a Way of Life," 245-263.

4. Nathan O. Hatch, *The Democratization of American Christianity* (New Haven: Yale University Press, 1989).

5. See, for example, Robert E. Webber, *The Younger Evangelicals: Facing the Challenges of the New World* (Grand Rapids: Baker Books, 2002) and Collin Hansen, "Young, Restless, Reformed," *Christianity Today* (September, 2006), 32-38.

6. Martin E. Marty, *Modern American Religion, vol. 1: The Irony of It All, 1893-1919* (Chicago: University of Chicago Press, 1986), 193, 251.

7. Edwin S. Gaustad and Mark A. Noll, eds., *A Documentary History of Religion in America: To 1877* (Grand Rapids: Eerdmans, 2003), 341.

8. Philip Schaff, *America: A Sketch of Its Political, Social, and Religious Character*, ed. Perry Miller (Cambridge, Mass.: Harvard University Press, 1961; orig. New York: Scribner, 1855), 16, 80-81, 234.

9. Peter D'Agostino, *Rome in America: Transnational Catholic Ideology from the Risorgimento to Fascism* (Chapel Hill: University of North Carolina Press, 2004), ix-15.

10. Daniel L. Johnson and Charles Hambrick-Stowe, eds., *Theology and Identity: Traditions, Movements, and Polity in the United Church of Christ* (New York: The Pilgrim Press, 1990), xi-xiii.

11. *New Conversations*, winter/spring, 1988, 13. Johnson and Hambrick-Stowe, eds., *Theology and Identity*, 139-149. Louis H. Gunnemann, *The Shaping of the United Church of Christ* (New York: The Pilgrim Press, 1977), 208.

12. *The Heidelberg Catechism with Commentary* (Philadelphia and Boston: United Church Press, 1963). *Book of Confessions* (New York: United Presbyterian Church in the United States of America, 1967).

13. Charles Hambrick-Stowe, ed., *The Living Theological Heritage of the United Church of Christ: vol. 3, Colonial and Early National Beginnings* (Cleveland, Ohio: Pilgrim Press, 1998), 416-421.

14. Ibid., 389-390, 433.

"Passing Through Many a Hard School and Test": Confessions, Piety, Liberty and the Lutheran Experience in the United States

Susan Wilds McArver
Lutheran Theological Southern Seminary

In the spring of 1811, John Dreher of South Carolina composed a lengthy letter to his apparently unconverted older brother Godfrey, a veteran of the Revolutionary War, and implored him to turn from his sins and accept Christ. "I was in hopes by this time you would reflect on your former life and turn to GOD who sent his only Son into the world to save sinners . . . not those who will live in their sins but only those who is willing to forsake sin," he wrote. Pleading with his brother to "Consider your poor soul and your dear children likewise," he asked Godfrey to consider "if you don repent hear on this side of the grave how will you stand before the Bear of God." Dreher concluded his appeal with some practical assistance: "Should you ever turn from your own ways in the way of God which I have a hopes and trust in God you will, I have sint you a small book, which gives you an instruction how to do, in this little book you will find how *Doctor Luther* done so too and every one that wants to be saved."[1]

Except for his final sentence, John Dreher's plea on behalf of his brother's immortal soul could have been written by almost any evangelical Christian during much of the nineteenth century. His impassioned appeal to the example of "Doctor Luther" as the paradigm for evangelical conversion, however, signifies the singularity of a denominational tradition that occasionally embraced, and sometimes resisted, the larger religious milieu of which it was a part.

Dreher's letter thus illustrates in capsule form the complexity of much of the experience of Lutheranism in the United States.[2] It is a story of variety, diversity, tension, and in a particularly appropriate Lutheran way, paradox. It is a Church made up of the sons and daughters of Germans, Swedes, Norwegians, Danes, Finns, Icelanders, Slovaks and African American slaves, and extends from the East Coast and the Caribbean to Canada, Alaska and Hawaii. They have been in this country since the 1600s and represent the fourth largest denomination in the United States, and yet curiously, they still seem at best a "semi-visible people."[3] Mark Noll probably spoke for many when he observed that the Lutherans could be considered "a type of mildly exotic ethnics—sort of like the Mennonites, only more of them."[4] Non-Lutherans unfamiliar with their history and presence are still more likely to associate them, if they do at all, with the stories of Garrison Keillor, their liturgical and musical traditions, their well-regarded social service agencies, or incorrectly with a well-known civil rights leader of the 1960s.

Part of the reason Lutherans are so hard to identify is the very complexity of the story they have lived. The dizzying array of their ethnic origins has meant that one almost needs to be well-versed in over a dozen languages and cultures to begin the most rudimentary examination of their history, and their numerous divisions, mergers, and controversies have seemed archaic and inscrutable to outsiders. Lutheran scholars, in an attempt to bring some order out of the chaos, have proposed various models and metaphors for describing the intricacy of the experience. They have suggested, for example, that the Lutheran story can be understood best through utilizing flow charts illustrating the mergers of many ethnic groups into one. Others have compared the strands of Lutheranism in this country to the braids in a woman's hair, to streams flowing into a river, or to a luxurious plant that has been transplanted from the Old World to the New and subsequently has thrived—or been subdivided, choked and trampled. Considering its confusion of acronyms and ethnic identifies, others have suggested less attractive metaphors: a can of alphabet soup, a crazy quilt, or even a person with multiple personality disorder. The Lutheran tradition and story in America, in other words, has developed in some interesting ways, few of them linear.[5]

The resulting complexity is not one that has lent itself easily to recounting within the larger canonical story of religion in America.[6] Lutherans have more often than not been largely pushed to the sides of the major story. Traditionally, many scholars have simply mentioned the Lutherans as one group among many who entered the United States during the great European migrations of the mid-to-late-nineteenth century, and then have consigned them to the Midwest and Great Plains without further comment. The experiences of earlier generations of American Lutherans during the colonial era in the Middle Colonies and South, if mentioned at all, are usually rolled into the "other" category of American religious experience, where groups as varied as the Quakers, Jews, Dunkers, Moravians, Catholics, and Lutherans find themselves lumped together as amorphous "dissenters" from the more "established" traditions. Lutherans appear in the historiography of American religion, in other words, as outsiders, as people who do not neatly fit the paradigms of the larger picture of religious development in this country. While more recent historiography has begun to revise this canonical retelling of the story in a way that acknowledges the reality of diversity and pluralism within the American religious experience, the study of Lutheran history has largely not yet reaped the benefit of this more expansive view.[7]

Part of the problem, Lutheran scholars must admit, is of their own making. In a predisposition not unique to their own tradition, they have tended to speak largely among themselves and have not proven particularly adept at weaving their own story into the larger story of religion in the United States.[8] Over the last century and a half, Lutheran meta-narratives have ranged widely across the historiographical spectrum to proclaim variously that Lutherans are either superior to all other church bodies, the same as all other church bodies, more American than all other church bodies, or most recently, just obviously and distinctively *different* from all other church bodies. Preferring to converse in a familiar vocabulary addressed to its own rather extended family than to translate that experience in intelligible ways to others outside the family circle has at least ensured at least two things. It has ensured both that other Lutheran scholars and readers will understand, if not always agree with, the concerns, issues, and passions of the author, and at the same time, it has guaranteed that hardly anyone outside of the Lutheran family will care. The complicated Lutheran story, therefore, has remained largely one told within, and not without, the tradition.

This complexity begins, though it does not end, with Lutheran theology, which has always stood as a defining measure of the tradition. Lutheranism has traditionally been defined by a series of theological propositions first articulated by its founder, Martin Luther (1483-1546). Driven by a deep-seated struggle within his own soul for a certainty of salvation, Martin Luther eventually came to an understanding that "the just shall live by grace through faith alone," and that no good work or individual merit could earn any sinner his or her own salvation. This Lutheran emphasis on the grace of God and not on the work or belief of the individual remains a bedrock conviction of the tradition. Other distinctive marks of Lutheran theology include an emphasis on *sola Scriptura*, the reality of living simultaneously as both saint and sinner, an emphasis on the vocational implications of the priesthood of all believers, a sacramental understanding of baptism and eucharist, a distinction between law and gospel, and a two kingdoms theology. These beliefs have both united Lutherans with other Protestants and at the same time separated them from the mainstream of the American Reformed tradition.

Lutheranism's central teachings were eventually inscribed in the *Augsburg Confession*, a document written in 1530 to clearly outline areas of both agreement and disagreement with the Catholic and Reformed Church of its day and which eventually became the defining theological text of the new denomination. Eventually, the *Augsburg Confession* was combined with other constitutive documents into *The Book of Concord* of 1580.

Martin Luther was concerned that a right understanding of the gospel be restored. This theological insistence was driven not by a love of abstract principles, however, but by his passion as a pastor: The *Ninety-Five Theses* of 1517 revealed his concern for confessional purity primarily as it affected the lives of his people. The *Theses* illustrated his apprehension that the wrong interpretation of the gospel being taught to his parishioners was depriving them of the assurance of God's love and grace, and thus the ability to live in and respond to that love.

These two emphases—an emphasis on correct theology *and* an emphasis on the daily Christian life lived in response to God's gracious action—were combined in Luther's thought and writings. At the same time, however, these two concerns created a tension that has continued to exist in Lutheranism to this day, between confessional theology and the practice of living. It is a tension that has played out in various ways as at different times and in different places, one or the other of these leanings has tended to predominate, sometimes to extremes. Over time, Lutherans by and large may have agreed that the *Augsburg Confession* was their defining document, but exactly what they meant by that continued to be up for discussion. What exactly did it mean, in the end, to "affirm the Confessions"?

In the immediate aftermath of Luther's death, the orthodox party insisted that to "affirm the Confessions" meant to assent to certain doctrinal truths. Trying to protect Lutheranism from encroachments from the right and the left, the orthodox emphasized right belief over right action.

In response, the "Pietists" emerged and critiqued the orthodox as cold, lifeless and formal, and called for a reformation not only of theology, but of life—a life transformed by a working, vital faith.[9] Armed with such popular devotional literature as Philip Jakob Spener's (1635-1705) manifesto *Pia Desideria* ("Pious Desires"), published in 1675, and the institutional strength of the University of Halle, Pietism quickly became an important source not only of Lutheran renewal, but eventually of evangelical revival.[10] Pietism also created a Lutheranism less concerned with ideological labels than with practical effects and one that stressed cooperation between Christian denominations in the pursuit of a greater Christian good.

Jaroslav Pelikan has noted the irony that in America the Lutheran experience proceeded in almost exactly opposite ways from the trajectory experienced in Europe. In the Old World, the Reformation was followed by a period of Lutheran Orthodoxy, then as a reaction, Lutheran Pietism. In the American context, the process was exactly reversed: Pietism, at its height in the eighteenth century when Lutheran immigrants began to arrive in large numbers, was the early predominant strain of Lutheranism in this country. By the early nineteenth century, a reaction against this Pietism emerged in the confessional movement, and only in the twentieth century have the fundamental principles of the Reformation been recovered. This theological background—and controversy—is one that Lutherans brought with them to this country.

But no theological tradition exists in pure platonic form. Both Christianity as the parent and Lutheranism as its child are Incarnational faiths, and theology is incarnated in flesh-and-blood people bound by time and space. The Danish philosopher Søren Kierkegaard reportedly once suggested that we meet ourselves on a ship already launched, a journey already underway. He meant by that statement that all people are born into a family, a culture, and a tradition, all of which had their beginnings and did their shaping work long before individuals came onto the scene at any particular point in the story.

Kierkegaard's observation can prove a fruitful metaphor when considering the case of Lutheranism in the United States. In fact, it can serve as both metaphor and as literal fact, for Lutherans did arrive in this country most often by sea.

The Lutheran "ships" departing from Europe held certain structural similarities in common. All, for example, subscribed in some way—often in competing ways—to the *Augsburg Confession*. But at the same time, these metaphorical vessels left from different ports at different times and took different routes to the New World, encountering varying scenery on the way. The passenger manifestos included Germans and Norwegians, pastors and lay folk, men and women, children and grandparents, university graduates and peasants. The passengers brought with them catechisms, novels, almanacs, Bibles, devotional literature, and theological tomes. These ships, their passengers, and their cargo, in other words, were already outfitted with different cultural and linguistic norms and with habits and idiosyncrasies that defined those on the respective vessels long before they ever reached American shores.

Upon arrival, passengers disembarked, taking their baggage with them. Some immigrants clustered together with their fellow passengers as they spread inland from the sea, providing an opportunity to reinforce the culture, language and folkways they had left behind. Other passengers scattered upon arrival, settling among neighbors very different from themselves. As a result, some carefully unpacked the items from their trunks and set them on the shelves of their new lives, exactly as they had been in the Old Country. Others put certain items under glass, on the mantelpiece, or in the front parlor, all in pride of place, but rarely utilized them in everyday life. Some interspersed their items on shelves with other objects acquired in the New World. Others consigned items in their baggage to the attic, where they were never seen again. And still others lost their luggage on the transatlantic crossing—or dumped the bags as soon as they arrived.

Each of these variables meant that once the ship landed in the New World, one could guarantee that those disembarking would have varied experiences of that world and the place of Lutheranism in it. In the Old Country, one was Lutheran by birth. In the New World, however, immigrants had a chance to forge both a new national and a new religious identity, combining the baggage they brought with them on board and the materials they found on land. As Henry Melchior Muhlenberg (1711-1787), the colonial patriarch of Lutheranism in this country wrote in 1753, "Any one coming from Europe, who brings some good with him into this land, must pass through many a hard school and test here. . . The laws of the province are mild, glorious, and good; the privileges, and especially the liberty of conscience, are priceless."[11] Yet the universality of human sinfulness, Muhlenberg believed, meant that no good field would grow up without weeds.[12] Muhlenberg spent almost half a century attempting to reconcile the "glorious and good" that the "liberty of conscience" offered, with the "hard school and test" the United States also provided. Muhlenberg was among the first to consciously wrestle with the difficulty, but he was certainly not the last.[13]

All of this has meant, then, that it is difficult to speak of a single Lutheran identity or Lutheran experience in this country. What can be spoken of more accurately is the existence of *many* Lutheran identities and experiences. Those identities have differed over time and space. They have varied by ethnic origin, point of departure, time of arrival, gender, race, theological worldview and historical context—just as all identity does. The original Lutheran settlement patterns, compared rather inelegantly but accurately by Martin Marty to a giant dumbbell laid across a United States map, proved enormously influential.[14] In the seventeenth and eighteenth centuries, Lutherans settled in Pennsylvania, New York, Delaware, Virginia and the Carolinas. In the nineteenth century, they clustered in the upper Midwest. And there Lutherans pretty much stayed. Lasting geographical denominational boundaries of strength and weakness are visi-

ble to this day, following in the wagon tracks of these original settlers. The old-
est continuing Lutheran church in the western hemisphere, founded in 1666 on
St. Thomas Island in the Caribbean, therefore, looks vastly different from the
newest Lutheran church on the continent in St. Paul, Minnesota, founded over
three centuries later.

It is not possible in the course of a single essay to examine in detail the entire history of Lutherans' encounters with the New World. Two different sound-
ings, however, taken at points 1500 miles and a century and a half apart, can
illustrate the complexity and the tensions between confessional theology and the
daily practice of living that Lutherans have struggled with in this country. Confessionalism does not—or at least it should not—exist without concern for the
Christian life, while pietism does not—or at least it should not—exist without
theological integrity. The first of these two examples examines that tension primarily from the confessional side, the other is drawn from Lutheranism's more
Pietistic side. While these incidents are specific to a certain time and place,
therefore, they can provide windows into the larger issues all Lutherans have
faced, both then and now.

SOUNDING # 1: THE HENKELS

Beginning in the 1600s and accelerating into the 1700s, Lutheran immigrants began to pour into the New World, leaving their homelands for a variety
of economic, political, social, and sometimes religious reasons. Unlike the New
England Puritans, who immigrated complete with their own pastors and communities, the first Lutheran immigrants usually came without them, and for
years had to make do with the most rudimentary traditional Christian services, a
situation which left them all too often to their own creative devices.

At first, the pioneers were scattered, settled communities were few, and the
parish church was weak and ineffective, if it existed at all. Under such conditions, those who sought religious instruction often were forced to take it where
they could find it. The rough and ready character of the frontier made sharing of
worship space and ministers a matter of religious survival. Most often, the desire
for a minister who could speak in their own tongue was more important for these
early Lutheran settlers than were theological niceties, and German Lutherans
were thus often first served by a variety of German Moravian or Reformed pastors—and not a few charlatans who preyed on the vulnerable—and occasionally
formed combined Lutheran/Reformed congregations.[15] The German language
and customs, therefore, defined the earliest German settlers, not denominational
affiliation. The arrival of Henry Melchior Muhlenberg in 1742 as a missionary
from Halle went a long way toward providing the fledgling church with pastors,
worship forms, and structures.[16]

The revivals known as the Second Great Awakening, which began in the
East and on the frontier around 1800, marked a pivotal moment. To a widely
scattered society with irregular preaching services and sporadic ministerial sup-
ply, camp meetings and revivals unquestionably brought many rural inhabitants
a spiritual message they were hungry to hear. Following an emotional conversion, the new Christian sought to live a life of extreme holiness, self-discipline,

and prayer. In addition, the isolation experienced in daily life made the noisy excitement of the revivals an entertainment event not be missed. Evangelicalism soon permeated American culture, and as one scholar has observed, this "simpler, more direct approach" to heaven proved popular with the predilections of a people living independently on the frontier.[17]

The question for Lutherans and all other non-evangelical traditions in this period was how to respond to this massive theological and social movement. For many rural Lutherans in the East, the inability to receive anything like regular preaching and the means of grace led many to embrace revivalism, perhaps literally, as an answer to prayer. While it may seem counterintuitive that *any* point of contact at all could be found between the sacramental theology of Lutheranism and the emotional "decision theology" of revivalism, many Lutherans found revivals not at all antithetical to their theological self-understandings. The American revival tradition had been fed and nurtured in its origins at least in part by German Lutheran pietism, and pietism's emphasis on holy living and personal renewal provided a point of contact for Lutherans who encountered evangelicalism in the new national context. Thus, many Lutheran pastors in the United States agreed that revivals in and of themselves were not necessarily suspect, provided they were conducted decently and in good order and were not considered a substitute for catechetical instruction.

Three influential Lutheran leaders in the eastern United States spread their considerable influence in favor of this "American Lutheranism." In the Southeast, John Bachman, pastor of St. John's, Charleston, South Carolina and a colleague of the naturalist John James Audubon, and Ernest Hazelius, Prussian born and educated and the sole member of the theological faculty of the Lutheran Southern Seminary, joined with Samuel Simon Schmucker of Gettysburg Lutheran Seminary in the North. These leaders believed that Lutherans should explore revivalism in an attempt to create an ecumenical, inclusive Christian community for the New World, a position they felt was consistent with that of the original sixteenth-century reformers.[18] While the so-called "Americanist party" still considered adherence to the *Augsburg Confession* central to their self-definitions as Lutherans, those allied with Hazelius, Bachman, and Schmucker were more willing to allow freedom from a "literal sense" of the document. In an America still largely rural and frontier, it seemed to many good Lutherans that it was far more important for Lutherans, Baptists, Methodists and Presbyterians to work together as Christians in a land where church attendance was still phenomenally low and infidelity high, than to accentuate the points of disagreement that divided them.

On the other hand, the Henkel family of North Carolina, a family including many Lutheran pastors and led by patriarch Paul and his son David, became increasingly alarmed at the sight of Lutherans occupying "mourner's benches." These leaders asked if Lutherans could accept the *form* of the surrounding evangelical revivals without also undercutting Lutheranism's traditional theological *substance*: a total reliance upon God's grace, coupled with an emphasis on the sacraments and catechesis. This party emphasized a return to confessional, sacramental theology that opposed the Americanist party. To the Henkels and other like-minded confessionalists, those advocating revivals were asking Lutherans to make a "decision for Christ" and therefore commit the unpardonable Lutheran sin: doing a good work to earn their salvation. To the Henkels, revivals seemed examples of "spiritual fanaticism run wild,"[19] and such pastors worked cease-lessly—and not always successfully—to convince Lutherans to adhere to more traditional understandings of Lutheran doctrine. As a result of the controversy, many Lutheran churches in the Southeast eventually left their mother synods and followed the Henkels into a "Tennessee Synod" in the 1820s and 1830s.[20]

It was an argument that raged across eastern American Lutheranism throughout the nineteenth century. In the Northeast, Samuel Schmucker's even-tual proposal thirty-five years later of a *Definite Synodical Platform* (1855) that called for a "recension" of the *Augsburg Confession* and the abandonment of certain errors contained in it eventually brought the subject to a head, culminat-ing in the creation of rival Lutheran seminaries, one in Gettysburg and the other in Philadelphia, PA, only one hundred and fifty miles apart.

Yet this story, which is so often recounted as a controversy merely located in theological disagreement between pastors, can also be told from other per-spectives. The controversy that eventually tore the eastern Lutheran Church apart had undeniable theological roots, yet the collision was not simply a colli-sion between confessional and American theology. Personal, political, social, and even economic divisions played a role in the bitter dispute that affected lay people as much as it did their pastors.

In the Southeast, for example, young David Henkel, the catalyst for much of the controversy, was so personally obnoxious and abrasive in making his points about the distinctions between Lutheran and evangelical theology that he alienated all in his path, reportedly contending, for example, that allowing Lu-theran and Reformed boys and girls to intermarry was as bad as allowing horses and cows to mate.[21]

More importantly, the controversy also clearly exemplified the larger po-litical and social class struggles in the new nation. The proposal in 1820 by the "Americanist party," for example, to create a "General Synod of the Evangelical Lutheran Church in the United States," a loose federation composed of Luther-ans in the East, unleashed a torrent of explicitly anti-Federalist, Jacksonian lan-guage from the Henkel party. David Henkel called for purifying the Lutheran church, a purification that rejected ties with any centralized, national power and which tied him with other "democratizers" of his age.[22] Significantly, his rheto-ric and the eventual creation of the confessional Tennessee Synod mirrored the formation of two other groups emerging at the same time and in the same geo-graphical location but at the opposite end of the theological spectrum: the Primi-tive Baptist movement and the Methodist Protestants. The Primitive Baptists formed out of a similar fear of a centralized power. The Methodists responded to a perception that the changing church hierarchy no longer met the needs of the poorer "plain folk" members of the church.[23] It is surely no accident that Lu-theran churches in Charleston, South Carolina, for example, whose elegant and wealthy members held little in common theologically, economically, or socially with more rural Lutherans in the interior of North and South Carolina, expressed no interest at all in the controversy.[24] Clearly, the debate reflected larger trends going on in the culture of the time.

Economic facts may also have played some part in the controversy. Henkel's attack on the creation of a General Synod may have arisen at least partially out of his concern for his own family's Henkel Press, a publisher of large volumes of material for conservative Lutherans. The Henkel Press would have been in direct competition with the church press of the larger body had North Carolina become a part of the General Synod.[25]

One can test the impact of confessional identity as translated into the lives of laypeople by examining their response to the controversy. Lay persons too became intimately involved in the conflict. Paul Henkel once reported being threatened by a layman with a club when he attempted to explain a more "Lutheran" understanding of baptismal regeneration to a hostile congregation apparently more used to a far less sacramental interpretation. The Church Council of another congregation, exposed for the first time to the Lutheran *Book of Concord* when they obtained a translation of the book into English from the Henkel family press, evicted its pastor when they discovered that he refused to subscribe to the book.[26]

This crisis proved enormously disruptive to eastern Lutheranism for over a century, but it also served a positive function in ways which probably could not be appreciated at the time. As Rob Kroes has pointed out in his study of Dutch Calvinists, religious divisiveness can still serve a cohesive function.[27] This controversy forced eastern Lutherans to define their place in the new nation vis-à-vis their evangelical neighbors. Even those who did not join with the more confessional Tennessee Synod or later in the northeastern General Council had to justify themselves and explain why they were still "true Lutherans" even if they did interpret the *Augsburg Confession* more leniently. Ultimately, over the course of a century, the answer given by the majority of Lutherans was a reaffirmation of their distinctive denominational theology and a de-emphasis on revivalism.

Theology, economics, politics, and social class all became intertwined to create and exacerbate this crisis. Examining only one of these factors alone is not enough to account for the fundamental divide this controversy engendered. But an examination of all of them illuminates a basic division within the ranks of American Lutheranism, a division precipitated by confessional disagreement, aggravated by larger issues within the fledgling United States culture, and which has recurred under different times and in different dress, time and time again throughout its history.

SOUNDING # 2: NORWEGIAN WOMEN'S GROUPS

On the other side of the country, another group of Lutheran immigrants arrived toward the end of this controversy to face challenges of their own. Norwegian immigrants arriving in the mid-to-late nineteenth century tended to transport large communities, complete with their own pastors, and settle together in enclaves in rural, isolated areas of the Midwest. Unlike the situation of Lutheran settlers over a hundred years earlier who had found themselves more scattered and more in contact with their English neighbors, the nature of this later group's settlement patterns meant that Norwegian Lutherans retained many of their identifying cultural, language and theological characteristics well into the twentieth century.

Norwegian Lutherans, however, like the largely Americanized German Lutherans of the East, also arrived divided along theological lines. Some arriving from Norway sought to replicate the Norwegian state church and culture. Others intentionally rejected the "high church" of their homeland in favor of a "low church" Pietism, typified in groups such as the Haugian Synod.

One way to examine this experience, however, is to start not with theological debate and institutional struggle, but with the more direct religious experience of Lutheran laypeople. For example, DeAne Lagerquist's study of Norwegian-American Lutheran women traces the lives of a population who remained largely unable to influence the bitter theological divisions articulated by Lutheran clergy and male members. Instead, by tracing the ages and stages of women who lived quiet yet spiritually meaningful lives in their homes, churches, and communities, Lagerquist examines what it meant to be Lutheran, Norwegian, and female to a generation of women in the Midwest. Her portrayal outlines ways in which Norwegian and Norwegian American women actively contributed to the process of Americanization of the family.[28]

The cultural and social location of these women affected the way they interpreted the religious teachings they heard from their pastors. As they interacted more and more with their American context, they slowly began to adopt patterns of church life similar to other Protestant women in the nineteenth century, particularly in their experience in forming church women's groups. These groups became important vehicles for transforming religious identity in the New World. Examining the large body of material these women began to write and publish themselves for use in their own women's organizations gives a window into the spirituality of these ordinary Lutheran lay women.[29]

Norwegian Lutheran women's literature embodied a "distinct spirituality as well as practical guidelines for daily religious practice and discipline" for women living out their roles as wives, daughters, and mothers.[30] Consistently throughout the literature, women found opportunities for "sacralizing . . . day-to-day parenting and homemaking. Women who cared for children never had to be without a religious interpretation of their daily lives and a community of women who spoke the same theological language and devised together rituals for interpreting, reinforcing and celebrating their spirituality of child nurture."[31] In so doing, women found that their devotional practices made their Christian faith "part and parcel of a woman's everyday life and concerns."[32]

While their pastors, and perhaps even their husbands, seemed pre-occupied with identifying and preserving right Lutheran doctrine, in other words, Norwegian women's religion proved far less theoretical and far more connected with the trials, tribulations, and joys of their day to day lives. The literature written, published, and composed by women themselves was far less concerned with confessional exactness and "doctrinal and synodical integrity" as it was with the lived experiences of a woman's daily life. These laywomen went to church, heard the preaching of their pastors, and listened to the explication of the sacraments, but then translated these received symbols into the concrete experiences of their daily lives. This was not necessarily the Lutheranism these women had been taught in the Old World. But the formation of American-style women's organizations provided new opportunities for redefinition and discovery in the new American context.

Lutheran women in the East, already further along in the Americanization process by the late nineteenth century, went even further in these new religious self-understandings. Eastern women's groups often became the most active parts of the church in terms of mission activity and outreach. Indeed, scholar Christa Klein noted long ago that paying attention to the story of Lutheran women's voluntary organizations might nuance our present characterization of historic Lutheranism as quietistic and aloof from social concerns.[33]

The examination of Lutheran identity through the lens of Lutheran women's groups thus provides yet another way of studying the Lutheran experience in the United States. Recognizing the importance, even the centrality of religion in the lives of these lay women, such a study leads to new ways of understanding how the American and the Lutheran experience intertwined. For these Norwegian women, Lutheran theology manifested itself in daily life, not in institutional mergers or divisions.

Just as an examination of socio-economic facts deepens our understanding of the "Americanist/Confessionalist" controversy in the East, so examining the religious self-understanding of Norwegian Lutheran women illuminates our understanding of the Americanization of immigrant communities in the Midwest.

CONCLUSION

As the twentieth century dawned, a series of mergers began to bring many of the varying strains of ethnic Lutheranism into larger united bodies. In the Midwest, Norwegian Lutherans were the first to successfully create a new body through merger in 1917, with the East Coast Lutherans close behind in 1918, belatedly reuniting northern and southern Lutherans who had been divided since the Civil War. Mergers accelerated throughout the twentieth century until 1988, after which three major bodies remained: the Evangelical Lutheran Church in America (ELCA), the Lutheran Church Missouri Synod (LCMS) and the Wisconsin Evangelical Lutheran Synod (WELS).

Yet the mergers creating modern Lutheranism have not been easy. While the LCMS and the WELS still largely represent a homogeneous ethnic entity, the ELCA merger brought together Lutherans from over a dozen ethnic varieties. Each merging group brought with it different pieties, experiences of the American context, and emphases in its theological interpretations of Lutheranism. It has sometimes felt as if the original passengers of a dozen different ships are now crowded into one.

In those areas of the East where German Lutherans had lived since the seventeenth and eighteenth century and had the most contact with their Anglo-Saxon neighbors, churches from New York to the Carolinas made the change from German to English both before and shortly after the Revolutionary War. In areas of the Midwest where Scandinavian Lutherans tended to settle near each other in more close-knit groups, acculturation into the American environment took consequently longer and continued into the twentieth century.

Although the situation is more complex than in the mid-nineteenth century, clearly the old confessional Lutheran/American Lutheran debate continues in a different form. But as these two examples have illustrated, Lutheran identity has varied over time and place.

Although these Lutherans existed in a context defined by their denominational affiliation and existing institutional structures, they also existed as Southerners or Midwesterners, as farmers or lawyers, as men or as women. All of these impacted upon the way people heard and received their tradition, and all of them thus affected the resulting history of the denomination.

Lutherans have historically labored to find a balance between an emphasis on theological confessionalism and an emphasis on the importance of living out the gospel day to day—and probably always will. That reality continues into the present as different groups struggle to maintain that tension as they address modern-day concerns and issues. Where that struggle will take the modern church is unknown, but it is clear that its history will continue to inform its struggle.

Notes

1. John Dreher, Saluda, South Carolina, to Captain Godfrey Dreher, Jr., 19 April 1811, in *Dutch Fork Digest: A Genealogical Newsletter of the Dutch Fork Chapter of the South Carolina Genealogical Society* 7 (July–September 1992): 84. Original spelling maintained, emphasis added.
2. This essay treats the experience of those Lutherans who eventually went into the Evangelical Lutheran Church in America in 1988. A separate essay in this volume by Dr. Mary Todd treats the experience of the Lutheran Church-Missouri Synod.
3. Martin Marty, *The Lutheran People*, rev. ed. (Madison Heights, Mich.: Cathedral Directories, 1989), 4.
4. Mark A. Noll, "Ethnic, American or Lutheran? Dilemmas for a Historic Confession in the New World," *Lutheran Theological Seminary Bulletin* 71 (Winter 1991): 17.
5. DeAne Lagerquist has discussed several of these metaphors in *The Lutherans* (Westport, Conn.: Greenwood Press, 1999).
6. For a discussion of how Lutherans have been handled in the historiography of religion in America, see Richard W. Dishno, "American Lutheran Historiography: A Regionalist Approach," in *American Lutheranism: Crisis in Historical Consciousness?: Essays and Reports of the Fourteenth Biennial Meeting of the Lutheran Historical Conference, October 27-29, 1988* (St. Louis: Lutheran Historical Conference, 1990), 29-49; and L. DeAne Lagerquist, "Does it Take One to Know One? Lutherans and the American Religious Historical Canon," *Dialog* 25 (1986): 201-206.
7. R. Laurence Moore, *Religious Outsiders and the Making of Americans* (New York: Oxford University Press, 1986) was one of the first to argue this point, calling into question the "Consensus School" of American historical writing, which he observed domi-

nated American religious historiography long after being discarded as inadequate by secular American historians (14).

8. See Christa Klein's discussion of this issue in "Denominational History as Public History: The Lutheran Case," in Robert Bruce Mullin and Russell Richey, eds., *Reimagining Denominationalism: Interpretive Essays* (New York: Oxford University Press, 1994), 307-17. Lutherans are not unique in this regard, of course. Mullin and Richey discuss the universal aspect of this tendency among religious historians of every denomination in their "Introduction" to *Reimagining*, 5-6.

9. Paul Kuenning, *The Rise and Fall of American Lutheran Pietism: The Rejection of an Activist* Heritage (Macon, Georgia: Mercer University Press, 1988), 7.

10. Mark Noll has traced this lineage in *The Rise of Evangelicalism: The Age of Edwards, Whitefield and the Wesleys* (Dower's Grove, IL: Intervarsity Press, 2003). See also Kuenning, 10-11.

11. Henry Melchior Muhlenberg, I: 376.

12. Muhlenberg proved acutely aware that "'if the seed has not yet taken strong and deep root and gained the upper hand, it is in danger of being rooted out or of being smothered by the weeds of erratic opinions,' from competing religious groups far more prolific than in Germany" (Reumann, 15-16, citing Muhlenberg, I: 376).

13. Mark Noll has noted, in a way similar to Muhlenberg, that almost all immigrants to the new world faced eventually the same dilemma: "whether America's liberal, democratic, commercial, mobile, and individualistic values [would] inevitably erode the particular structures of inherited religious tradition." Mark Noll, *The Old Religion in a New World: The History of North American Christianity* (Grand Rapids: Wm. B. Eerdmans, 2002), 236.

14. Martin Marty, "In Search of American Lutheran Identity," in *Evangelical Studies Bulletin* 21 (Spring 2004): 1.

15. Kathleen Neils Conzen discuses this tendency among Lutherans and Reformed to share worship space and pastors in "Germans," in Stephan Thernstrom, ed., *Harvard Encyclopedia of American Ethnic Groups* (Cambridge, Mass.: Harvard University Press, 1980), 409.

16. Kroes has noted the same result among Dutch Calvinists in *The Persistence of Ethnicity: Dutch Calvinist Pioneers in Amsterdam, Montana* (Urbana: University of Illinois Press, 1992), 1-11.

17. Bost, 49. See 48 ff. for Bost's discussion of Lutherans and the revivals.

18. Paul Kuenning, who has discussed this issue extensively, prefers the term "moderate confessionalists" over "American Lutherans," feeling this term more accurately describes a party that subscribed to the Lutheran confessions, but in a less rigid way than "strict confessionalists" did. See Kuenning, *The Rise and Fall of American Lutheran Pietism: The Rejection of an Activist Heritage* (Macon, Georgia: Mercer University Press, 1988), 1. Kuenning has argued strongly that American Lutherans found common ground with American evangelicals based on their own pietist traditions. See 77 ff. and Bost, 52, particularly n. 21, and 55. John Bachman was one of E. Brooks Holifield's "gentlemen theologians." See E. Brooks Holifield, *The Gentlemen Theologians: American Theology in Southern Culture, 1795-1860* (Durham, N.C.: Duke University Press, 1978). Raymond M. Bost, "The Reverend John Bachman and the Development of Southern Lutheranism" (Ph.D. diss., Yale University, 1963) is the best and most extensive treatment of Bachman. On Hazelius, see Raymond M. Bost, "Establishing the South Carolina Synod," in *History of Synod*, 175 ff.

19. Bost, 37.

20. A full recent treatment of the controversy may be found in Raymond M. Bost and Jeff L. Norris, *All One Body: The Story of the North Carolina Lutheran Synod, 1803-1993* (Charlotte: Delmar Printing Company, 1994), 45 ff.

21. Bost, *All One Body*, 62.

22. Robert M. Calhoon, "Confessionalism and Denominationalism in Early Southern Lutheranism," paper presented to the Congregational Heritage Workshop, Region Nine, Evangelical Lutheran Church in America (ELCA), 13 June 1994, Lutheran Theological Southern Seminary, Columbia, South Carolina. Richard Dishno has also explored use of this language in "A Regionalist Approach," 40-42.

23. Dishno, 42. Bill Cecil-Fronsman, *Common Whites: Class and Culture in Antebellum North Carolina* (Lexington, Kentucky: University Press of Kentucky, 1992), 198 ff.

24. It is not known how St. John's numerous free and slave African American members responded to the controversy.

25. Bost, 62-63.

26. Socrates Henkel, *History of the Evangelical Lutheran Tennessee Synod* . . . (New Market, Virginia: Henkel & Company, 1890), 13-14.

27. Kroes, *The Persistence of Ethnicity*.

28. DeAne Lagerquist, *In America, the Men Milk the Cows: Factors of Gender, Ethnicity, and Religion in the Americanization of Norwegian-American Women* (Brooklyn: Carlson Publishing, 1991), 197.

29. Betty DeBerg, "The Spirituality of Lutheran Women's Missionary Societies, 1880-1930," in "Missionary to America: The History of Lutheran Outreach to Americans," ed. Marvin Huggins, *Essays and Reports 1992* 15 (St. Louis, Missouri: Lutheran Historical Conference, 1994), 142-160.

30. Ibid., 143.

31. Ibid., 156.

32. Ibid, 159.

33. Klein refers briefly to this in her discussion of "Piety: Evangelical and Catholic," in her essay "Lutheranism," in *Encyclopedia of the American Religious Experience*, ed. Charles H. Lippy and Peter W. Williams, 3 vols. (New York: Charles Scribner's Sons, 1988), I:446, and has discussed the idea more fully in conversations with the author.

Contesting the Faith:
The Internal Struggle of
American Lutheranism

Mary Todd
Ohio Dominican University

What does it mean when some within a confessional tradition appropriate the word *confessional* as a means of identifying themselves over against the majority of their co-religionists, who they claim are not confessional? The question is more than rhetorical or semantic; it in fact describes the situation in American Lutheranism today.

The traditions included in this project are defined as confessional, meaning they subscribe to historic confessions, or statements of faith. Additionally, each is a tradition whose European roots were transplanted by immigrants into American soil. To that end, because the historic documents collected in 1580 as the *Book of Concord* serve next to Scripture as the confessional base of the Lutheran tradition, the logical premise is that Lutherans are by definition confessional, therefore any reference to "confessional Lutherans" would seem redundant at best. Despite that claim, the term confessional continues to be used instead as an intentional self-referent badge of difference within the tradition, borrowing from the nineteenth century language and practice of conservative Lutherans new to the United States.

The current situation reflects only the most recent debate among Lutherans in America, whose history has been marked by repeated struggles and competing claims over the confessions themselves. Both Lutheran and non-Lutheran scholars have observed that this fourth-largest denomination—identified by Roof and McKinney in the "moderate Protestant" category[1]—seems strangely marginal in American life given its more than eight million adherents and its longevity on the American scene.[2] Lutherans are either largely absent from or "mentioned in passing" in most narratives of the American religious experience.[3] What is it that has kept Lutherans from greater prominence or influence? Mark Noll, commenting on the unsteady path of Lutherans in America, observes that "Lutherans seem to have both easily accommodated to American ways of life . . . and never accommodated to American ways."[4] While it may be partially true that the answer lies in an uneasy accommodation, another possibility exists—that conflicts over the interpretation, application, and authority of their confessional statements have kept Lutherans from fully engaging their culture, a necessary step toward offering a uniquely Lutheran contribution to both the secular and religious American landscapes. Simply put, for most of their history, Lutherans in America have been at odds over the very things on which they supposedly agree. While some have seen such disagreement as a mark of vitality, most will admit that incessant infighting only serves to divert energy from other work. Internal conflict has unfortunately caused American Lutherans to miss the opportunity to enrich American life in any distinctly Lutheran way.

THE LUTHERAN CONFESSIONS

Lutheran self-understanding is based on adherence and subscription to Scripture and the sixteenth-century confessional writings that explicate it. The primary statement incorporating the principles of Lutheran doctrine is the *Augsburg Confession* of 1530. Following a series of disputes among Lutheran reformers about interpretations of that confession, a larger collection of documents, known collectively as the *Book of Concord,* was published in 1580. These "organically related"[5] documents include the three ecumenical creeds (*Apostles', Nicene,* and *Athanasian*), Luther's *Small* and *Large Catechisms* (1529), the *Augsburg Confession* and its *Apology* (1531), the *Schmalkaldic Articles* (1537), the *Treatise on the Power and Primacy of the Pope* (1537), and the *Formula of Concord* (1577). The centerpiece *Augsburg Confession* outlines the Reformers' articles of faith as well as their "protestations" against the Church of Rome. Often referred to as the *Symbolical Books,* or simply the *Symbols,* the confessions serve as the normative exposition of or commentary on Scripture for Lutherans, who hold the Bible as the sole authority for faith and the only source and norm for teaching. At the center of the confessions is Luther's preeminent contribution to Protestant thought, the concept of justification by grace through faith alone, apart from works. The confessions are always to point beyond themselves to that truth: "The Gospel and the sacraments provide the only proper approach to an understanding of the Confessions," writes German theologian Edmund Schlink, who cautions against their legalistic use: "To expect the Confessions to yield concretely binding directives for all concrete situations . . . is to paralyze the Christian in his obedience to God."[6]

The concept of paradox—both/and—is essential to understanding Lutheran theology. Several key tenets of the faith depend on a creative yet unresolved tension between seemingly contrary notions. Lutherans strive to hold both law and gospel in balance without overdependence on one to the neglect of the other. When Luther spoke of being *simul justus et peccator* ("at the same time both saint and sinner"), he was describing one of the most challenging tensions for contemporary Lutherans—his concept of two kingdoms, in which Christians live simultaneously in the secular kingdom of the left and the spiritual kingdom of the right. Lutheran understanding of the Eucharist as the real presence—the bread and wine *are* Christ's body and blood—is a further example of a paradox at the heart of the church's faith. The both/and dialectic is not only a mark of Lutheran distinctiveness, but integral to Lutheran theology.

COMPLEXITIES

The question concerning the redundancy of the expression "confessional Lutheran" notwithstanding, a distinct confessionalism did in fact arise in the early nineteenth century in Germany that was brought to the United States by German Lutheran immigrants. A confessional movement within an already confessional tradition admittedly adds a complexity, not only for those outside the tradition who wish to understand its history, but for Lutherans seeking to understand their tradition as well.

In twenty-first century America, the heirs of confessional Lutheranism are the Missouri and Wisconsin Synods and as many as fifteen other very small church bodies. D. G. Hart considers confessional Protestants such as the Missouri Synod "the lost soul of American Protestantism," those church bodies within larger Protestant traditions that he believes maintain the true heritage of the faith because they resist notions of relevance and instead emphasize creed, polity, order and liturgy.[7] Hart acknowledges that confessionalism as he defines it is not only divisive and intolerant but ethnocentric, pejorative, and separatist. Still, he defends the position over against the activism of what he calls the pietist or conversionist Protestant majority, which Hart holds responsible for having "worn away the confessional identity" of mainline Protestant denominations.[8] Challenging Robert Wuthnow's familiar analysis, Hart argues that "the central struggle throughout Protestantism's history has been between confessionalism and pietism, not evangelicalism and liberalism."[9] Because he is less interested in how faith traditions have adapted in America, Hart applauds these "religious outsiders" for remaining faithful to their heritage despite societal pressures to Americanize.

What Hart overlooks is the possibility of further layers of distinction within the confessional Protestant traditions he champions, such as those described by Dean Lueking in his 1964 study of the Missouri Synod's mission enterprise. Lueking finds two distinct and disparate strands of confessionalism within the synod, both present from its beginning. Defining the strands as "contrasting ways of conceiving of the church and its mission," Lueking identifies an evangelical confessionalism whose accent is on the gospel and that is ecumenical and mission-minded at heart, a conviction that sees the Lutheran Confessions as a unifying bridge to the rest of Christianity rather than a wall of separation.[10] Evangelical confessionalism stands in implicit tension with the dominant scholastic confessionalism for which the Missouri Synod is better known. Deeply influenced by both Pietism and seventeenth century Lutheran orthodoxy, the center of scholastic confessionalism is its emphasis on correct belief (*reine Lehre*). Because truth and error are incompatible, "those who refused to drop conflicting views on any of the wide range of doctrines considered essential" were declared by scholastic confessionalists to be errorists who had to be corrected. Mission, then, took on a different meaning to scholastic confessionals with their insistence on confessional loyalty: "Correcting the erring was far more appealing and immediate than meeting the demands of witness to those utterly unfamiliar with Christian truth."[11] Lueking's insights into the nuanced distinctions between confessional Lutherans within one Church body inform the study both of its own history and the larger history of American Lutheranism itself.

CONFESSIONALISM IN AMERICA

The confessionalism that German Lutherans brought with them to America began in Germany in the early nineteenth century in reaction to the rising rationalism of the time. The German Awakening, or *Erweckungsbewegung*, paralleled but was hardly as extensive as the Second Great Awakening that was rearranging the American religious landscape during the same period. Confessionalists desired a renewal of the faith through a neo-orthodoxy combined with a renewed spirit of Pietism, stressing a heart religion over Rationalism's emphasis on thought and reason. Coupled with this shift in theological perspective was the threat of the state. These fundamentally conservative Lutherans—ometimes called Neo-Lutherans, sometimes Old Lutherans, but all fearing loss of the "old belief"—found untenable the blurring of doctrinal lines evidenced by the Prussian Union of Lutheran and Reformed in 1817.[12] Their desire to return to the *status quo ante*[13] led them to leave Germany for a new world where they could worship and live as they wished.

German Lutherans had first come to North America in the colonial period, but it was through the nineteenth-century emigrations that the contours of American Lutheranism took shape. The story is part of the rich religious drama of the antebellum period, the "spiritual hothouse" when American Christianity experienced its democratization, as historians Jon Butler and Nathan Hatch have described the era.[14] The spirit of possibility seemed boundless in the young nation and the fertile soil of the new territories offered space and place for the development of communities and identities. Americans were on the move. A sense of vigor and vitality animates the story of American religious history more so in this era than in any other. Some of that energy has to do with a cast of very interesting characters, especially those who started the "made in America" originals in the wake of the Second Great Awakening. Less well known, but equally interesting, are the stories of the first wave of immigrants from Europe who were arriving in America and settling in, some in the Old West. Each with its own personalities and story, many of these emigrations brought with them religious traditions they hoped to transplant in their new land. Their stories reveal that neither the emigrants, their traditions, nor the new nation, remained unchanged in the process.

In America the German emigrants were known as Old Lutherans, self-declared confessional Lutherans who looked to the historic confessions of faith in the *Book of Concord* for correct theological understanding. They had left Germany in circumstances not unlike the Massachusetts Bay Puritans in 1630, religious migrants who believed it impossible to stay in their native land and preserve the true faith. Two migrations each followed a charismatic leader who promised freedom from the persecution the believers—more accurately, the clergy—had known under the state consistories. A Prussian pastor, J. A. A. Grabau (1804-1879), who had been imprisoned twice for his refusal to comply with the regulations imposed by the Prussian Union, led a company of 1,000 emigrants to America in 1839, most to Buffalo, New York, but some further west to Milwaukee, Wisconsin. In 1845, they formed the Buffalo Synod, also known as the "Synod of Exiles from the Lutheran Church of Prussia."[15] In Saxony, despite the fact that Rationalism was actually on the decline and there was no similar threat of union, Pastor Martin Stephan (1777-1846) nevertheless organized a group of 665 emigrants who left Bremen in November 1838 and reached St.

Louis in February 1839, having lost at sea a ship carrying most of their goods and fifty of their company.

The Emigration Code of the Saxon community had carefully laid out its plans for governance once it reached the United States. Again like the Bay Colony Puritans, the Saxons intended for their society, or *Gesellschaft*, to be a theocracy. An emigration committee had written exhaustive travel, settlement, ecclesiastical and civil codes, including the use of a common fund for all expenses. Stephan, who had himself made bishop aboard ship, was clearly the principal figure in this hierarchical system. But Stephan's vision was never realized. Within weeks of the purchase of property in Perry County, Missouri, one hundred miles south of St. Louis, to which many of the company had relocated from St. Louis, Stephan was deposed and exiled by rowboat to southern Illinois after several young women admitted sexual involvement with the bishop. The little enclave of emigrants drifted leaderless and fought among themselves for two years until C. F. W. Walther (1811-1887), the youngest of the clergy, convinced them that they had not sold their souls to Stephan after all, but were in fact a church by virtue of the preaching and administration of the sacraments in their midst. But in the process the Episcopal polity they had intended to transplant in the Missouri hills surrendered to believers determined never again to submit to a hierarchical structure.

Germans respected the clergy for being among the most educated members of the community. The relationship between pastor and people acknowledged both rights and respect, as well as Luther's two-part understanding of ministry—the priesthood of believers and the set-apart ordained office of Word and Sacrament. With regard to church governance, Luther practiced a policy of *Realpolitik*.[16] Because Walther in all matters depended on Luther, both for a theological doctrine and for the practical application of that doctrine in the congregation, were Luther whispering advice into Walther's ear, he would likely have said: "Let the situation determine the rules by which the church is governed." By far the prevailing position in the Saxon community was their insistence that they would not fall prey again to clerical despotism as they had under Stephan. A system of checks and balances grew from that experience that left the laity to direct the practical affairs of the congregation and the pastor the ministry of Word and Sacrament. Walther may have compromised on church polity to keep the Saxon community alive, but he remained uncompromising in holding the clergy to a binding and unconditional subscription to the Lutheran Confessions.

During the Perry County community's period of distress, Grabau, leader of the Prussian emigrants, wrote to the Saxons proposing that the two confessional groups jointly found a seminary. Three years later, the Saxon clergy finally responded by telling Grabau they could not agree with his elevation of the ordained ministry, a position similar to Stephan's. Comparing their experience to "children who have been burned," the Saxons claimed they had learned firsthand the dangers of a hierarchical system such as Grabau advocated.[17] They now understood the ministry not as station or status, as it had been in Germany, but as office. Grabau was outraged, claiming the Saxons had misread Luther, and he threatened the "would-be-Lutherans" with excommunication from his pulpit if they did not repent their error.[18] And so it came to be that these Saxons and Prussians, who in Europe had shared a common conservative faith, could find no common cause in their adopted homeland. They would instead, observed Philip Schaff, be divided into "enemy camps . . . . vying with each other in their church papers from week to week with an antipathy and bitterness which in truth is not an honor to Lutheranism and Christianity and does not in the least command respect from the Anglo-American."[19] Differing interpretations of the confessional documents to which they both subscribed became the source of bitter polemics and led to the founding of rival synods.

Walther, by now in St. Louis, was in search of other like-minded Lutherans through the newsletter he began publishing in 1844, *Der Lutheraner*. His underlying question was always, with whom can we be in fellowship? Walther never missed an opportunity to put other Lutherans on notice that the Saxons in Missouri understood themselves to be not only the one true church but the guardians of confessionalism in America. He was quick to challenge American Lutherans of the General Synod who had embraced the "new measures" of evangelicalism and revivalism, accusing them of compromise and "pseudo-Lutheranism."[20] Those accused in its pages thought the publication to be nothing more than the sniping of a "narrow and bigoted spirit."[21] But German missioners in Ohio, Michigan, and Indiana who had become disaffected with the Ohio Synod (primarily over the use of English, as well as Reformed tendencies regarding the Eucharist) rejoiced when they read *Der Lutheraner*. The missioners were known as "Loehe men," having been sponsored by a confessional Lutheran pastor in Bavaria, Wilhelm Loehe (1808-1872), and sent from Germany to America to serve the increasing numbers of German immigrants in the 1840s. Loehe had also financed a seminary in Fort Wayne to train his "emergency helpers" in the Midwest.

Loehe was what Dean Lueking would call an evangelical confessionalist due to his dedication to mission in multiple forms. Loehe's support of North American missioners is perhaps equaled by his involvement in creating a Bavarian network of institutions, including homes, hospitals and schools, and training laypeople—deaconesses in particular—to serve in them. Loehe was "the Neo-Lutheran who linked the ecumenical substance of the Lutheran Confessions with the call for mission at home and abroad."[22] Despite never traveling to America, Wilhelm Loehe was a formidable ally whose support was courted by various of the German immigrant groups as they attempted to establish themselves in their new land. In the absence of the state involvement they had known under the consistory system in Germany, any local structure they created had to conform to a Lutheran understanding of church and ministry. That was all they knew. Their confessionalism assured that the Old Lutherans would stand in contrast to the "deeds not creeds" spirit of evangelicalism by putting their emphasis on creeds or confessional statements.

When Loehe learned of the constitution adopted in 1847 by the Missouri Synod, he feared the German clergy had fallen prey to the "mob rule" of American democracy.[23] "Look at the composition of your congregations," he wrote,

"The unlimited right of suffrage on the part of the congregation is not only non-apostolic but also downright dangerous."[24] He had warned his missioners against the new measures of revivalists and the unionist tendencies of Lutherans who wished to speak English, but he hadn't thought to warn them about alliances with Lutherans who held different ideas about church and ministry. In response to Loehe's concerns that he had been overly influenced by American democratic principles, Walther protested: "We did not pattern the doctrine of the Church after the conditions prevailing here, but we established the Church according to the doctrine of our Church."[25] But Walther was unable to convince Loehe, and in 1854 the Bavarian pastor lent his support to the formation of the new Iowa Synod instead of either the Missouri or Buffalo synods. Loehe and the Iowans took issue with Walther's insistence that there were no "open questions" in the confessions. Not only did they see a distinction between essential and nonessential matters, but they believed, since "there never has been absolute doctrinal unity in the church," that total agreement should not be a condition of fellowship.[26] But Missouri disagreed, as "dogmatic rigor was of the essence," and so it grew "adamant in combat."[27] Again, the common cause of the confessions they shared in Germany would be no guarantee of relationship in their new homeland.

In Milwaukee in 1850, another group of German Lutherans organized themselves as the Wisconsin Synod. At first they were among those who felt the sting of Walther's pejoratives, as their founder, Johannes Muehlhaeuser (1803-1867), disdained Old Lutherans and "dismissed the Lutheran Confessions as 'paper fences.'"[28] But within two decades of its founding, Muehlhaeuser's position lost out to a confessional stance almost identical to Missouri's, and the two German church bodies became "sister synods." By 1872, along with four other ethnic synods, they had created the Synodical Conference, a union designed primarily for mission efforts.

The conditions of their emigration required the German Lutherans to reconstitute the relationship between their theological identity or self-understanding and their church government. In addition, like some, but not all, emigrant groups, they retained the language of their old homeland in the new. Missouri and Wisconsin Lutherans did so not only for familiarity and tradition, but because they believed the faith could only be transmitted in the language of the fathers. The churches thereby resisted the assimilation of their people as well as the extension of its mission into the surrounding culture. By defying other ethnic Lutherans who offered differing interpretations of their shared confessions as well as American Lutherans over against whom they defined themselves, these German synods gave notice that they meant to be different. And if there is one defining feature they share, aside from the fact that neither has ever merged with any other Lutheran synod, separatism and insularity are marks of distinction for Missouri and Wisconsin Synod Lutherans. They have come to be known not for their "peculiar teachings on justification by faith but for their refusal to pray with others."[29]

Polemics would be the language introduced to America by the Old Lutherans, spoken in the German they believed to be the only proper means of transmitting the faith. Polemics are fighting words that offer a beleaguered minority a sense of identity as it defines itself in contrast to others. As ethnic synods drew lines in the sand, they established patterns that would influence their future relationships. The refusal of the confessional Lutherans in Milwaukee to accept German clergy from the United Rhine Mission Society because the men served both Lutheran and Reformed believers led those clergy to found the Wisconsin Synod [WELS] in 1850. Disagreements between German and Scandinavian congregations in Minnesota led to the formation of the Minnesota (German) Synod and the Augustana (Scandinavian) Synod in 1860. Each synod considered itself confessional, but constant controversy about how that claim was understood kept them separate. While immigrant numbers, and thereby Lutheran numbers, grew, so did the number of ethnic synods. Between 1840 and 1875, nearly sixty separate synods were founded. German Lutherans founded the Missouri Synod, the Buffalo Synod, the Iowa Synod, the Wisconsin Synod and more. Scandinavians included Happy Danes and Sad Danes, Norwegians and Augustana Synod Swedes, white Finns and red Finns. By the end of the century Lutherans were found in over 100 synods in twelve major groupings. The fact that all carried the name Lutheran hardly diminished the hostility some of these groups expressed toward one another.

The occasional cooperative efforts between and among these various groups were tentative and frequently temporal. The longest sustained cooperative venture, lasting nearly 100 years, was the Synodical Conference, comprising six confessional synods who wished to sponsor mission initiatives. Founded in 1872, it was only eight years old when wracked by the "Predestination Controversy" that officially ended only when the Ohio and Norwegian Synods left the Conference in 1883. When division happened, it was often bitter, always accompanied by mean-spirited language and mutual condemnations, and lingered long after in the hearts and minds of both sides. Lutheranism entered the twentieth century no more united than the passengers on the immigrant ships they'd traveled on, as their own historians recount: "Immigration had an isolating and introverting effect upon Lutherans in their relationships to each other and to American Protestants."[30]

DIFFERING OPINIONS FROM AMERICAN LUTHERANS

In the midst of the immigrant waves of the nineteenth century, Lutherans longer established in the United States were challenged by a leading theologian who desired to advance the Americanization of the tradition. Samuel Simon Schmucker (1799-1873), a professor at the new Gettysburg seminary (founded in 1826) and most responsible for organizing the General Synod, embraced several features of the evangelicalism that was transforming American Protestantism in the antebellum period. Schmucker, "convinced early in his career that confessions could be helpful in defining an American Lutheranism," felt strongly that not only did the *Augsburg Confession* as a summary of Lutheran belief need to be adapted for American Lutherans, but that Lutherans themselves needed to adapt to the changes in the social context that surrounded them.[31] Seeking a truly American church, his convictions led him to introduce the Definite Synodical Platform in 1855, a revision or "rescinsion"—Schmucker's own word—of the *Augsburg Confession* that removed five "errors" from the *Confession*, thereby reducing the document to what he considered the essentials of the faith.

Not only because it tampered with the confession itself, but particularly because the excised items all had to do with the sacraments of the church, the Definite Platform was strongly opposed by the Old Lutherans, who shared an insistence and dependence on the sufficiency of the Lutheran confessions along with their intention to transplant the doctrinal purity they felt was being lost in Europe in their new land. Old Lutherans, who denounced the Definite Platform as evidence of the rationalism they had come to America to flee, were resolute as to their *quia* subscription to the confessions—they accepted the confessions *because* they agreed with Scripture—whereas American Lutherans admitted to a *quatenus* formula, accepting the confessions only insofar as they conform to Scripture.

Schmucker's attempt at reducing the tenets of the confession to a "common creed" was met with an equally virulent reaction by Lutherans within his own General Synod. A series of divisive developments led to the formation in 1867 of the General Council, dedicated to the *Unaltered Augsburg Confession*. Charles Porterfield Krauth (1823-1883), a confessional theologian from the new Philadelphia seminary, emerged as the leader of these American Lutherans who would stress the "reformatory conservatism" they understood Lutheranism to represent. Krauth, a self-declared advocate of "pure, unadulterated Lutheranism,"[32] may have called himself conservative, but Walther hardly considered him so, responding with his usual rhetoric of pejoratives. Writing for the new Synodical Conference in 1872, he distanced the Conference from both the General Synod and the General Council, accusing the Council of a "lack of confessional loyalty" and labeling the General Synod "a worthless, hollow and deceased church body."[33]

As the nineteenth century came to a close, the Missouri Synod's conviction that it was the one true church was reaffirmed by the leadership who followed the long tenure of C. F. W. Walther. The sermon preached at his 1887 funeral declared that the synod possessed "the truth—the whole unvarnished truth," and Walther's successor, Franz Pieper (1852-1931), later threw down the gauntlet that "whoever contests our doctrinal position contends against the divine truth."[34] Not all Lutherans shared the high view Missouri held of itself, however, and bitter feelings ran deep. Interestingly, these same years saw the first thawing of relations among some of the Scandinavian synods: When the United Norwegian Lutheran Church in America was founded in 1890, one of the partners in merger was a group known as the Anti-Missourian Brotherhood.

WOULD THE TWENTIETH CENTURY BE DIFFERENT?

Most histories of Lutheranism present the twentieth century in contrast to the nineteenth with regard to the question of Lutheran unity. Whereas the nineteenth century found a multiplicity of ethnic synods, each carving out a distinctly separatist confessional stance, the twentieth century finds many of those synods seeking common ground, eventually joining together, working through differences, and expressing an increasingly ecumenical spirit. The desire for unity, however, was burdened by what historian Eric Gritsch considers "the enduring American Lutheran question: Does confessional unity require theological conformity?"[35]

While the trajectory of Lutheran unity is clearly evident in the history of the mergers—which culminated in the 1987 formation of the Evangelical Lutheran Church in America (ELCA), incorporating two-thirds of American Lutherans—to focus on the end result glosses over the reality of persistent and perpetual contention and controversy over the course of the century. The first decades are well known to religious historians for the Fundamentalist-Modernist controversy that reached national attention in the Scopes trial of 1925. Lutherans remained on the sidelines while chaos reigned in other denominations, but revealed in subsequent parochial developments that similar division was present in their own tradition:

- Internal criticism of the dogmatic theology of the Wisconsin Synod in the 1920s by members of the faculty of its Wauwatosa Seminary, including church historian J. P. Koehler (1859-1951), led to the suspension of several clergy in the "Protest'ant Controversy". The Wauwatosa Theology, while not critical of the synod, posited the value of a historical-exegetical approach to scripture. The "Protest'ant Conference", organized in 1927, remains yet, a small but independent remnant of the church.

- The Missouri Synod began serious fellowship talks in the late 1930s with the new American Lutheran Church (ALC), founded in 1930 as an amalgam of the Iowa, Ohio, and Buffalo Synods. An almost immediate conservative backlash led to a polemical new publication, *The Confessional Lutheran*, and a growing mean-spiritedness in the synod. In 1945, forty-four prominent Missouri churchmen issued a statement decrying what they considered the legalism and lovelessness in their church body and the narrow interpretation of Scripture with regard to fellowship. *The Statement of the Forty-Four* was withdrawn in 1947 "for the sake of peace," but the factions it revealed would return to haunt subsequent history.

- The Wisconsin Synod, increasingly unhappy with its Missouri sister's receptivity to other Lutherans, especially its dialogue with the ALC in quest of a common confession, broke with Missouri and left the Synodical Conference in 1961, declaring itself "the largest Lutheran body in the world that has remained loyal to the Word in these days of apostasy."[36]

- By 1962, as a result of numerous mergers, most Lutherans in the United States were members of three primary Lutheran Church bodies: the American Lutheran Church (ALC), the Lutheran Church in America (LCA), and the Lutheran Church-

Missouri Synod (LCMS). The 1965 agreement by these three bodies to form a pan-Lutheran agency called the Lutheran Council in the USA (LCUSA), successor to the National Lutheran Council that had been organized during the first World War, fueled the desire of the conservative minority in the Missouri Synod to challenge the new spirit of openness in the synod, a development they blamed on the failure of the synod to discipline the signers of the 1945 Statement.

- The decision of the American Lutheran Church and the Lutheran Church in America to ordain women to the pastoral office in 1970 led the Missouri Synod to ask the ALC to reconsider its decision, as the two bodies had just the year before entered into altar-pulpit fellowship. The ALC declined to do so, its president appealing to the 1971 Missouri convention that their differences should not divide the church: "What shall we do when we both act out of our convictions of what is taught in the Bible?"[37] Missouri officially broke the fellowship agreement ten years later.

- The Missouri Synod in the 1970s was wracked by controversy over what was being taught at its St. Louis seminary. The dispute over historical-critical interpretation of Scripture and the authority of an advisory synod and its president led to the creation of a seminary-in-exile, schism, and the formation of a new church body in 1977, the Association of Evangelical Lutheran Churches (AELC). From its founding, the AELC, true to Lueking's evangelical confessional tradition, sought unity with other Lutherans, and in 1987 the Evangelical Lutheran Church in America (ELCA) was formed by the merger of the AELC, ALC and LCA.

- In 1996 a virtual grassroots movement calling itself Word Alone was organized within the ELCA out of concern over a proposal for full communion between the ELCA and the Episcopal Church in the USA. The proposed Concordat was narrowly defeated at the 1997 Churchwide Assembly but the revised *Called to Common Mission* was adopted two years later. Word Alone supporters objected to the historic episcopate that would now be required in clergy ordinations on the grounds that it was contrary to the Lutheran confessions.

- In 2001 the Missouri Synod in convention declared that it could no longer consider the ELCA an orthodox Lutheran church body, in large measure due to concern over the ELCA's "theological direction," including the ecumenical accord it had recently reached with several Reformed church bodies, and in particular the 1999 Joint Declaration on the Doctrine of Justification between a majority of world Lutherans and the Roman Catholic Church.

- In 2001, only weeks after the September 11th tragedy, twenty-one Missouri Synod pastors filed charges against the bishop of the Atlantic District of the Missouri Synod, Dr. David Benke, declaring that his participation in the Prayer for America event at Yankee Stadium was a violation of the synod's prohibition of both unionism (praying with other Christians) and syncretism (praying with non-Christians). Dr. Benke's eventual acquittal remains a contested matter to some in the synod.
- In 2005 self-defined confessional Lutherans of the Missouri Synod filed a lawsuit against the president of the synod, charging him with fraudulently manipulating his own reelection at the 2004 convention.
- At its 2005 Churchwide Assembly, the ELCA, faced with serious differences over homosexuality, overwhelmingly passed a unity resolution before voting on the sexuality issue in an effort to forestall a split in the church body. The resolution urged adherents to "concentrate on finding ways to live together faithfully in the midst of disagreements."[38]

LUTHER'S FAVORITE QUESTION: "WHAT DOES THIS MEAN?"

Today ninety-five percent of Lutherans in the United States belong to two primary church bodies. One, the Evangelical Lutheran Church in America, is twice the size of the other, is less than twenty years old and still struggling in its attempt to blend the disparate traditions and institutional memories of its predecessor church bodies. The smaller church body is The Lutheran Church-Missouri Synod. The tangible difference between these two churches is evident in their attitudes and policies toward the service of women, but a larger issue is the very real difference in their attitude and openness to other Christians, with the underlying question: "With whom shall we pray?"

Many Lutherans believe that to be Lutheran is to be ecumenical, in accord with Article VII of the *Augsburg Confession*: "For the true unity of the Church, it is enough [*satis est*] to agree concerning the teaching of the Gospel and the administration of the sacraments." Others strongly disagree, convinced that there must be consensus, if not full agreement, on doctrinal issues before any sort of fellowship—prayer, altar, or pulpit—can occur. With each side holding that its position is in accord with the confessions, this difference in Lutheran opinion offers a strong example of Lueking's model of contrasting strands of confessionalism.

Observers both inside and outside of Lutheranism have attempted to reduce the differences among Lutherans to dichotomous either/or distinctions. Some have located the demarcation between orthodox and Pietist traditions, others between depth of subscription to Scripture and the confessions. At the beginning of the twenty-first century, Lutheranism in America remains far more complex doctrinally than such facile distinctions would indicate. Sharp divisions in each of the two major church bodies along conservative/moderate lines presuppose only continued struggle over identity, not eventual realignment.

What explains the long history of contention among Lutherans in America? In 1871 Charles Porterfield Krauth wrote:

> The life of a church may be largely read in its controversies. As the glory or shame of a nation is read on its battlefields, which tell for what it periled the lives of its sons, so may the glory or shame of a church be determined when we know what it fought for and what it fought against, how much it valued what it believed to be the truth, what was the truth it valued, how much it did and how much it suffered to maintain that truth, and what was the issue of its struggles and sacrifices.[39]

Krauth believed that controversy contributes to the vitality of the church. David Gustafson, critical of the 1987 merger establishing the ELCA, admiringly argues that Krauth and the confessional party he led in the controversy over the Definite Platform *cared enough* about truth and the Lutheran church's future in America that they were willing to fight over the vital issues."[40] It is not being argued here that differences of opinion cannot or should not exist among those who share a religious tradition. Indeed, Lewis Coser contends that "a certain degree of conflict is an essential element in group formation and the persistence of group life."[41] Mark S. Hanson, presiding bishop of the ELCA, would agree: "It seems unwise for a church body bearing the name of Martin Luther, the reformer, and empowered by the witness of Scripture to expect or even desire to be without dissent."[42] Lutheranism in the United States has in fact grown in spite of relentless haggling over a book called *Concord*.

It could be argued that the seemingly endless debates over the confessions are no more than attempts to clarify Lutheran identity, to answer the question, "who are we?"—though most often that question is asked in comparison to another, one of who we are not. It could also be argued, as this essay suggests, that controversy serves to deflect the attention of the church from its primary mission—the gospel.

Philosopher John Roth believes that Americans are kept at odds by the very things on which they agree, notions such as liberty, equality and justice. While not all define those terms the same way, Americans tend to agree that those concepts represent the essence of what the nation stands for. In a similar sense, Lutherans are kept at odds by the very things on which they agree—the understanding of law and gospel, of the authority of Scripture and of ministry, of fellowship, even of the word "confessional," divide Lutherans today, as they have divided Lutherans over the course of their existence in America.

Is it perhaps the nature of Lutheran theology—the paradoxical affirmations themselves—that guarantees the persistence of controversy in the life of the church? Or is it that Americans find it difficult to embrace notions of ambiguity, such as those represented by the both/ands that are so singular to Lutheran theology? Paradox requires us to hold two seemingly, though not necessarily, contrary notions in tension without resolving the tension. America seems much more comfortable with an either/or dualism that insists we land on one side of an issue or another, where complexity and ambiguity are discouraged. The resilience of a national political system dominated by only two parties certainly reinforces such binary thinking.

Might the catechetical format of questions and answers introduced by Luther, by which young or new Lutherans are taught the faith, contribute to the difficulty Lutherans have in embracing ambiguity? Lutherans have no tradition like the Jewish *midrash* that allows for variant points of view in theological opinion. Neither are they gathered under one church and magisterium as Roman Catholics are; there is no Lutheran Rome to speak once or for all, nor a Lutheran counterpart to the Catholic Common Ground Initiative that seeks dialogue on polarizing issues.

In the persistent and perpetual conflict among Lutherans about their confessions, neither ultra-orthodox nor liberal considers the other an authentic Lutheran, defining them pejoratively instead as sub-Lutheran, if not outright un-Lutheran. Endemic conflict alters the focus of a group and narrows its mission, as Wayne Saffen suggests in his meditation on religious arguments:

> Religious argument satisfies
> The need to be right.
> It saves no one.
> Only saving action saves.
> . . . .
> Religious argument evades the task.
> Religious questions prolong debate.
> That is why they are asked.[43]

And so the struggle for the soul of the Church goes on. While family quarrels are hardly the exclusive domain of Lutherans, and can be found in the histories of most ethnic traditions, they seem a permanent aspect of Lutheranism in America. The long-held Lutheran conviction that "the Church must always be reforming itself" hardly translates that the church must always be fighting itself, or that contention and controversy are necessary components of reform. For a tradition whose confession is grounded in the both/and, we might expect Lutherans to be better equipped theologically to hold variant viewpoints without dissolving into warring factions.

Those members of this confessional tradition who consider themselves the only true confessionals would retort that faithfulness, not compromise, is the distinguishing mark of confessionalism as they fight the good fight of faith. But as the battle of over who is the more authentic Lutheran continues to be joined, Carl Braaten's observation seems fitting, as he finds it "ironic that a church can become absolutely legalistic about a set of documents that condemns legalism and not see the point."[44] And yet the Lutheran legacy of controversy continues.

Mark Noll has challenged Lutherans to finally make the contribution to America that he believes is inherent in their confessions and in the voice of Luther himself, in which "we hear uncommon resonances with the voice of God."[45] But to do so, they would first have to listen, not only to Luther but to each other. After nearly 400 years of Lutheranism in America, is it too late? DeAne Lagerquist thinks not: "The story of American Lutheranism is . . . the long haul of faithfulness in the midst of imperfection, of starting over and trying again. This is the difficult task of being both/and: both Lutheran and simultaneously American."[46] By holding to both, might American Lutherans offer a model of balance to an increasingly pluralist and divided America, a balance to temper the extremes on both ends of the religious spectrum?

Notes

1. Wade Clark Roof and William McKinney, *American Mainline Religion: Its Changing Shape and Future* (New Brunswick NJ: Rutgers University Press, 1987), 87-90.
2. Mark A. Noll, "Ethnic, American, or Lutheran? Dilemmas for a Historic Confession in the New World," *Lutheran Theological Seminary Review* 71 (Winter 1991): 17-43, and "The Lutheran Difference," *First Things* 20 (February 1992): 31-40. Even the dean of American religious historians, Martin Marty, himself a Lutheran, ponders whether Lutherans are "exotic enough to inspire mere curiosity on the part of non-Lutherans." Marty, *Health and Medicine in the Lutheran Tradition: Being Well* (New York: Crossroad, 1986), 8. See also L. DeAne Lagerquist's observation in her fine survey of American Lutheran history, *The Lutherans*, student edition (Westport CT: Praeger, 1999), 1: "Lutherans in the United States don't expect anyone who isn't one of them to notice them."
3. Roger Finke and Rodney Stark, *The Churching of America, 1776-1990: Winners and Losers in Our Religious Economy* (New Brunswick NJ: Rutgers University Press, 1992), 21.
4. Mark A. Noll, "American Lutherans Yesterday and Today," in *Lutherans Today: American Lutheran Identity in the 21st Century*, ed. Richard Cimino (Grand Rapids: Wm. B. Eerdmans Publishing Company, 2003), 4. Robert Benne takes issue with Noll's lament over the lack of the "Lutheran attitude" in American public life in *The Paradoxical Vision: A Public Theology for the Twenty-first Century* (Minneapolis: Fortress Press, 1995).
5. Edmund Schlink, *Theology of the Lutheran Confessions* (Philadelphia: Muhlenberg Press, 1961), xxv.
6. Schlink, xxi.
7. D. G. Hart, *The Lost Soul of American Protestantism* (Lanham,MD: Rowman & Littlefield Publishers, 2002).
8. Hart, xxv.
9. Ibid., 183.
10. F. Dean Lueking, *Mission in the Making: The Missionary Enterprise Among Missouri Synod Lutherans, 1846-1963* (Saint Louis: Concordia Publishing House, 1964). It should be noted that Lutherans use the term "evangelical" quite differently from those who call themselves evangelicals. The Lutheran root in German is *Evangelium*, the Gospel, which proclaims the central doctrine of justification by grace through faith; usage of the term dates to the Protestant Reformation and its emphasis on *sola scriptura* (scripture alone).
11. Lueking, 13-17.
12. For the development of these movements of protest and renewal among Lutherans in Germany, see Walter H. Conser, *Church and Confession: Conservative Theologians in Germany, England, and America, 1815-1866* (Macon, George: Mercer University Press, 1984).
13. Theodore G. Tappert, ed., *Lutheran Confessional Theology in America, 1840-1880* (New York: Oxford University Press, 1972), 9.

14. Jon Butler, *Awash in a Sea of Faith: Christianizing the American People* (Cambridge, Mass.: Harvard University Press, 1990); and Nathan O. Hatch, *The Democratization of American Christianity* (New Haven: Yale University Press, 1989).

15. Conser, 259.

16. Carl S. Mundinger, *Government in the Missouri Synod: The Genesis of Decentralized Government in the Missouri Synod* (St. Louis: Concordia Publishing House, 1947), 6.

17. G. H. Loeber, *Hirtenbrief* (New York: H. Ludwig & Co., 1849), 75.

18. Philip Schaff, *America*, in Carl S. Meyer, ed., *Moving Frontiers: Readings in the History of the Lutheran Church-Missouri Synod* (St. Louis: Concordia Publishing House, 1964), 185.

19. In Meyer, 184.

20. Carl Mauelshagen, "American Lutheranism Surrenders to Forces of Conservatism" (Ph.D. diss., University of Minnesota, 1936), 94.

21. Mauelshagen, 93.

22. Eric W. Gritsch, *A History of Lutheranism* (Minneapolis: Fortress Press, 2002), 181.

23. Mundinger, 189.

24. Mundinger, 200.

25. C. F. W. Walther, *Church and Ministry*, Preface to the First Edition, trans. J. T. Mueller (St. Louis: Concordia Publishing House, 1987), 7-10. Originally published in 1852 as *Kirche und Amt.*

26. Iowa Synod's Principles of Fellowship, in Meyer, 284.

27. James D. Bratt, "Protestant Immigrants and the Protestant Mainstream," in *Minority Faiths and the American Protestant Mainstream*, ed. Jonathan D. Sarna (Urbana: University of Illinois Press, 1998), 122.

28. Mark Braun, *A Tale of Two Synods: Events That Led to the Split between Wisconsin and Missouri* (Milwaukee: Northwestern Publishing House, 2003), 20.

29. Martin E. Marty, *Modern American Religion*, volume 1: *The Irony of It All, 1893-1919* (Chicago: The University of Chicago Press, 1986), 178.

30. August R. Suelflow and E. Clifford Nelson, "Following the Frontier, 1840-1875," in *The Lutherans in North America*, ed. E. Clifford Nelson (Philadelphia: Fortress Press, 1980), 171.

31. E. Brooks Hollifield, *Theology in America: Christian Thought from the Age of the Puritans to the Civil War* (New Haven: Yale University Press, 2003), 403.

32. Conser, 265.

33. Laurie Ann Schultz Hayes, "The Rhetoric of Controversy in the Lutheran Church-Missouri Synod with Particular Emphasis on the Years 1969-1976" (Ph.D. diss., University of Wisconsin, 1980), 171.

34. Nelson, 377.

35. Gritsch, 221.

36. Braun, 344.

37. Missouri Synod, *Proceedings*, 1971, 102, cited in Mary Todd, *Authority Vested: A Story of Identity and Change in the Lutheran Church-Missouri Synod* (Wm. B. Eerdmans, 2000), 221.

38. http://www.elca.org/ScriptLib/CO/ELCA_News/encArticleList.asp?article=3160

39. Charles Porterfield Krauth, *The Conservative Reformation and Its Theology* (Philadelphia: J. B. Lippincott & Co., 1871), 147, in Tappert, *Lutheran Confessional Theology in America*, 223-224.

40. David A. Gustafson, *Lutherans in Crisis: The Question of Identity in the American Republic* (Minneapolis: Fortress Press, 1993), 179, emphasis added.

41. Lewis Coser, *The Functions of Social Conflict* (New York: The Free Press, 1956), 31.

42. "Discerning Dissent," *The Lutheran* (July 2006), 58.

43. Wayne Saffen, "Religious Argument," in *The Third Season: Pentecost* (Philadelphia: Fortress Press, 1974), 57-60.

44. Carl Braaten, *Principles of Lutheran Theology* (Philadelphia: Fortress Press, 1983), 29.

45. Noll, "The Lutheran Difference."

46. Lagerquist, 16-17.

Presbyterian Confessional Identity and its Dilemmas

James H. Moorhead
Princeton Theological Seminary

When the great confessional traditions of western Christianity were born in the wake of the Reformation, they wished to plant Christianity within the entirety of European life. With the partial exception of the Anabaptists, these traditions neither observed nor understood many of the distinctions assumed in the early twenty-first century. They did not make our sharp separations between secular and sacred, public and private, or church and state. They were not, of course, naive. They did not confuse the authorities who controlled the current world and those who had power in the age to come; and they distinguished the civil sword from the ecclesiastical. But they did assume that, despite these important distinctions, there existed a *corpus Christianum*—a single Christendom—which the authorities of both this age and the next served. There was, in short, one comprehensive Christian civilization.[1]

Those who created the various post-Reformation traditions also believed that the success of Christian civilization rested on correct theology. And here was the rub. They could not resolve who held the proper theology. After years of theological and eventually military conflict—in the Thirty Years War on the Continent and later the English Civil War—none of the post-Reformation traditions—Catholic, Reformed, Lutheran, Anabaptist, Anglican, or their minor permutations—commanded assent in all of Europe. The various confessional traditions had to reach some form of accommodation with each other. This adjustment might assume different manifestations: an established church with various forms of tolerated dissent, or in the creation of territorial churches. It might involve the blurring of theological lines in order to maintain greater public consensus and influence; or conversely, it might entail the preservation of the distinctiveness of a confessional traditional by withdrawal from larger public concerns.

Of course, a complete history of the Presbyterian confessional tradition in America cannot be told solely in terms of the dialectic between the maintenance of theological particularity and engagement with the larger culture. But for one short essay, it is perhaps enough to try to sketch a broad overview of ways in which this dialectic—a legacy of post-Reformation Europe as well as a product of "Americanization"—has shaped Presbyterian confessional identity in the United States.

THE MULTIPLE ROOTS OF COLONIAL PRESBYTERIANISM
Presbyterians are usually and rightly seen as products of the magisterial

Reformation—that is, of the branch of the Reformation that relied upon the support of the magistrate or civil authorities and thus took for granted its churches would be established and protected by law. Although remnants of this expectation lingered among Presbyterian immigrants to the New World, many of them had already experienced in the Old World realities preparing them to accept something less. In England, Presbyterians, originally hoping to reconstitute the national church according to their own principles when the Westminster Assembly met in the 1640s to draw up a confession of faith, catechisms, and a directory of worship, failed to achieve this goal when the Civil War temporarily ended the Stuart monarchy and brought Lord Protector Oliver Cromwell to power. With the various groups that supported him too divided on the exact features of a properly reformed national church, Cromwell opted for a policy of considerable toleration of various Protestant factions. Once the Stuart monarchy was restored in 1660, the status of Presbyterians declined further. Various laws severely curtailed their right to worship. Following the so-called Glorious Revolution that brought William and Mary to the throne in 1688, the legal situation of Presbyterians in England improved in that they, along with a number of other bodies, achieved toleration of their activities though not full civil equality.[2]

In Ireland—then part of the English dominions—he Scots Presbyterians who had settled there, especially in the northern areas known today as Ulster, also lived with religious uncertainty. After the Restoration, the officially established Church of Ireland was Anglican in tone and ritual, sometimes willing to tolerate Presbyterian labors and sometimes eager to suppress them. The anomaly of the Presbyterian position was underscored by the fact that their ministers received a royal grant of four hundred (later six hundred) pounds even as the marriages they performed were often regarded as invalid and the offspring of such unions as illegitimate!

Only in Scotland—united through the crown with England but until 1707 having a separate Parliament—did Presbyterians achieve their original goal of creating a reformed national church. Yet even there, the road to that end was tortuous, the process productive of schisms, and the result (to some) far from perfect. After the reformation of John Knox and his associates in 1560, Presbyterianism underwent efforts under the Stuart monarchs to force greater conformity with Anglican practices. Even when William and Mary permitted Presbyterians to reestablish their national church on a more thoroughly Presbyterian basis, there remained practices—such as the traditional right of lay patrons to nominate ministers—that were out of accord with simon-pure Presbyterian theory. Moreover, various divisions kept all Presbyterians from constituting a single national church, though they came closer in Scotland than anywhere else.

In these diverse environments, what would be the distinctive mark of their unity? One obvious answer supplied by the tradition was adherence to the *Westminster Standards*, written by the Westminster Assembly in the 1640s at a time when, the authors hoped, these documents would serve as a guide for a common theology and practice throughout Ireland, England, and Scotland. Once that hope failed, the *Westminster Confession* functioned in somewhat different ways among Presbyterians in diverse places.

In Scotland after the accession of William and Mary permitted a significant "re-Presbyterianizing" of the established church, all clergy were required to declare their adherence to the *Westminster Confession*—an oath made more rigorous in 1711 when candidates for ordination had to aver that they did "sincerely own and believe the whole doctrine of the Confession of Faith . . . to be the truths of God, contained in the Scriptures of the Old and New Testaments." Yet rigorous subscription in theory did not always mean so in fact. For example, when John Simson, a professor of divinity at Glasgow, was charged with holding Socinian and Arian views, he was, though eventually suspended from the ministry, allowed to continue teaching. Similarly, the Presbytery of Auchterarder imposed a series of rigid doctrinal tests to ensure ordinands' absolute conformity to Westminster; but when a candidate appealed a negative decision by the presbytery, the General Assembly sustained his appeal. Sorting out precisely what was happening amidst the fog and furor of these controversies is not always easy; but whatever the accuracy of specific charges or rebuttals, a new theological temper was clearly emerging: a mood in which rigid subscription did not necessarily mean adherence to every particular of Westminster or perhaps even to the underlying assumptions of the confession.[3]

For Presbyterians in Ireland, the theological debates moved into a debate over the more fundamental question: was it proper for a church judicatory to require subscription to *any* creed? Although the Synod of Ulster had mandated subscription to Westminster in 1705, the call of a minister to Belfast in 1720 not only created a brouhaha about his orthodoxy but also sparked a debate in which some clergy argued that church bodies did not have a right to impose adherence to a confession of faith. At first the Synod tried to compromise the issue by passing the so-called Pacific Acts which, while requiring adherence to the Westminster standards, nevertheless allowed that dissent from particular parts of the creed would not necessarily disqualify a minister or ordinand. By 1725, this compromise had failed; and the Synod gathered all the ministers who refused to subscribe into a single presbytery, and the following year, expelled that body from their fellowship.[4]

In the same years, English Presbyterians and Independents (Congregationalists) engaged in a similar controversy over creedal subscription. After Presbyterian churches had expelled ministers allegedly holding heterodox views on the trinity, the two groups met together at Salter's Hall, London, in 1719, to discuss the issues in question. The conference discussed the rights that ministers, congregations, and church judicatories had in such matters, but reached no definitive judgment. While suggesting principles for resolving such questions, the conference rejected creedal subscription. Presbyterians, by one historian's count, said no to creedal subscription by two to one at the Salter's Hall conference.[5]

By the early eighteenth century, then, debates over adherence to Westminster had become common among English-speaking Presbyterians, though the precise approach to the issue varied from place to place. In Scotland where Presbyterians (at least the largest group thereof) constituted an established church, the debate seldom turned on *whether* subscription was advisable but rather on *what* it meant, the rigorists of Auchterarder Presbytery, for example, drawing rather different conclusions than the more moderate majority of the General Assembly. In England, Presbyterians overwhelmingly rejected subscription perhaps because they feared, as only one of several dissenting religious bodies, that required creedal allegiance would be used to press them into conformity. By contrast, the Irish Presbyterians, while dissenters experiencing legal disabilities in some respects like those of their coreligionists in England, nevertheless maintained close ties to Scotland where most of their clergy were trained and by whose religious and cultural currents they continued to be shaped. Here where Presbyterian experience was a curious hybrid of experiences partly like those of the English and partly like those of the Scots, debates over subscription would be especially sharp.

These controversies took place in a new world. Intellectually the Enlightenment was changing the context of creedal subscription. Viewing God in terms of reasonableness, benevolence, and morality, Enlightened thinkers stressed the capacity of humans to understand and obey this rational deity. God, to the extent that He intervened in human affairs at all, coerced no one into belief but sought to persuade people, one by one, of the supreme reasonableness of his rule. In this conception lay a new understanding of the church, perhaps best expressed by John Locke, in *A Letter Concerning Toleration* in 1689. "A church then, I take to be a voluntary society of men joining themselves together of their own accord, in order to the public worshipping of God, in such a manner as they judge acceptable to him, and effectual to the salvation of their souls." The understanding of the church was one, as Peter Brooke suggests in his history of Ulster Presbyterianism, in which "the Kingdom of Christ was not a corporate body with an authority derived from Christ, but the kingdom of the individual conscience. Each man was individually accountable to Christ for his own spiritual life." While this argument could readily be—and often was—used as an argument against subscription to Westminster, some turned it into a case for the legitimacy of subscription. Brooke notes, for example, that one person in favor of mandating adherence to Westminster argued that this requirement violated no one's rights since a person was free to leave the Synod and join another religious body.[6]

The assumption that there were multiple religious societies which one could legitimately join was itself a product of a monumental social and religious change. The fracturing of western Christendom into various camps, especially in areas (such as the United Kingdom) where a single church did not even command full territorial hegemony, altered the meaning of confessional traditions. Thus adherence to the *Westminster Confession of Faith* would not entail, as its authors originally intended, the establishment of a common order and polity uniting all of those who took the name of Christ in England, Ireland, or Scotland. To subscribe to the *Confession* would now be to demarcate oneself from others who called themselves Christians in some other fashion. Yet there remained within the confessional tradition aspirations to influence society at large. In a sense, much of the story of Presbyterian confessionalism in America would be a narrative of the ways in which its adherents tried to navigate between the wish to maintain the particularity of their creed, liturgy, and polity and their wish to be at the center of their society as its shapers and representatives.

THE BIRTH OF THE AMERICAN PRESBYTERIAN CONFESSIONAL TRADITION

All of the Presbyterian groups from the United Kingdom—and the Congregationalists to whom they were closely related theologically—helped to shape American Presbyterianism. When the main body of the Puritan migration from England landed in the Massachusetts Bay area in the 1630s, most of these immigrants were Independents or Congregationalists, but a few had Presbyterian sympathies—a fact that became more apparent when some New Englanders moved to Long Island where they founded Presbyterian churches. Others came from Scotland and settled in colonies such as New Jersey and North Carolina. By most accounts, however, the largest single group to affiliate with colonial Presbyterianism were the Ulster Scots, most of whom landed in Philadelphia during the 1720s and later, moving from there into the hinterlands of Pennsylvania and then down the Great Valley (the Shenandoah) into Virginia and beyond.[7]

The Presbyterians who migrated to North America came from contexts which, despite their faith's origins in the magisterial Reformation, did not give them a uniform anticipation that their churches would enjoy the favors of the state. The places they settled on the western shores of the Atlantic further diminished expectations that they would enjoy legal privileges. The early Presbyterian settlements on Long Island, in New Jersey, Maryland, Delaware, or Pennsylvania were in places without establishments of religion. For reasons of either pragmatism or principle, these middle colonies had eschewed the notion of established churches, and these areas enjoyed probably the highest degree of religious pluralism of any section of Britain's American dominions. Thus Presbyterians from the various parts of the United Kingdom settled in precisely those places which were most likely to reinforce the aspects of their experience inclining them to see themselves as but one body of Christians among others and to expect no special favors from the state.[8]

The diverse elements of Presbyterianism were cobbled together in a haphazard fashion. Churches calling themselves Presbyterian existed at least from the late 1600s, but the first presbytery—the Presbytery of Philadelphia—was not formed until 1706, and this body was not organized into a Synod and subdivided into additional presbyteries until ten years later. Neither of these bodies had a formal constitution or confession of faith.

In the 1720s, at about the same time as the similar discussions in the

United Kingdom, the Synod considered the possibility of requiring its ministers to indicate their assent to the *Westminster Confession*. Those who called for creedal subscription saw it as a necessary guard against the infiltration into the church of some of the errors arising out of the Enlightenment. John Thomson, pastor in Lewes, Delaware, asked: "Now a church without a confession, what is it like?" He replied that such a church was "in a very defenseless condition, as a city without walls" because it had "no bar provided to keep out of the ministry those who are corrupt in doctrinals." As it had in Ireland and England, the call for subscription produced opposition. Jonathan Dickinson, the New England born pastor of the Presbyterian Church in Elizabethtown, New Jersey, preached to the 1722 synod on "the true boundaries of the church's power." He rejected confessional subscription on the grounds that the church could not go beyond Scripture in determining rules for doctrine or discipline; to do so would be "a bold invasion of Christ's royal power."[9]

In 1729, the Synod of Philadelphia sent Thomson's proposal for subscription to committee. The committee was a balanced one including both Thomson and Dickinson and others of their respective persuasions, and it produced what most historians have considered a balanced—and ambiguous—report that the Synod enacted. Subsequently known as the Adopting Act, the legislation required all ministers to subscribe to the *Westminster Confession of Faith*, but concessions were made to those who had opposed this policy. On the one hand, its preamble echoed the anti-subscriptionists who exalted individual conscience over churchly authority, but on the other, the act said that church courts did have the responsibility to defend "the faith once delivered to the saints." In fact, the document can be interpreted as a compromise between the two viewpoints that Peter Brooke sees at war in Ulster Presbyterianism in the same era: "the Kingdom of Christ . . . as a corporate body with an authority derived from Christ" versus the notion of "the kingdom of the individual conscience." The careful balancing was also apparent in the kind of subscription that the synod mandated. Ordinands and ministers did not need to affirm every jot and tittle of Westminster, only its "essential and necessary articles." But what were the articles so basic and essential that everyone had to give assent? The Adopting Act did not say. The determination of the matter was left for church courts to decide on a case by case basis. By drawing boundaries of uncertain scope and by allowing latitude in their interpretation, the synod's action resembled the Pacific Acts passed by Irish Presbyterians.[10]

Significantly, when the members of the Synod reconvened, in the afternoon following the passage of the Adopting Act, in order to make their own subscription and to record any reservations they might have, the one part of Westminster to which they indicated exception were clauses relative to the power of the civil magistrate in matters religious: the Synod "do not receive those articles in any such sense as to suppose the civil magistrate hath a controlling power over synods with respect to the exercise of their ministerial authority; or power to persecute any for their religion."[11]

The Synod's action can be understood as manifesting both continuity with the Presbyterian past and the novelties of a new world. On the one hand, the arguments and solutions hammered out in 1729 bore the marks of the debates that had already taken place within the United Kingdom. But unlike the British Isles where confessional subscription either identified Presbyterians as an established church or, alternately, marked off Presbyterians as dissenters, adherence to Westminster had a different meaning in Pennsylvania, Maryland, and Delaware where there was no establishment and where the various churches coexisted on a fairly equal basis. Here confessional subscription was a way by which Presbyterians maintained their distinctiveness in a pluralistic environment. If Patrick Griffin is correct, the push for confessional consolidation also derived from very practical questions of identity and order. Subscription "arose," Griffin avers, "in response to the plight of frontier settlers reeling from poverty, drunkenness, and violence, searching for stability." To maintain the integrity of its own identity in this chaotic world, the Synod was adopting, at least in part, an enclave mentality; and it was deemphasizing its role in shaping the whole of society—witness the concessions on the role of magistrate. Yet the transformation was far from complete, for Presbyterians had scarcely chosen to inhabit a sectarian close. The exact boundaries of confessional identity had been left vague to allow different points of view to cohere—after all, what were those "essential and necessary articles"?[12]

Scarcely had the church found resolution (or at least temporary compromise) of the subscription question when it was plunged into the Great Awakening. Presbyterians had been experiencing a movement stressing experiential piety and spiritual rebirth for some years before the visit of the young Anglican preacher George Whitefield to the colonies in 1739-41 served as a catalyst for a more general revival. At the center of the renewal movement within Presbyterianism was William Tennent, Sr., and his sons, especially Gilbert Tennent. The elder Tennent founded a school near Neshaminy, Pennsylvania, for the training of ministers—it was derisively dubbed the "log college" by opponents. Through his pupils, Tennent encouraged a style of preaching that would expose the self-righteousness of the unconverted, enable them to see their dire sinful condition, and thus be led to a true piety based on spiritual rebirth.[13]

The revival had a mixed impact on the confessional identity of Presbyterians. There was no repudiation of Westminster's doctrines, and the deeply experiential revivalism of the era continued a tradition of awakening, usually in conjunction with the observance of the Lord's Supper, that stretched back more than a century to Scottish and Ulster roots. Yet on balance, the Great Awakening probably did begin a process of moving American Presbyterians toward a Pietist instrumentalism that valued the regular preaching, ordinances, and polity of the church only to the extent that these promoted the individual soul's encounter with God. The controversies set loose within Presbyterianism by the revival—controversies which split Presbyterians between 1741 and 1758—may also have brought the tradition into disrespect. "The internecine spectacle that ensued," Patricia Bonomi has observed, "the loss of proportion and professional decorum, contributed to the demystification of the clergy, forced parishioners to choose between competing factions, and overset traditional attitudes about deference and leadership in colonial America."[14]

Shortly after the reunion of the church in 1758, Presbyterians perforce gave more thought to their public role as the revolutionary crisis deepened. Despite the fact that many Presbyterians played important roles on behalf of the struggle for independence (and despite a subsequent patriotic hagiography that has wished to magnify this role), there were pockets of those remaining loyal to the crown just as there were many who were eager to avoid taking sides. Yet on balance, Presbyterians appear to have been more supportive of the revolution than not, and once it was successfully accomplished, the denomination had to consider what its confessional identity and mission would be in a republican society increasingly dominated by the ideals of the Enlightenment.

The denomination gave an instructive hint when it drew up plans to reorganize itself under a General Assembly that met in the first year (1789) the new federal constitution was in effect. The introduction to the new plan of government declared: "Every Christian Church . . . is free to declare the terms of admission to its body, and to declare what it thinks are the rules laid down by Christ for his Church. If in doing this it makes the laws too lax or too narrow, it wounds, not outsiders, but only itself." The Presbyterian Church in the USA included among those rules the requirement that clergy avow their acceptance of the scriptures as "the only infallible rule of faith and practice" and adoption of "the confession of faith of this church [the *Westminster Confession*], as containing the system of doctrine taught in the holy Scripture." There was no mention of those elusive and heretofore undefined "essential and necessary articles," though arguably the phrase "system of doctrine" might be understood as conferring a measure of liberty in subscription. Moreover, the church now revised the *Westminster Confession* by removing passages suggesting that the magistrate might rightly suppress blasphemy or heresy and make sure that worship was kept pure. In this fashion, the denomination *seemed* to opt to keep confessional purity by reducing itself to one voluntary society among others in a free society while leaving the public realm free of the church. That conclusion, however, would be premature, for the revised *Confession* also contained the statement: "Yet, as nursing fathers, it is the duty of the civil magistrates to protect the church our common Lord, without giving the preference to any denomination of Christians above the rest." "Implicit in this thinking," Fred J. Hood has observed, "was that in some way Protestant Christianity, as distinguished from any single denominational expression of that religion, was to be the established religion of America." Presbyterians, while determined to maintain their own confessional identity, had not given up the remnants of the notion that they might be part of a broader Christian coalition shaping society into a *corpus Christianum*.[15]

As Presbyterians were beginning to rethink their identity in a changing culture, a major event transpired in the arrival of John Witherspoon from Scotland in 1768 to assume the presidency of the College of New Jersey (later

Princeton University). Witherspoon's tenure was significant not only because of his important political and ecclesiastical involvement—he was the only clergyman to sign the Declaration of Independence and the first moderator of the Presbyterian General Assembly—but also because he helped set in motion some of the key intellectual trends by which the church would think through its identity in the decades to come. Witherspoon, while rather traditional in his theological commitments, espoused major tenets of the Scottish moral philosophy. By the early nineteenth century, in part because of Witherspoon's instrumentality, the Scottish philosophy had become virtually ubiquitous through higher education in the United States. As employed by most American thinkers, it created an intellectual platform on which Christian orthodoxy, commitment to republican culture and polity, and a confidence in the commonsense moral and rational intuitions of humanity were presumed to unite. Events would soon put that judgment to the test.[16]

THE TRIALS OF PRESBYTERIAN CONFESSIONAL IDENTITY IN THE YOUNG REPUBLIC, 1790-1865

In the early nineteenth century, Presbyterians made major efforts to extend their ministry and influence in the young nation. In the Plan of Union (1801), Presbyterians and Congregationalist permitted congregations composed of members of one denomination to call a minister of the other and also allowed the formation of union churches composed of people of both denominations. By 1808, Presbyterians allowed Congregationalist churches and associations to become part of the Presbyterian Church while keeping many of their own distinctive practices. In New York state and in the Western Reserve in Ohio, substantial numbers of originally non-Presbyterian congregations were brought into the denomination. Although this practice might dilute Presbyterian identity, it drew little opposition at the time, for the two denominations seemed relatively close in theology, and the policy strengthened Presbyterianism numerically.[17]

Presbyterians also tried to shape the nation through participation in voluntary societies. In the first quarter of the nineteenth century, Protestants concerned about the promotion of specific causes—for example, foreign and home missionary work or the distribution of Christian literature—created voluntary benevolent societies. Non-denominational in character and outside formal ecclesiastical structure, these organizations were controlled by boards composed of individuals (often lay people) who represented only themselves, not their churches. The voluntary societies thus embodied a task-oriented ecumenism that brought Protestant Christians together in an *ad hoc* fashion. Although these organizations were formed locally as well as nationally, it was at the national level that they gained great notoriety. A group of organizations, often with interlocking directorates, became known collectively as the evangelical united front or as the benevolent empire. To name only a few, these institutions included the American Board of Commissioners for Foreign Missions (1810), the American Bible Society (1816), and the American Home Missionary Society (1826).[18]

Although the benevolent empire had a broader constituency than the Presbyterians and Congregationalists, these two denominations provided the vast
majority of the leaders and workers for the voluntary societies. Fred J. Hood has
argued that the voluntary societies were intended "as intermediate institutions
between the denominations and the civil government." That is, the founders of
the societies saw them as the means by which, in a society rapidly disestablish-
ing its churches—the last such establishment in Massachusetts was ended in
1833—Christians could continue to sway public opinion and mores and maintain *de facto* Protestant hegemony. Presbyterian Robert Baird, writing at mid-
century, gave expression to this hope. After describing a number of the efforts
of the benevolent societies, particularly of the Bible Society, he observed:

> The impression prevails among our statesmen that the Bible is emphatically
> the foundation of our hopes as a people. Nothing but the Bible can make men
> the willing subjects of law; they must first acquiesce with submission in the
> government of God before they can yield a willing obedience to the require-
> ments of human governments, however just these may be. It is the religion of
> the Bible only that can render the population of any country honest, industri-
> ous, peaceable, quiet, contented, happy.

In short, the *corpus Christianum* lived in the new republic, and the voluntary
societies were an important means whereby that reality would be perpetuated.[19]

So, too, were the religious revivals, often collectively called the Second
Great Awakening, which swept many parts of the nation from the 1790s
through the 1830s. These revivals included many different manifestations. For
example, they encompassed people in Connecticut Congregational churches
who were experiencing spiritual renewal in their week to week Sunday worship
amidst "stillness, silent weeping, and melancholy"; but the revivals also included frontier camp meetings, such as the famous gathering at Cane Ridge,
Kentucky, in 1801, where men and women shrieked, rolled on the ground, or
fainted as they were "slain in the spirit." Timothy Dwight, president of Yale
College, preaching for spiritual awakening in college chapel during the 1790s
was an instrument of awakening; yet, so also were the numerous Methodist
class meetings in whose small groups believers gathered weekly to share their
spiritual experiences. Depending upon the interpreter to whom one turns, the
Second Great Awakening fulfilled extraordinarily varied social functions: it
was a means by which defenders of the culturally established denominations
(Congregationalists and Presbyterians) tried to exert social control, it was an
organizing process by all sorts of religious bodies revitalizing and extending
themselves, it was an instance of Christianity turning populist. Possibly it was
the means whereby a new middle class inculcated in working people the habits
of time, thrift and self-discipline appropriate to the new market economy; or
perchance the revival offered those same workmen the tools for resisting the
emerging capitalist order. The fact that a plausible case can be made for each of

these interpretations suggests that revivalism was contested terrain, that it was performing multiple functions for different groups. Yet on balance, revivalism was probably a force more innovative than traditional. To change the metaphor, conservatives might try to ride the animal, but it remained a balky creature not easily tamed.[20]

The career of sometime Presbyterian (and later Congregational) evangelist Charles G. Finney illustrates the point. Trained to be a lawyer, this upstate New Yorker experienced a conversion experience, read divinity with his pastor, and then was ordained an evangelist in 1824. After winning his credentials as a successful promoter of revivals in his home region, he went on to conduct similarly successful awakenings in major cities of the east coast, including New York City. He eventually became a professor of theology at Oberlin College, though he continued for the rest of his career to divide his time between the campus and evangelistic tours. Characteristic of his preaching was a willingness to innovate and be pragmatic: for example, he readily imported into Presbyterian churches so-called "new measures," such as the anxious bench, pioneered by Methodists. For Finney, the key issue was always whether a practice or a doctrine worked: did it bring about the conversion of sinners and lead them to subsequent sanctification? In him the instrumental character of revivalism reached its zenith. Tradition, liturgy, doctrinal formulations, catechesis—all were expendable unless they enabled Christians to bring others to Christ and promoted holy living. Despite the fact that elements of his piety and thought continued to give evidence of his Presbyterian background, Finney not only jettisoned much of the *Westminster Confession of Faith* but also became virtually Arminian in his theology and eventually argued for the possibility of complete sanctification in this life.[21]

While Finney was by no means typical of all Presbyterian supporters of revival, he did illustrate its cutting edge and the reason that many who would preserve the Presbyterian tradition became uneasy with the movement. Theologically, very few marched to his nearly Arminian and sanctificationist theology, but there were voices, especially in New England, which seemed to be re-working Reformed theology in ways that appeared to conservatives subversive of the Westminster theology. For example, since the late 1700s the New Divinity disciples of Jonathan Edwards had re-conceptualized the atonement in governmental terms rather than penal substitution, had emphasized the natural (as opposed to moral) power of humans to avoid sin, and rejected the imputation of Adam's sin to his posterity. By the early nineteenth century, Nathaniel William Taylor of Yale appeared to be enlarging human agency even further. Through the Plan of Union with the New England Congregationalists, these ideas, conservatives feared, were gaining access to Presbyterian pulpits. Thus people like Finney seemed to a growing Old School, or conservative party, to represent the dangerous trajectory along which theological changes were moving.[22]

Yet even so, Nathan Hatch has observed, the theological differences might not have led to schism had not "bold and daring innovations set the Old School

proponents on edge. They saw dubious theology wedded to inflammatory practice." They feared the "new measures" in revivalism, the so-called "promiscu-
ous meetings" in which women were allegedly permitted if not encouraged to
speak, and the failure of many Plan of Union churches to observe proper denominational procedure. The Old School increasingly distrusted the voluntary
societies, which they themselves had once supported, for usurping dangerous
powers over the church. Innovations that had once seemed to be means of extending Presbyterian influence—revivals, benevolent societies, and the Plan of
Union—now appeared to threaten the very integrity and identity of Presbyterianism. A concerted effort by Old Schoolers secured them a majority in the
General Assembly of 1837—a majority they used to expel the so-called New
School portions of the denomination which they saw tainted with "the restless
spirit of radicalism." To restore what they perceived as the purity of the Presbyterian confessional tradition, the Old School was prepared to turn aside to some
degree from the public arena and to settle for a smaller domain but one with
more secure boundaries. In so doing, they were falling in with a larger religious
trend of "resurgent churchly traditions" typified by "high church" Episcopalians stressing the distinctiveness of the Episcopal tradition, Lutherans of the ilk
of C. F. W. Walther similarly emphasizing the *Book of Concord*, and even Old
Landmark Baptists claiming that their movement alone stood in continuity with
the apostolic Church. As James D. Bratt has recently observed, "new voices" in
the 1830s and '40s were offering people "communities of belonging where they
could rest assured. These bodies needed to be marked by clear boundaries. . . .
If the world would not roll on swiftly to the millennium some sanctuary within
it might be found." In the decades after their expulsion, even the New School
Presbyterians found themselves placing renewed emphasis upon their Presbyterian identity.[23]

Yet the world refused to leave Presbyterian confessionalism alone. Conflicts over slavery—and ultimately a civil war—invaded the Presbyterian enclave. Before the issue had become exceedingly controversial, the General Assembly declared in 1818 that the peculiar institution was "totally irreconcilable
with the spirit and principles of the Gospel of Christ." Subsequently the Assembly tried to avoid the question of human bondage, especially after 1833 with
the emergence of the more radical forms of antislavery thought generally
known as abolitionism. Both New School and Old School Presbyterianism contained abolitionist elements, but these were more numerous in the New School
denomination which was *slightly* more inclined to speak against slavery. After
the 1837 rupture, the Old School, containing both northern and southern members, placed a virtual embargo on the subject. "The church of Christ is a spiritual body," declared the 1845 Assembly, "whose jurisdiction extends only to the
religious faith, and moral conduct of her members. She cannot legislate where
Christ has not legislated." Since Christ had not declared slavery to be sinful,
neither could the church. In the Southern portion of the Old School, the notion
of the so-called "spirituality of the church" became especially marked through
the influence of theologian James H. Thornwell who argued, at least on occa-

sion, that the church's disengagement from non-religious concerns should be so total that the church *qua* church should not even endorse humanitarian organizations. Some have argued that the southern church's view of the spirituality of the church was never as thoroughgoing as the southern tradition has traditionally claimed, at least not until the failure of the Confederacy and the onslaught of Reconstruction made the doctrine a useful club to beat interfering Yankee churchmen. In any event, it is clear that the doctrine was ignored when it was convenient to do so. For example, the prominent Old School New Orleans Presbyterian minister, Benjamin M. Palmer, urged in November, 1860, as secession loomed, that his fellow Southerners should "ascertain the nature of the trust providentially committed to us." What was that trust? "I answer, that it is *to conserve and to perpetuate the institution of domestic slavery as now existing.*" By contrast, the Northern Old School Assembly in 1864—the Old School denomination had split along sectional lines at the outset of the war—told its congregations:

> The recent events of our history, and the present condition of our Church and country, furnish manifold tokens that the time has at length come, in the providence of God, when it is His will that every vestige of human slavery should be effaced, and that every Christian man should address himself with industry and earnestness to his appropriate part in the performance of this great duty.[24]

Differing patriotisms had proven thicker than shared theology. For a body that had previously claimed that it could speak on public issues only on the basis of specific scriptural warrant, the Northern Old School's assembly's appeal in 1864 to "events of our history" as the grounds for the duty of "every Christian man" seeking to help end the peculiar institution seemed a shockingly thin argument. It even verged on outright political partisanship, for in the Northern presidential election campaign then taking shape it was clear that Republicans would be going to the country on a platform calling for the end of slavery, the Democrats on one which either opposed outright or evaded such a stance. Yet it was even more shocking that the Southern Old School, having taken a stronger stance on the "spirituality of the church" than its northern counterpart, could be so confident that providence had given the Confederacy the task "to perpetuate the institution of domestic slavery as now existing." Of course, historical interpreters who dismiss religious commitments as mere froth on the waters of politics, economics, or other "secular" matters will be inclined to smile knowingly, "What else would you expect?" Maybe they are right. Yet at another level there was perhaps a consistency—even a theological harmony—for the respective positions that southern and northern Old Schoolers had taken. For Presbyterians, confessional identity had always been about at least two things: the maintenance of correct doctrine *and* the church engaged in a meaningful way with its larger culture. Presbyterians were certainly doing the latter; the tragedy was that Christian orthodoxy, commitment to republican culture and polity, and a confidence in the commonsense moral and rational intuitions had given the Christians of North and South two different visions of what that meant.

NEW ISSUES OF CONFESSIONAL IDENTITY AND ITS
DECENTRALIZATION, 1865-1925

By the close of the Civil War, the major bodies of Presbyterians, North and South, had achieved unity within their respective regions. The handful of New Schoolers who resided in the South, having broken with their northern counterparts in 1857, united with the southern Old School in 1862. Similarly, the Old and New Schools in the North achieved reunion by overwhelming margins in 1869-70. While this merger was partly due to a relaxation of theological animosities and a discovery that the two sides did share much common doctrinal ground, there is no doubt that the sense of having participated in a common enterprise to preserve the Union played no small part in the two groups' *rapprochement*. Since the issues faced by the reunited northern church were more dramatic and to some extent prefigured the same path that the South would follow, albeit more slowly and with less open conflict, the remainder of the essay will concentrate on the reunited northern church.[25]

In the 1870s and later, a new set of disputes emerged among Presbyterians about the meaning of their confession and subscription to it. In at least two respects, however, these controversies differed in nature from the preceding ones. First, older conflicts often turned on matters, the settlement of which tended frequently to mark off differences between the Reformed or Presbyterian views from other confessional traditions. However, the new controversies concerned matters that challenged beliefs in many different traditions simultaneously. The so-called higher biblical criticism increasingly won a hearing among Americans after the 1880s, and with it came a host of questions about the nature and extent of the Bible's authority. A more self-consciously liberal theology drawn from the inspiration of European figures such as Kant, Schleiermacher, and Ritschl, as well as home-grown thinkers such as Horace Bushnell, began to emphasize the possibility of growth or change in theology, often gave priority to religious experience in the determination of doctrine, implied that the essence of true faith was a life lived in a vital relationship with God and not a set of propositions about God. This modernism touted the virtue of self-conscious adaptation of the faith to the spirit of the age, whether measured by humanity's allegedly improving consciousness or advances in the sciences; liberals also tended either to play down the supernatural elements of Christianity or to collapse transcendence into immanence. In such ways, they understood themselves to be making the essence of the Gospel understandable for their age. Their opponents, of course, saw matters differently; and often turned to the *Westminster Confession* as a way of refuting these liberal beliefs.[26]

At the same time, there was a widespread dissatisfaction with elements of the *Westminster Confession*, often among people who otherwise had little sympathy with liberal or modernist beliefs. For example, in 1889 after receiving a number of requests to consider the possibility of revising the *Westminster Confession*, the General Assembly polled the presbyteries, more than sixty per cent of which favored some change. The presbyteries—as well as the theological newspapers and journals discussing the question—most frequently cited several areas where they wished to see revision: Many were discomfited by Westminster's section "Of God's Eternal Decree" and, balking at the notion of reprobation, wished a section affirming God's love for all humanity. Likewise, in an era in which zeal for foreign missions was booming, many felt the absence of a statement on the need to evangelize the world was glaring. So, too, many found troubling implications in the chapter "Of Effectual Calling" which included the declaration: "Elect infants, dying in infancy, are regenerated and saved by Christ through the Spirit." Some found here an implication that not every infant might be among the elect, and they deemed even the hint of damned infants morally insupportable. Yet the two-thirds majority needed for approval of revisions was not attained in 1892-93 when possible revisions were sent to the presbyteries.[27]

One of the likely reasons for failure was that the Church was simultaneously embroiled in a heresy trial. In 1891, Professor Charles A. Briggs delivered an inaugural address, entitled "The Authority of Holy Scripture," upon his transfer to a new chair at Union Seminary (NYC) where he had already been teaching for some years. The address vigorously advocated the critical study of Scripture and, in passing, dismissed the notion of biblical inerrancy. In the ensuing controversy, the General Assembly vetoed Briggs' election to the new professorship, Union Seminary renounced its affiliation with the Presbyterian Church, and Briggs was eventually ousted from the Presbyterian ministry. This case, coupled with a similar trial of Henry P. Smith of Lane Seminary (Cincinnati) and a later one of Professor Arthur C. McGiffert, created an atmosphere in which some feared that any revision of Westminster would open the floodgates to theological error.

In response to these cases, several General Assemblies chose to define "essential and necessary articles" of Westminster. In 1892, the Assembly declared biblical inerrancy to be an "essential and necessary article." In 1910, it added—and in two subsequent assemblies reaffirmed—this and other doctrines that it considered essential to the system of doctrine in the *Confession of Faith*: the virgin birth of Jesus, the substitutionary atonement, the bodily resurrection of Christ, and the fact that Jesus worked miracles. In this way, the Assembly was attempting to build a bulwark against the intrusion of certain forms of modernism into its seminaries and pulpits.[28]

Yet even as it used the *Confession* to restrict the influx of liberalism, the denomination also signaled its discomfort with Westminster. For example, revision of the *Confession* was finally achieved in 1903, with the addition of two new chapters—"Of the Holy Spirit" and "Of the Gospel of the Love of God and Missions"—as well as a concluding declaratory statement. The effect of these was to emphasize the importance of missions, to assert that nothing in the *Con-*

fession should obscure the fact that God loves all humanity, and that all who die in infancy are indeed saved. There was some disagreement as to whether the teaching of the *Confession* had been significantly altered by the changes, but few would have disputed the observation of a secular newspaper, the Philadelphia *Public Ledger*, that without disavowing the *Confession*, the additions were able "to render it [the Confession] instantly so much more congenial to the modern mind."[29]

Yet controversy was not over. In the wake of World War I and in the context of what George Marsden has shown to be a sense of cultural crisis, some conservatives in the so-called "Fundamentalist-Modernist controversy" renewed the struggle to force liberals from the Church. Although he was not their chief tactician, J. Gresham Machen, then an assistant professor at Princeton Seminary, was clearly the intellectual leader of this group. Contending in *Christianity and Liberalism* (1923) that Modernism or Liberalism was an entirely different faith than historic Christianity, Machen insisted that liberals should, in intellectual honesty, withdraw from the Presbyterian Church or, failing that outcome, be extruded. For a time it appeared that liberals might indeed be ousted; but events in 1925 changed the dynamics within the denomination. In that year the General Assembly elected Machen's Princeton colleague, Charles R. Erdman, as moderator. Although he was deeply conservative theologically, he believed that there was room for greater breadth of views within the denomination than did Machen. Erdman persuaded the Assembly to authorize the appointment of a special commission to examine the causes of unrest in the church. The commission's report, adopted by the assemblies of 1926 and 1927, proposed a means for composing the differences. Rejecting the claim that there was widespread departure from the historic faith of the denomination, the commission argued, in effect, that the efforts of previous assemblies to define *a priori* essential articles of the *Confession* were unconstitutional. The constitution lodged the right of determining what was an essential or necessary article in each presbytery as it, on a case by case basis, examined ordinands or received ministers. While the General Assembly had power on an appellate basis to review these decisions, it had no constitutional authority to issue general or blanket statements about what was or was not essential in the *Confession*. In effect, as Lefferts Loetscher argued, the commission proposed theological decentralization as the solution to the controversy, and the denomination largely accepted this solution. Henceforth, at least moderate liberalism would be secure within the Presbyterian Church. As for the conservatives, most of them stayed within the denomination, although Machen and something under one per cent of the denomination, after a struggle over an independent board of missions, withdrew in 1936 to form the Orthodox Presbyterian Church.[30]

Motivating the commission decision was something more than a narrow reading of the church's constitution. In the final paragraphs of its report to the assembly, the special commission pointed to the fact that the denomination had to find unity because of its great task to shape or influence the world beyond its borders:

If Christianity is not true it should be abandoned. But if it is true, as we know it to be true, without which the world cannot live, then this truth must be carried into every field of human life, into all types of human relationships for the righting of wrong and the achievement of good through the Kingdom of God. . . . Never was there a clearer or more commanding call that the Church advance in her organized corporate work at home and on foreign fields. . . . God has given our Church all the equipment she requires for the fulfillment of her task with respect to that purpose. Now let her rise and go forward.

Once again Presbyterians had affirmed a confessional identity that included devotion both to a particular set of beliefs and practices (not fully defined) and also to a mission shaping the wider society of which they were a part. Perhaps, then, it was not coincidental that in the same decade that it endorsed greater theological breadth, the Assembly undertook a major reorganization of its agencies in the name of a more effective ministry to the nation and world.[31]

THE REDEFINITION, THE RECOVERY, OR THE SCATTERING OF CONFESSIONAL IDENTITY, 1925-1967?

Yet precisely where did these decisions leave Presbyterian confessional identity? Loetscher, writing in 1954 and grateful for the lack of theological controversy that the church had experienced in the wake of the decisions of the 1920s, nevertheless worried that "memories and scars of the fundamentalist-modernist controversy still largely inhibit among Presbyterians the frank and realistic discussion of theological questions which the times and the present opportunity call for. 'The less theology the better' seems to be the lurking implication." The fact that decisions about the theology of ordinands and ministers had been left largely to the presbyteries to make—or not—as they saw fit raised questions about the extent to which the denomination's confessional tradition determined its current identity. Moreover, the way in which both so-called liberals and conservatives had used the Westminster standards during the conflict that culminated in the 1920s raised troublesome questions as to whether these documents were actually guides to their living faith, or simply a useful armory from which to draw at random weapons to use against opponents. Thus, for example, liberals might readily seize Westminster's assertion that God alone is Lord of the conscience or conservatives the declaration about the Bible as infallible rule of faith and practice and yet never really grapple with the larger theological assumptions or worldview out of which the entire document came.[32]

But even as the fires of the Fundamentalist-Modernist controversy were waning, a new theological perspective was making itself felt among Presbyterians. That theology usually called in America neo-orthodoxy exerted a powerful influence upon American seminaries in the 1930s. It was associated with such figures as Karl Barth and Emil Brunner in Europe and Reinhold and

H. Richard Niebuhr in America. Despite very major differences among the people denominated by this label, the movement shared a common mood of disenchantment with nineteenth-century liberal theology. It stressed classic Protestant themes such as the centrality of the Bible as the instrument of God's revelation, but it did so while rejecting fundamentalist notions of inerrancy. Neo-orthodoxy often emphasized other traditional themes such as the sinfulness of humanity, the transcendence of God, and Christ as the savior not merely the moral example of humanity. Yet unlike many fundamentalists, neo-orthodoxy's understanding of God's revelation was dynamic. To know God was not to affirm changeless propositions; it was to respond in trust to the encounter with the living God in Jesus Christ.[33]

This theological renaissance—manifested in the work of Presbyterian biblical scholars such as G. Ernest Wright, Floyd V. Filson, Otto Piper, and James Smart, and also popularized in the Faith and Life Curriculum for Sunday Schools—was translated into a major creedal change for Presbyterians. When the Presbyterian Church in the U. S. A. and the United Presbyterian Church of North America merged in 1958, the first General Assembly of the new denomination charged a committee with the task of preparing a "brief contemporary statement of faith"; but a year later the committee, chaired by Edward A. Dowey, requested and received a mandate to make a broader review of the Reformed confessional heritage. In 1965 the group proposed a *Book of Confessions*; and two years later, after some changes, it was officially adopted by the denomination. In the Book were included not only a contemporary statement (the *Confession of 1967*, popularly called *C 67*), but also documents from various periods of church history.[34]

The argument for a compendium of Reformed confessions as well as a contemporary statement of faith was summarized by Dowey. "The *Westminster Confession*, standing alone, is not modern enough to guide the present, nor is it ancient enough to represent the past." What was needed was a confessional basis that was simultaneously more representative of the basis and more specifically attuned to contemporary issues. The act of constructing a book of confessional documents in this fashion served to remind Presbyterians that confession did not primarily mean the affirmation of timeless propositions: it was the dynamic act, as the *Confession of 1967* said, of "bearing a present witness to God's grace in Jesus Christ."[35]

Throughout the document the emphases of the theological renaissance of the preceding thirty years resonated: the priority of God's activity in redemption, a recognition of human sinfulness, the Christocentric focus of revelation. Yet even as *C 67* turned away from nineteenth-century modernism, it gave little comfort to Fundamentalism. For example, although a phrase calling the Bible the "word of God written" was added largely to please conservatives, the overall thrust of the discussion of Scripture clearly pointed away from theories of inerrancy or infallibility. (In fact, *word* in the phrase "word of God written" was deliberately rendered in the lower case to make clear that Scripture's authority came solely from the fact that it witnessed to the "one sufficient revelation of God . . . Jesus Christ, the Word of God." Moreover, for the first time, a Presbyterian confessional document explicitly endorsed modern biblical scholarship.[36]

Making God's reconciling work in Christ its central theme, the confession called upon the church to join in that work. "To be reconciled to God is to be sent into the world as his reconciling community." The statement then cited specific issues in the contemporary world where the Christian community needed to witness to God's new creation: (1) racial and ethnic discrimination, (2) the dangers of nationalism in the achievement of peace, justice, and freedom, (3) the prevalence of "enslaving poverty" throughout the world, and (4) "anarchy in sexual relationships." Equally important was the tone of the statements which implied a commitment to prophetic judgment of existing inequities within society and which appeared to cast the church in the role of social critic. That prophetic stance was epitomized in a much debated passage in which the *Confession* asserted that the search for peace, justice, and freedom would require "fresh and responsible relations across every line of conflict, even at risk to national security." Moreover, the *Confession* warned that "the church which identifies the sovereignty of any one nation or any one way of life with the cause of God denies the Lordship of Christ and betrays its calling."[37]

EPILOGUE

The adoption of the *C 67* marked both continuity and novelty in the history of Presbyterian confessionalism. By emphasizing worldly issues, the document continued the long tradition that confessing the faith was not merely the creation of an enclave of right thinking believers but also an attempt to shape the whole of society in accord with the will of God. Yet far more than earlier confessional documents, the *Confession* dealt with social issues explicitly and sought to ground those concerns theologically. By including this statement in a *Book of Confessions*, the denomination also attempted to make its creedal foundation more nearly representative of the breadth of the Reformed tradition. The drafters of the *Confession of 1967* hoped, in the words of one of their number, that the document "recaptured and intensified" the dynamic Christocentric understanding of faith held by Luther and Calvin—an understanding subsequently overlaid with emphasis upon biblical inerrancy and upon rational assent to intricate systems of doctrine. But the document represented a break with a more recent tradition. Its authors were self-consciously rejecting as inadequate for the current age not only the *Westminster Confession* but also the interpretations placed upon that document by conservative Presbyterians in the nineteenth and early twentieth centuries.[38]

Although the church's new confessional basis was broader and theoretically less restrictive than Westminster, that fact may actually have worked against doctrinal laxity. Edward Dowey argued that during the time the denomination retained Westminster as its sole standard, many ignored it as a virtual dead letter. The intense discussion of theological issues prompted by the creation of *The Book of Confessions* may have helped to clarify viable modern confessional boundaries for Presbyterianism. Yet a counter-argument can also be made. Almost as soon as—and arguably even before—the denomination adopted *The Book of Confessions*, the neo-orthodox consensus that had sustained the enterprise was giving way to a plethora of theological perspectives—various neo-evangelical, liberationist, feminist, and other theologies—none of which to date has managed to command full assent throughout the church.[39]

Symptomatic of this ambivalent situation is the latest addition to *The Book of Confessions*. In 1983, the reunion of the southern and northern branches of the Presbyterian Church occasioned the drafting of *A Brief Statement of Faith—Presbyterian Church (U.S.A.)* adopted in 1991. Structured after the Trinitarian benediction of 2 Corinthians 13 and consisting of just over 550 words, the *Brief Statement* artfully weaves together classical theological themes of the Presbyterian tradition and contemporary social concerns such as feminism, environmentalism, and the need "to work with others for justice, freedom, and peace." The statement thus continues the dialectic at the heart of confessionalism and made more explicit since *C 67*—the effort to balance the particularity of the community's theological convictions and its engagement with the world. The *Brief Statement* also illustrates how precarious the current Presbyterian confessional consensus is. Because of diversities within the church, membership on the drafting committee was carefully balanced to reflect differences of theology, ethnicity, and gender; and the committee held numerous forums throughout the country to get the sense of the denomination at large. While this process resulted in a carefully balanced statement that won lopsided approval when the church voted, it is unclear that agreement would have held if Presbyterians had to move beyond the brief generalizations they adopted in 1991.[40]

Notes

1. For the idea of the various Reformations as efforts to replant Christianity in western culture, I am indebted to my colleague Scott H. Hendrix, *Recultivating the Vineyard: The Reformation Agendas of Christianization* (Louisville, Ky.: Westminster John Knox Press, 2004).

2. My discussion of Presbyterians in Ireland, Scotland, and England in this paragraph and the next several is informed especially by Patrick Griffin, *The People with No Name: Ireland's Ulster Scots, America's Scots Irish, and the Creation of a British Atlantic World, 1689-1764* (Princeton: Princeton University Press, 2001); Peter Brooke, *Ulster Presbyterianism: The Historical Perspective, 1610-1970* (New York: St. Martin's Press, 1987); Thomas McCrie, *The Story of the Scottish Church from the Reformation to the Disruption* (Glasgow: Bell and Bain, 1988 [1875]); and Marilyn J. Westerkamp, *Triumph of the Laity: Scots-Irish Piety and the Great Awakening, 1625-1760* (New York: Oxford University Press, 1988). I have also drawn in this section on research that appeared in a different form and in another venue: see James H. Moorhead, "'The Last Will and Testament of the Springfield Presbytery' from the Perspective of Presbyterian History," *Discipliana* 64 (Summer 2004), 35-48. The article was originally one of the Kirkpatrick lectures, sponsored by the Disciples of Christ Historical Society

and delivered on June 26, 2004, at the Cane Ridge Meeting House as part of the two hundredth anniversary commemoration of "The Last Will and Testament."

3. See, for example, David C. Lachman, *The Marrow Controversy, 1718-1723: An Historical and Theological Analysis* (Edinburgh: Rutherford House, 1988).

4. For further perspective on the significance of the schism and of the Irish impact on American Presbyterianism, see Elizabeth I. Nybakken, "New Light on the Old Side: Irish Influences on Colonial Presbyterianism," *Journal of American History* 68 (March 1982): 813-32.

5. Westerkamp, *Triumph of the Laity*, 77-80.

6. John Locke, *A Letter Concerning Toleration* (Buffalo: Prometheus Books, 1990 [1689], 22; Brooke, *Ulster Presbyterianism*, 89-91. Brooke's citation is from Gilbert Kennedy's 1724 argument that those who believed the Synod of Ulster lacked the power to make such a requirement were at liberty to depart from Presbyterianism and espouse Congregationalism. "No man," Kennedy observed, "by nature is bound unto any particular church or sect, but every one joins himself voluntarily to that society. . . . [I]f afterwards he discover any thing either erroneous in the doctrine, or incongruous in the worship of that society to which he has joined himself, why should it not be as free for him to go out as it was to enter?" I have also been influenced in my understanding of the pro- and antisubscription arguments by A. W. Godfrey Brown, "A Theological Interpretation of the First Subscription Controversy (1719-1728)," in *Challenge and Conflict: Essays in Irish Presbyterian History and Doctrine*, ed. J. L. M. Haire (Antrim: W & G Baird Ltd., 1981), 28-45. Amidst the vast literature on the Enlightenment, a still very helpful work is Henry F. May, *The Enlightenment in America* (New York: Oxford University Press, 1976).

7. For information on the development of early American Presbyterianism, see Westkerkamp, *Triumph of the Laity*, 136-64; Leonard J. Trinterud, *The Forming of an American Tradition: A Re-examination of Colonial Presbyterianism* (Philadelphia: Westminster Press, 1949), 15-37; Griffin, *The People with No Name*, 65-97; Ned C. Landsman, *Scotland and Its First American Colony, 1683-1765* (Princeton: Princeton University Press, 1985), 99-191; Duane Meyer, *The Highland Scots of North Carolina, 1732-1776* (Chapel Hill: University of North Carolina Press, 1957), *passim*.

8. Patricia U. Bonomi, *Under the Cope of Heaven: Religion, Society, and Politics in Colonial America*, updated ed. (New York: Oxford University Press, 2003), 133-38.

9. Dickinson is quoted in Bryan F. Le Beau, *Jonathan Dickinson and the Formative Years of American Presbyterianism* (Lexington: University Press of Kentucky, 1997), 31, 36.

10. *Minutes of the Presbyterian Church in America, 1706-1788*, ed. Guy S. Klett (Philadelphia: Presbyterian Historical Society, 1976), 103-04. In citations here and in the next paragraph, I have taken the liberty to bring capitalization and spelling in accord with contemporary use.

11. *Ibid.*, 104.

12. Griffin, *The People with No Name*, 123.

13. On the Tennents' role in the Awakening, see Milton J. Coalter, Jr., Gilbert Tennent, Son of Thunder: A Case Study of Continental Pietism's Impact on the First Great Awakening in the Middle Colonies (New York: Greenwood Press, 1986). See also Trinterud, Forming of an American Tradition, 53-108; Westerkamp, Triumph of the Laity, esp. 165-213.

14. Bonomi, *Under the Cope*, 139.

15. The introduction to the plan of government is quoted in Trinterud, *Forming of an American Tradition*, 297. See also *The Constitution of the Presbyterian Church (U.S.A.), Part I: Book of Confessions* (Louisville, Ky.: Office of the General Assembly, 1999), section 6.129; and Fred J. Hood, *Reformed America: The Middle and Southern States, 1783-1837* (University, Alabama: University of Alabama Press, 1980), 114.

16. Mark A. Noll, *Princeton and the Republic, 1768-1822* (Princeton: Princeton University Press, 1989).

17. Robert Hastings Nichols, *Presbyterianism in New York State: A History of the Synod and Its Predecessors*, ed. James Hastings Nichols (Philadelphia: Westminster Press, 1963), 70-86.

18. See, for example Charles Foster, *An Errand of Mercy: The Evangelical United Front, 1790-1837* (Chapel Hill: University of North Carolina Press 1960), 121-55; Clifford M. Drury, Presbyterian Panorama: One Hundred and Fifty Years of National Missions History (Philadelphia: Board of Christian Education, PCUSA, 1952), 52-76; Peter J. Wosh, *Spreading the Word: The Bible Business in Nineteenth-Century America* (Ithaca: Cornell University Press, 1994), 74.

19. Hood, *Reformed America*, 119; Robert Baird, *Religion in America,* ed. Henry Warner Bowden (New York: Harper and Row, 1970 [1856]), 153-54.

20. The description of the Connecticut revivals comes from David W. Kling, *A Field of Divine Wonders: The New Divinity and Village Revivals in Northwestern Connecticut, 1792-1822* (University Park: Pennsylvania State University Press, 1993), 5. On the frontier campmeetings, see John B. Boles, *The Great Revival: The Beginnings of the Bible Belt,* 2nd ed. (Lexington: University of Kentucky Press, 1996). For examples of these various interpretations of the religion of the Second Great Awakening, consult Clifford S. Griffin, *Their Brothers' Keepers: Moral Stewardship in the United States, 1800-1865* (New Brunswick: Rutgers University Press, 1960); Donald G. Mathews, "The Second Great Awakening as an Organizing Process, 1780-1830: An Hypothesis," *American Quarterly* 21 (Spring 1971): 23-43; Nathan O. Hatch, *The Democratization of American Christianity* (New Haven: Yale University Press, 1989); Paul E. Johnson, *A Shopkeeper's Millennium: Society and Revivals in Rochester, New York, 1815-1837* (New York: Hill and Wang, 1978); and William R. Sutton, *Journeymen for Jesus: Evangelical Artisans Confront Capitalism in Jacksonian Baltimore* (University Park: Pennsylvania State University Press, 1998).

21. See, for example, Charles E. Hambrick-Stowe, *Charles G. Finney and the Spirit of American Evangelicalism* (Grand Rapids: Eerdmans Publishing Company, 1996); and Keith J. Hardman, *Charles Grandison Finney, 1792-1875* (Syracuse: Syracuse University Press, 1987).

22. On the theological disputes, see George M. Marsden, *The Evangelical Mind and the New School Presbyterian Experience: A Case Study of Thought and Theology in Nineteenth-Century America* (New Haven: Yale University Press, 1970); 7-30; Mark A. Noll, *America's God: From Jonathan Edwards to Abraham Lincoln* (New York: Oxford University Press, 2002), 293-329.

23. Hatch, *Democratization*, 196; H. Shelton Smith, Robert T. Handy, and Lefferts A. Loetscher, eds., *American Christianity: An Historical Interpretation with Representative Documents*, 2 vols. (New York: Charles Scribner's Sons, 1960, 1963), 2: 66-118; James D. Bratt, "The Reorientation of American Protestantism, 1835-1845," *Church History* 67 (March 1998): 69. See also James H. Moorhead, "The 'Restless Spirit of

Radicalism': Old School Fears and the Schism of 1837," *Journal of Presbyterian History* 78 (Spring 2000): 19-33.

24. The pronouncement of the 1818 General Assembly and the statement from the 1864 northern Old School assembly are quoted in James H. Moorhead, *American Apocalypse: Yankee Protestants and the Civil War, 1860-1869* (New Haven: Yale University Press, 1978), 87, 127. The quotations from the 1845 assembly and from Palmer are found in Maurice W. Armstrong, Lefferts A. Loetscher, and Charles A. Anderson, eds., *The Presbyterian Enterprise: Sources of American Presbyterian History* (Philadelphia: Westminster Press, 1956), 200, 205. The discussion of the spirituality of the church draws on James Oscar Farmer, Jr., *The Metaphysical Confederacy: James Henley Thornwell and the Synthesis of Southern Values* (Macon, Ga.: Mercer University Press, 1986), esp. 188-89, 256-60.

25. On Presbyterian reunion, see Marsden, *Evangelical Mind*, 199-244.

26. On the rise of late nineteenth-century modernism, see William R. Hutchison, *The Modernist Impulse in American Protestantism* (Cambridge: Harvard University Press, 1976); and Gary Dorrien, *The Making of American Liberal Theology: Imagining Progressive Religion, 1805-1900* (Louisville, Ky.: Westminster John Knox Press, 2001).

27. Lefferts A. Loetscher, *The Broadening Church: A Study of Theological Issues in the Presbyterian Church since 1869* (Philadelphia: University of Pennsylvania Press, 1954), 39-47. I am also indebted to Kenneth J. Ross, "No Babies in Hell: Infant Salvation and Reformed Eschatology as It Influenced Debate in the First Attempt to Revise the Westminster Confession of Faith in the Presbyterian Church, U.S.A., 1889-1893," unpublished Ph.D. seminar paper, Princeton Theological Seminary, 1987.

28. Loetscher, *Broadening Church*, 39-74; Mark S. Massa, *Charles Augustus Briggs and the Crisis of Historical Criticism* (Minneapolis: Fortress Press, 1990), 85-109; George M. Marsden, *Fundamentalism and American Culture: The Shaping of Twentieth-Century Evangelicalism, 1870-1925* (New York: Oxford University Press, 1980), 109-18.

29. For the *Ledger* quote, see Loetscher, *Broadening Church*, 89. The southern Presbyterians added the very same chapters to the *Westminster Confession of Faith* in the 1940s, though in a different place within the text. See Ernest Trice Thompson, *Presbyterians in the South*, 3 vols. (Richmond: John Knox Press, 1963-73), 3: 492.

30. Loetscher, *Broadening Church*, 108-36; Marsden, *Fundamentalism and American Culture*, 171-84; Bradley J. Longfield, *The Presbyterian Controversy: Fundamentalists, Modernists, and Moderates* (New York: Oxford University Press, 1991), esp. 28-53, 128-161; and D. G. Hart, *Defending the Faith: J. Gresham Machen and the Crisis of Conservative Protestantism in Modern America* (Baltimore: Johns Hopkins University Press, 1994).

31. *Minutes of the General Assembly of the Presbyterian Church in the U.S.A.,* third series, vol 6., 1927 (Philadelphia: Office of the General Assembly, 1927), 85-86. For a treatment of the reorganization within the denomination, see James H. Moorhead, "Presbyterians and the Mystique of Organizational Efficiency, 1870-1936," in *Reimagining Denominationalism: Interpretive Essays*, ed. Robert Bruce Mullin and Russell E. Richey (New York: Oxford University Press, 1994), 264-87.

32. Loetscher, *Broadening Church*, 156.

33. In this section, I draw heavily upon research done for James H. Moorhead, "Redefining Confessionalism: American Presbyterians in the Twentieth Century," in *The Confessional Mosaic: Presbyterians and Twentieth-Century Theology*, ed. Milton J. Coalter,

John M. Mulder, Louis B. Weeks (Louisville, Ky.: Westminster John Knox Press, 1990), 59-83. See also Hutchison, *Modernist Impulse*, 288-311; and Sydney E. Ahlstrom, "Continental Influences of American Christian Thought Since World War I," *Church History* 27 (September 1958): 256-72.

34. W. Eugene March, "'Biblical Theology,' Authority, and the Presbyterians," *Journal of Presbyterian History* 59 (Summer 1981):113-30; William B. Kennedy, "Neo-Orthodoxy Goes to Sunday School: The Christian Faith and Life Curriculum," *Journal of Presbyterian History* 58 (Winter 1980): 326-70; *Report of the Special Committee on a Brief Contemporary Statement of Faith* (Philadelphia: Office of the General Assembly, 1965). The other documents adopted included the *Nicene Creed*, the *Apostles' Creed*, the *Scots Confession*, the *Heidelberg Catechism*, the *Second Helvetic Confession*, the *Westminster Confession* and *Shorter Catechism*, and the *Declaration of Barmen*.

35. Report of the Special Committee, 22; Book of Confessions, 9.01.

36. Book of Confessions, 9.27, 9.30.

37. *Ibid.*, 9.44-9.47.

38. Arnold B. Come, "The Occasion and Contribution of the Confession of 1967," *Journal of Presbyterian History* 61 (Spring 1983): 21.

39. I base my assessment of Dowey's views on comments which I heard him make on many occasions.

40. James H. Moorhead, "Presbyterians Confess Their Faith Anew," *Christian Century* 107 (July 11-18, 1990): 145-48. It is perhaps worth noting that the Southern Presbyterian Assembly had in the 1970s proposed its own book of confessions (including a contemporary statement of faith); but the proposal, while winning the support of a majority of the presbyteries, fell short of the number required for adoption.

Eternally True, Variably Useful:
How Confessions Worked In Some
American Reformed Churches

James D. Bratt
Calvin College

Of the many unintended consequences attending Napoleon Bonaparte's invasion of central Europe, few would have seemed less likely than a resurgence of confessional consciousness in the Protestant churches there. Apart from his own religious indifference, the emperor had reduced the church to the service of the nation at home, and if not a consistent philosophical rationalist, he meant to bring rational efficiency to the conduct of government and society abroad. Inevitably, his armies spread Enlightenment assumptions and revolutionary spirit in their self-understood liberating mission. None of this was friendly to established religion, much less to dogmatic theology or hunger for tradition. That very hostility, however, helped bring traditional religion into a more positive light once liberation had been exposed as conquest and once the creation of new structures became necessary in the wake of the armies' departure. In that context a revival—"revéil"—of religious earnestness quickened in the younger generation, offering a new turn for the old faith in the wake of failed revolutionary hopes. To feed their zeal many would tap old veins of dogmatic theology, finding in Reformation writers fresh lessons for a dispirited age.[1]

The influence of the French wave was not so easily expunged, however, nor, for the religiously zealous, was the old regime it had drowned necessarily inspiring. If piety and the attendant works of charity had risen in some quarters during the eighteenth century, rationalist accommodations in theology and civil accommodation, even cooptation, in polity had spread as well. The "legitimate" rulers of the post-1815 era in fact could and sometimes did avail themselves of Napoleonic examples in "restoring" their regimes on a now more efficient and effective basis. Sooner or later those regimes would also take recourse to the spirit as well as system of "nation"-building to survive. Those who put new hope in religion, therefore, had to answer certain key questions. Was the revival of religion to redeem the church or the nation, or both at once? What role did theology per se have in the project? And how was theology, particularly the theology of the sixteenth-century Reformation, to be understood in a nineteenth-century context? Was it a heritage of truth given to the saints once for all in timeless language, or was it a set of monuments from a seminal stage in the Church (and/or nation's) history, monuments meant not for imitation, much less for worship, but for instruction, properly inspiring comparable efforts at this new stage of historical development?

Thus, as the slightest dip into its literature reveals, the confessional re-newal of the nineteenth century came deeply entwined with debates over history and the character of the church. Somewhat less obviously—indeed, contrary to the hopes of some advocates then and some historians later—it also came con-nected to politics.[2] The connection was not predictable, in that traditionalists sometimes endorsed the restorationist state, sometimes suspected it, sometimes foreswore politics, and sometimes only opposed the current regime in the name of another one, historical or hypothetical. But as it did with the "Church ques-tion" and "historical question," the "confessional principle" necessarily sidled up against the "political principle." This was most evident in Germany, where the confessional initiative in particular and the theological enterprise in general were the most advanced of their age. Whatever more they became, these were rooted in responses to King Frederick William's effort (duplicated by other rul-ers in other territories) to unite the Reformed and Lutheran communions in his territories for purposes of Prussian nation-building; and they necessarily dealt with the understanding of history that Georg F. W. Hegel spelled out at the Uni-versity of Berlin in the interest of understanding Prussia's—more broadly, the "German principle's"—place in the dialectical unfolding of the World Spirit.[3]

This paper does not explore the German confessional renewal itself but its analogues and influences in American immigrant fellowships where one of Germany's finest sixteenth-century originals, the *Heidelberg Catechism*, had significant impact: namely, the German and Dutch Reformed churches. Under-standing the latter, further, requires attention to post-1815 developments in the Netherlands. The circumstances in which the confessional impulse had to work differed markedly across these sites according to the prevailing ecclesiastical and political regimes and the disparate out-workings of the dynamics of democ-ratic revolution. Certain common impulses can be detected among Reformed confessionalists across all these venues: a yearning for rootage that lent stability and substance to individual faith, the insistence upon clear standards by which to judge corporate doctrine and life, the concern for sustaining a heritage in which youth could be nurtured and the elderly consoled, the creation of a collective memory to bridge the distance across generations and the separation in space between an erstwhile homeland and the new land where the immigrants now found themselves. Yet between and within each of these communities the church question and the history question received very different answers. The political question proved unavoidable because of the substance of the confessional heri-tage itself; as Reformed people these groups all inherited the family compulsion for political and cultural involvement.

The immigration that fostered whole new networks of Dutch Reformed churches in the American Midwest began with an agrarian crisis in the 1840s but was shaped by the religious policy of the restorationist regime of Willem I. Now "king," no longer "*stathouder*," of a Netherlands that had been expanded to incorporate present-day Belgium, Willem showed the mentality of an Enlight-ened despot and availed himself of French models of centralization to make his new realm cohesive and orderly. His measures included the incorporation of the Dutch Reformed Church (*Nederlandse Hervormde Kerk*, or *NHK*) into the apparatus of state without the advice or consent of the old church's synod, replacing that body with a fifteen-member committee that reported to the king via the Department of Protestant Worship, and reversing the venerable Presbyterian, bottom-up lines of initiative with top-down hierarchical controls.[4] The only function left to the church's own discretion was doctrine, which nonetheless was commanded to permit mutual tolerance of all opinions. Over time, and in the interests of religious renewal, some reforming elements in the church won the acceptance of, then the mandate that hymns be sung at every service, trumping the old practice of exclusive psalmody. The new order, in short, involved every part of church life—liturgy, theology, and polity; in each domain it replaced the traditional with the innovative; and in the interests of regularity, it forbade dissent or the exercise of local option that had made the old republic workable, also in religious affairs.

Many in the Dutch wing of the Reveil acceded to these changes out of respect for the House of Orange, to maximize Protestant solidarity in the face of the expanded realm's Catholic majority, or out of their own priority upon interior religious concerns. Some stoutly traditionalist clergy dissented, however, and they were joined by some newly-minted pastors of Reveil affiliation to make public protest in the 1830s—precisely in the wake of the fiasco of Belgian secession that attended Willem's ham-handed administration there. These preachers rallied a considerable number of rank-and-file who had long been affiliated with local conventicles devoted to prayer, mutual encouragement and admonition, and the reading of the "old writers" of the Dutch pietist "Later Reformation." Indignant at the heterodoxy they saw flowing into the church from university theology departments, offended by the "humanistic" hymns in worship, frustrated by the loss of local control or appeal, they started defying parish boundaries to pursue "orthodox" baptism for their children and sermons for themselves. Formal separation from the national church soon followed. The populist character of the *Afscheiding* (Secession) was evident from the disparaging comments made about it by the local worthies whom it challenged, from socio-economic evidence later tabulated by historians, and above all by the movement's lightening spread: five years after its first eruption in 1834, the Seceders numbered only half a dozen ministers but 128 churches.[5]

The confessional component in these maneuvers had several aspects. First, it furnished a strict standard against heterodoxy. The Seceders were adamantly of the opinion that the three doctrinal standards of the church—the *Belgic Confession*, the *Canons* of Dort, as well as the *Heidelberg Catechism*—were authoritative *quia*, because, and not merely *quatenus*, in so far as, they were in conformity with the Scriptures; and they took the *NHK*'s prolonged, indecisive debates over the question as conclusive evidence of its lack of soundness.[6] The standards themselves, and especially venerable commentaries on them, provided grist for the edifying discussions Seceder home-and-church circles continued from conventicle practice. But the confessional emphasis also exposed a division in Seceder ranks. On the one side, those from the Northern provinces made doctrinal soundness the crucial test of church membership and sought to establish uniformity across all congregations under the direction of the church's Syn-

odical assemblies. The Northerners, that is, envisioned a purified version of the
national church. Seceders from the eastern-central parts of the Netherlands, on
the other hand, put greater emphasis upon pious experience and were willing to
allow some local variations in a more decentralized polity. A third option obtained in the southwestern, riverine section of the country where millennialist
and biblicist strains derived from Anglo-evangelicalism added to the mix. Once
the emergency of seceding was over and the churches had to decide how to
structure their new fellowship, the Northern school prevailed over the others,
giving the new union a pronounced confessionalist cast.[7]

It was leaders of the movement's marginalized wings, Albertus C. van
Raalte from centrally-located Gelderland, and Hendrik P. Scholte, from Zeeland
in the southwest, who led the vanguard immigration to the American Midwest in
the 1840s, settling in western Michigan and south-central Iowa, respectively.
Not just the confessional but the political question came into play in this decision. Since religion and regime were so closely identified in the Netherlands, the
act of seceding from the church meant a real psychological distancing of self
from nation—or, as the Seceders understood it, distancing the self from a nation
whose departure from the ways of God was being chastised in the 1830 loss of
Belgium and the 1840s' economic stagnation. Such alienation could and did lead
on to emigration; Seceders were far more likely to leave for the United States
than was any other Dutch religious cohort, and the minority parties among them
were the first to leave in number. Beyond providing the ideological permission
and initial leadership for emigration, Seceders carved out the enduring networks
of communication and transfer in the transplantation process so that this group,
in its various permutations, would have a far greater impact in Dutch America
than in the Netherlands.[8]

Just as secession had led to immigration, so in the new country immigration soon led to another secession, with different confessional mentalities again
defining the process. Both for practical and ideal reasons, Van Raalte affiliated
the churches of the west Michigan *diaspora* with the denomination descended
from the colonial-era settlement in New York and New Jersey, eventually
named the Reformed Church in America (RCA). This body, while still mindful
of its particular theological heritage, had significant interplay with the moderate
evangelical party in American Protestantism, which just around 1850 was ap-
proaching the high-water mark of its numbers and national influence. Van
Raalte's experiential-ethical emphases within the Reformed tradition matched
up well with this milieu, while the venerable denomination offered the resources
that would enable the newcomers to prosper. It promised as well a route of entry
into the larger culture to balance off the geographical segmentation that Van
Raalte had chosen for safety's sake in the first generation. Soon dissidents appeared in his "colony," however, resenting Van Raalte's agglomeration of economic as well as religious roles and harboring suspicions of where the new
American affiliation might lead them. They offered in token thereof disturbing
signs they had observed in eastern RCA churches: baptisms celebrated in private
homes instead of the congregation, a lack of regular preaching from the *Heidelberg Catechism*, racial segregation at communion, the tolerance of Masonry

among church officers, above all, the singing of hymns and doubts about the warrant of the Netherlands Secession. The mix of concerns from polity, liturgy, and theology resembled that of 1834, so that the protesters who left the RCA in 1857, composed at the start of but four congregations and one minister, traded volubly and in time successfully on the Secessionist model to provide in most Dutch-American settlements across the Midwest a "Christian Reformed" neighbor and rival to the local RCA congregation, and an alternative application of Reformed confessional understanding.[9]

In the same decades the German Reformed in America also experienced a new infusion of confessional consciousness—not from immigrants, however, but at the hand of a grandson of a signer of the United States Constitution, John Williamson Nevin. The denomination itself was somewhat less venerable than the Reformed Church in America, having been sown by the German migration to Pennsylvania in the first half of the eighteenth century. It had maintained its language and its solidarity partly through a political alliance with the flintier Scots and Ulster Presbyterian immigrants who came to Pennsylvania in even greater numbers, but the generations of revolutionary agitation and reconciliation, together with a lack of fresh immigrants from Germany, led to a deep settling-in in the land, and led some church leaders to look to the intense revivalism of the 1830s to quicken the somnolent souls they spied in the denomination's pews. If some there indeed qualified for the label, others were happy with the weekly round of rural life, a quasi-German liturgy, and generally Reformed loyalties espoused from the pulpit.[10]

Nevin himself was sure that the revival system was just that—a whole system rising from faulty premises to hurtful consequences, that the half-measures of custom would not prevail against it, but that only a fully fleshed-out alternative, fed from the taproot of the Reformed confessions and conveyed by an integral liturgy, was equal to the task. He came to this conclusion, and to the German Reformed house, over long experience. Reared in the traditional Ulster Presbyterian usages of south-central Pennsylvania, Nevin had suffered, he would later call it, a miscarried new birth at the hands of a revivalist while at Union College. He next undertook the rigorous training in Westminster theology via Scottish "Common Sense Realism" on offer at Princeton Seminary before launching on a career as theological professor and evangelical reform activist at Western Seminary in present-day Pittsburgh. Two blows in 1837 jolted him off that track: the "spiritual juggleries" of a visiting Finneyite revivalist, and the wholesale split in the Presbyterian Church.[11] Though he sided more with the Scots-Ulster Old School prosecution against the more Yankee New School defendants in the church struggle, he was deeply dismayed by the split as such, and he associated it with the histrionics of hyper-revivalism which Old School devotees typically shunned. In Nevin's eyes both events were excrescences of atomism, a willful defiance of the wisdom and witness of community and tradition. Both followed a sort of rationalism, the revivalists' being a manipulative technique to spur a predictable "conversion," the Old Schoolers' being a confidence in abstract words at the cost of the spirit and history behind them. Despite the Old Schoolers' pretense of preserving it and the Finneyites' protest of reviving it, Nevin concluded, neither had true regard for the church. Furthermore, both schisms and sensationalism would go on multiplying without let, for on the premises offered, the one party could not attain a purity clear enough nor the other an experience intense enough to settle on anything lasting, and their respective rationalisms would eventually make both prey to the destructive, disbelieving type soon to arrive from Europe.[12]

The antidotes Nevin offered were Church and history, and the German theological scholarship he drafted off in proposing them were mirrored in his 1840 departure to teach at the German Reformed Church's seminary at Mercersburg, Pennsylvania. But he soon discovered the twin plagues of 1837 breeding there as well—in the revivalist campaigns some denominational leaders were sponsoring, and in the allure among German circles of the announcement by John Winebrenner that he had founded a new pure Church of God upon the premises of the Bible alone. The dual challenge galvanized Nevin to translate his superior command of the new German scholarship into one of the most sophisticated theological projects of his era, the Mercersburg theology.[13]

From Friedrich Rauch, his colleague at Mercersburg, Nevin absorbed a Hegelian psychology that treated the individual as part of a trans-personal spiritual identity. From reading J. A. Neander, Nevin learned the German historicist approach that constituted for him "an actual awakening of the soul."[14] Prior to these steps he had adopted an intuitional epistemology. With these three his Romantic-Idealist equipment was complete and the empiricist-atomistic mindset of Scottish Common Sense was put to rout. As "Common Sense" was the regnant philosophy in virtually all of American academia, as well as the operational matrix of American religion, both sophisticated and common-folk, both rationalist and revivalist, Nevin was presenting something of a cultural revolution. But he did so in the interests of what he considered to be authentic, traditional Christianity. In American Protestantism as it was Nevin saw a profound devolution from that standard, evidenced by a lack of genuine personal holiness and an increasing desperation to make conversion convincing. At the root of the problem lay a false notion of salvation. American evangelicals gazed on a distant Jesus who, whether temporarily snared by artifice (revival) or fixed by reason (Princeton), still remained a distant fund of forgiveness in an abstract calculus of justification.[15]

Nevin offered instead a radically Christological and ecclesiological alternative: understanding the Church to be Christ's continuing presence on earth, the Incarnation—Christ's personal entry into history—as the defining event of all history, and the sacraments as the means of enduring union with Christ that would secure believers in genuine holiness and incorporate them in the new order into which God was redeeming all creation. His churchly substance was rooted in historical method. Nevin returned to the Reformation, demonstrating how much of its heritage—even within the Reformed stream—had been lost to "Puritan" and Princetonian reductions in America. Following Calvin's own clues, he then delved deeply into patristic writers and practices to try to settle questions of polity and liturgy as well as doctrine. Nevin's conclusions brought him to the verge of conversion to Catholicism; at the end he demurred, although he did agree with John Henry Newman that the much-bruited Anglo-Catholic position was an untenable halfway house. The German Reformed was as authentic a stop as any, Nevin concluded, for it was built on the Reformed catholicity of Calvin and stood a fair chance of someday being the mediator that would bring together Lutheran and Reformed, then, perhaps, Protestant and Catholic.[16]

One might expect confessional statements proper to take a marginal place in this project since the 1837 Presbyterian schism had ultimately arisen from wrangling over the Westminster standards. But in fact Nevin hailed a different Reformed confession—the *Heidelberg Catechism*—and a different notion of what confessions entailed as central to the solution that church and history offered. His first writing upon moving to Mercersburg aimed at rebuilding *Heidelberg* in German Reformed consciousness and practice, and his preaching at the local church proceeded through its prescribed course of Lord's Days. Nevin found the *Heidelberg* a superior statement because of "its reserve in regard to high Calvinism on the subject of the decrees" over which so much of the Presbyterian dispute had proceeded and its positive disposition toward "the sacraments and good works." Rather than delivering up the "cold workmanship of the understanding" á la Princeton's *Westminster*, it was "full of feeling and faith . . . of fresh, simple childlike trust." In terms of the culture war engulfing the denomination, the *Heidelberg* was characteristically German and thus opposed to "the Puritan atmosphere with which we are surrounded." Even more, it opposed the spirit of "mere private judgment and individual will" that lay at the bottom of the American Protestant malaise. Nor was the *Catechism* merely doctrinal; it entailed a whole liturgy of "altar, organ, and gown" and observance of the church year with its regular cycle of festivals.[17]

In sum, the *Heidelberg* embodied the "Spirit" of the apostolic "Catholic Church. . . . In no other Reformed symbol probably are the great constituents of the true and proper character of this [ancient] confession, liberty and reverence for authority, the sense of the individual and the sense of the general, more fairly and happily combined." Stabilizing the church amidst the swirl of innovation and controversy, the *Heidelberg* was especially useful for the education of the young. As Nevin expounded in the concluding chapter of his great critique of revivalism, *The Anxious Bench*, nothing would better serve to bring lasting Christians into the fold than consistent nurture in the "system of the catechism," which at once taught and embodied the way of the church—that is, the believer's saving union with Christ.[18]

Ultimately, however, the *Heidelberg* proved to be a halfway house back to the Church's primal confession, the *Apostles' Creed.* Nothing demonstrated the provincial and fundamentally sectarian character of American Protestantism more clearly in Nevin's estimate than the utter neglect the *Creed* had suffered in those circles. He himself had not learned it either at home or at seminary, and estimated that not one in ten of the American theological professoriate could recite it without stumbling. Discarded by "puritans" as papist formalism, the *Creed* in fact lay at the foundation of the church, Nevin argued. It was simply the extension of Peter's original confession of the messianic status of Christ, and it remained for all time "the rule and frame of all sound theology." The *Creed* scotched the authority of private judgment and transcended modern abstract, rationalistic constructions of the faith, whether of the pious or skeptical variety. At the same time, within its framework every age could make its own distinctive contribution to the proper development of doctrine. Finally, like the *Heidelberg Catechism*, the *Creed* did not end as a doctrinal formulary but led through itself back to "the idea of the Church, the mystery of Christianity," namely, the union of believers with Christ and with each other beyond any partial interest over the long span of space and time.[19]

Clearly, while supporting their distinctiveness, Nevin was speaking well beyond German Reformed circles. Nathan Hatch regards him first among the critics of the "democratization of American Christianity" that he, Hatch, so ably anatomized as the product of the very traits Nevin most protested: radical individualism, populist rationalism, disregard for history, and suspicion of institutions.[20] That fellowships so constituted were themselves prey to a new authoritarianism, to pretenses of innocence and universal warrant, Nevin was early to point out. His critique of hard-sell, mobile revivalists put him in the ranks of contemporaries who feared the penetration of the market revolution into all spheres of American life. His remedies on the religious side mirrored a dawning regard in civil and cultural domains for the virtues of stability, continuity, and the salience of institutions, a trend that would increasingly prevail over the next century.[21] Nevin did not believe that proper Christian initiatives should simply mirror secular developments, however; rather, in a remarkable article from 1850 entitled "Catholicity" he argued that Christ's redemption would work from the Church into every domain of human existence, bringing family and state and "the various domestic and civil relations that grow out of them" to their divinely ordained perfection. Art, science, business and trade—all would come into the redemption initiated by Christ as the second Adam. If Christianity "forms the true and proper wholeness of mankind, the round and full symmetrical *cosmos* of humanity," then a segmented ecclesiology and quietist politics seemed out of the question for Reformed people.[22]

But how should Christian engagement with the world proceed, particularly when the political side of that world was dissolving into the rancor and chaos of the American 1850s? Nevin never mounted an answer; in fact, he quit public life for much of that decade, perhaps out of a sense that the needed set of answers could not be tried. When he did return to teaching, at Franklin and Marshall College in Lancaster, his lectures on history remained Idealist and philosophical with little to say about the Civil War that was raging along the nearby Mason-Dixon Line. Likewise he returned to the ecclesiastical lists amid these portents of world-historical change that had shredded the unity of most American churches—to fight for liturgical reform in the German Reformed Church. An appropriate churchly initiative indeed, but hardly one commensurate with the cosmic scope promised by the German method.[23]

Ironically, it would be Nevin's immigrant colleague at Mercersburg, Philip Schaff, who would find the levers of promise and power in America. Ironic because Schaff arrived on the American strand bearing the word of peace and reconciliation in the summer of 1844, just when Protestant mobs were assaulting

Catholics in Philadelphia and a generic mob lynched Joseph Smith at an Illinois jail. In such a context Schaff's ordination sermon in Germany sounded most apt: he had pledged there to take to the shallow, brawling American scene all it needed by way of churchly heft and scholarly sophistication. Likewise his inaugural address at Mercersburg emphasized how much the Reformation had grown out of its Catholic heritage. But while Nevin was interested in history to recover forgotten theological resources against the partialities of the present, Schaff was more intent upon history's patterns of development. He soon discerned where the American course was headed: not to the conflagration of the Civil War, the prospects of which he embarrassingly discounted in an article published exactly as the guns at Sumter flared, but to the forefront of world history under practical genius and industrial might civilized by a generically Protestant ethos.[24]

Schaff was virtually ordained by experience to see the most salient pattern of change to be a reconciliation of contraries. Born into a Reformed family in German Switzerland, he became immersed in the various pietist circles—but also the discordant theological *milieux*—of Tübingen, Halle, and Berlin where he took his successive educational degrees. Contrary to Nevin, the longer he lived amid American Protestantism the more he liked it. He especially liked it when, owing to wartime disruptions, he left Mercersburg and the German Reformed bypath it represented to go to New York City and the Presbyterian power situated in the once pro-revival, New School-descended Union Theological Seminary. There he spent the rest of his long career, the scholar-statesman-organizer of an emerging American Protestant mainline.[25]

Throughout these changes Schaff was loyal to the Hegelian dialectics he had absorbed from his German teachers F. C. Baur, F. A. Tholuck, and J. A. Neander. He arrived at Mercersburg with their model of Church history, which identified a Petrine thesis in Roman Catholicism that had been countered by a Pauline antithesis in the Reformation and awaited a Johannine synthesis of the two. The young Schaff thus relativized Protestantism, to the deep chagrin of one wing of the German Reformed Church, a chagrin deepened when his opponents brought him up on heresy charges only to demonstrate that they knew little, and he a great deal, of the church's confessional documents.[26] Yet Schaff did not sail on from that point toward High Church harbor, but began promoting America as the place where key antinomies—between freedom and order, vitality and stability, innovation and tradition—might be resolved into a third way full of creative power. That is, Christendom's old problems might finally be solved in America. Schaff took his own mission to be supplying the side that his adopted land lacked: theological ballast, a sense of tradition, and ecumenical respect.[27]

His method was two-fold. First, his ecclesiastical statesmanship brought representatives of the leading Protestant bodies together on projects of common appeal like the New York Sabbath Committee and the American Revised Bible translation. His favorite along this line was the resuscitated Evangelical Alliance (1867), which had originated in 1846, just after his "Romish" inaugural, as a pan-protestant, anti-Catholic united front. Second, he channeled his German training into some of the lasting monuments of American church historical scholarship: the *History of the Christian Church* (8 vols., 1858-1910), *The*

Creeds of Christendom (3 vols., 1877), the *Schaff-Herzog Encyclopedia of Religious Knowledge* (3 vols., 1882-1884), and *A Select Library of the Nicene and Ante-Nicene Fathers* (14 vols., 1880-1886). His organizational monument still endures in the American Society of Church History.[28]

Schaff's attitude toward confessional materials themselves bore out these hopes and methods. He honored Protestantism for subordinating all creeds to Scripture and by insisting that, beneath the plethora of Protestant statements, there lay substantial "evangelical" agreement on all the essentials of "orthodoxy." Yet he insisted that confessions were necessary, debunking the "no creed but Christ" pretense of some evangelicals as well as the anti-creedal crusade of the American restorationists earlier in the century. Besides being inevitable, confessions were vital for defining the "bonds of union" in a given church fellowship and for "the instruction of children . . . [via] a solid and substantial religious education, in distinction from spasmodic and superficial excitement."[29] Finally, confessions were valuable as markers along the Church-historical way, being deposits of the special insight each age had to contribute to the whole. This path was one of progress, however, a progress that had led to the American evangelical consensus at present and that augured "the great work of the future—the reunion of Christendom in the Creed of Christ."[30]

Schaff's historical study *The Creeds of Christendom* in effect relativized all of them (save the *Apostles' Creed*, he allowed in passing) by the very respect with which he regarded each and by his confidence in the ineluctable "advance" of the times. He thus emphatically supported the late nineteenth-century campaign in the northern Presbyterian Church to revise the Westminster standards. Honoring Calvinism for having boldly engaged the theological difficulties around divine sovereignty that other fellowships dodged, Schaff nonetheless found Reformed confessions from the seventeenth-century scholastic age (*Westminster* but also the *Canons* of Dort) to be excessively focused on decretal theology and to follow "metaphysical" premises by hard logic to conclusions— about reprobation, infant damnation, and limited atonement in particular—that Scripture never or only ambiguously taught. Besides, he declared, it was time to recognize that "old Calvinism is fast dying out. It has done a great work, and has done it well, but cannot satisfy the demands of the present age." That age demanded, nicely, only what the overriding tenor of the gospel also manifest, the priority of God's love even over his justice, and the generosity of a grace that was intended for all. It would not be bad, Schaff concluded, if everyone concerned operated inconsistently; let "pious Calvinists preach like Arminians, and pious Arminians pray like Calvinists."[31]

It was Calvinism's political heritage, notably, that Schaff found non-negotiable. "The essence of Calvinism is the sense of the absolute sovereignty of God and the absolute dependence of man; and this is the best school of moral self-government, which is true freedom." To which he appended a political-confessional footnote: "The principles of the Republic of the United States can be traced, through the intervening link of Puritanism, to Calvinism, which, with all its theological rigor, has been the chief educator of manly characters and promoter of constitutional freedom in modern times." Accordingly, Schaff gave himself heartily to causes that promised to uphold the Christian *public* character of the United States: generically Protestant public schools, legally enforced sabbatarianism, specifically anti-Mormon prohibitions of plural marriage, and the generally anti-Catholic prohibition of alcoholic beverages. If confessions were contingent upon history, the character they bred was vital to sustain in unity and order Schaff's promised land, a nation that had once come apart in his backyard at Mercersburg and that now burgeoned as an industrial empire from its corporate capital in New York.[32]

Dutch immigration to the United States rebounded after the Civil War and peaked in the early 1890s, just before the great crash that signaled the vicissitudes to which that new industrial order was subject. In the Dutch-American churches which multiplied with these new arrivals, the role of the confessions and the question of Calvinism's relation to public life were stirred most potently by Abraham Kuyper, a Dutch theologian-statesman-organizer of the same caliber as Schaff.[33] Kuyper in fact was educated in the same methods and menu as Schaff, also did his doctoral work in Church history, and celebrated Calvinism as a political— confessional— indeed a "life-principle" whose ultimate manifestation on the world-historical stage was the United States. Far from reading history as a course of progressive synthesis, however, Kuyper's dialectics held an eternal antithesis between Calvinism (more broadly Christianity) and all its contraries. The most threatening enemy of his own day he deemed to be naturalism, first as philosophy but no less as a way of life, as a cultural system that elevated materialism and a social matrix that bred oppression. The part of the believer in this conflict was to pray and preach by personal faithfulness, of course, but even more—and here was Kuyper's distinct contribution—to band together in Christian organizations in every domain of life, there to work for justice as laid out by the "ordinances of God" in creation and Scripture. Theirs was to be a principled pluralism, Kuyper insisted, with no special privileges, but also no structural debilities, for Christians. A stronger call to public life and cultural engagement could hardly be imagined, nor a model more conducive to combative rhetoric and solidarity in social organization.[34]

Yet the theoretical root of this system, and its source in Kuyper's own experience, was Reformed dogmatics. Kuyper had been schooled in the glory of the "Reformed principle" and the intricacies of sixteenth- and seventeenth-century Reformed authorities by the pioneering Dutch Modernist J. H. Scholten at Leiden; and after a season spent in the earnest piety and mediating theology that was Schaff's lasting harbor, Kuyper turned back to those writers as his own meat and drink. Amid the toils of life and the rising storm of unbelief, rock-ribbed Calvinism provided the only sufficient shelter.[35] He then entered upon a career of promoting this conviction among the Reformed *kleine luyden* ("little people"), first of all via one of the Netherlands' first mass-circulation newspapers. The weekly theological column he published in the Sunday number thereof accumulated over his half a century of writing into a body of commentary upon all the cardinal doctrines of Reformed Christianity. He began in the 1870s with treatments of the covenants and election; moved in the 1880s to *The Work of the Holy Spirit* and a massive commentary on the *Heidelberg Catechism*; climaxed at the turn of the century with his most innovative and controversial work, a three-volume treatment of *Common Grace*; before ending on deliberations about the kingship of Christ and (during World War I) eschatology.[36] Each Sunday issue also included a devotional column that manifest an affective intimacy with the Bible which also came through in his theological work. But in his theology Kuyper consistently followed the lead of the "Calvinistic principle" rather than conventional hermeneutics, provoking critics right and left to dub his not traditional but "neo-Calvinism."[37]

When Kuyper's influence began to tell in Dutch America around the turn of the century, it provoked as much resistance as enthusiasm. The leadership in Reformed Church circles increasingly identified over the next decades with American Progressive crusades that assumed a generous definition of "Christian" politics, while the laity there, as well as the preponderance of laity and clergy in the Christian Reformed Church, held more closely to the confessionalist-pietist heritage of the Secession. Since most of the new immigrants entered the CRC, the conflict over Neo-Calvinism centered there and served as a contest over group identity and prospects in the American world.[38] Nicely, the battle opened on Reformed theology's signature tenet of election. The Kuyperians generally accepted their master's supralapsarian position for its logical consistency with the Calvinist principle of divine sovereignty and for releasing believers from preoccupations with their interior spiritual condition to work for King Jesus in the public world. The infralapsarian opposition was led by Foppe M. Ten Hoor, professor at the denomination's Theological School at Grand Rapids, and Lammert J. Hulst, a venerable pioneer pastor self-taught in Seceder confessional ways. Appealing to the *bloemtijd*, the seventeenth-century glory years, of Reformed theology, they disparaged Kuyper as a neophyte and innovator. They criticized his philosophical heavy hand for mangling the more nuanced and variable, but also preponderantly "infra," testimony of the tradition. And they made a telling argument about social class and its spiritual correlations. Ten Hoor explained:

> the Secession emerged from the spiritual life, born out of the need of the soul
> . . . . It was a reformation of poor, lost sinners who felt the need of redemption through Christ and who fled from the dead churches of Rationalism in theReformed Church [*NHK*]. . . . It was a reformation of the foolish, the weak, the ignoble, accounted nothing according to the world . . . [and opposed by] all that is rich and learned and mighty.

To which Hulst added: "Does not experience teach what fruit is produced whenever preachers concern themselves with worldly affairs? Their religious tasks are neglected; their preaching and their intercourse with church members become worldly. . . . Truly, now is no time to put the emphasis on general [i.e., Kuyper's common] grace and to reject particular grace."[39]

The confessionalists won this particular battle when the CRC Synod of 1906, following the mother Church's lead in the Netherlands, declared "infra" to be the standard position and "supra" a tolerable exception. But for the next twenty years the contest between the two parties continued, complicated by internal variations on either side. This era concluded with the forced Americanization dictated by World War I hysteria and left the more strictly confessionalist party in power. They would retain hegemony well into the 1950s, when the residue of another world war worked its way into the denominational system. Leading the party in this period would be Henry J. Kuiper, from 1928 to 1956 editor of *The Banner*, the Church's English-language weekly and its principal locus of communication and control; and Louis Berkhof, Ten Hoor's successor as professor of systematic theology at (now) Calvin Theological Seminary and codifier of its orthodoxy in the three-volume *Reformed Dogmatics* (1932), digested for student use into the *Manual of Reformed Doctrine* (1933).[40] Over these two long eras, then, prewar and interwar, we can observe another sort of confessional regime than the ones viewed so far. The Christian Reformed rejected the developmental model of Nevin and Schaff and took the Reformed standards to be univocal, unchanging truth; compared to the original Secession, they were less oppressed than ignored by formal power and commanded a segmented enclave that experienced increasing prosperity over time; and they sought neither to counter nor to endorse the purposes of the civil regime, yet finally could not escape the pull of politics.

Most Christian Reformed confessionalists were also pietists by virtue of the attention they devoted to the personal inward state. They assumed all people to be fallen and depraved and relatively few to be elect, meaning that close scrutiny about one's progress in realizing the covenantal promises of baptism held the highest priority, to be matched by close monitoring of one's "walk with the Lord" upon successful resolution of this first step. Personal experience did not ride on its own, however, but was to be channeled through and instructed by theological standards. The Psalms played a crucial role here, being the only music permitted in the Dutch-language churches until the 1920s, and the officially preferred choice thereafter. The Psalms were also commended as a template for private devotions. The *Heidelberg Catechism* came a close second, combining as it did didactic purpose and pastoral tone. Through these "objective" lenses, pastors and professors taught time and again, one's merely "subjective" impulses had to be refracted, could be transcended. The *Catechism* was reduced to simplified form for children, was covered in a five-volume set of sermons compiled by H. J. Kuiper over two decades, was treated in 400-page commentaries by esteemed ministers—and neither writers nor readers on the subject ever seemed to wear out.[41]

Mirroring this interior spirituality was a tightly gathered, strictly demarcated ecclesiology. That pattern was expectable of an immigrant church, but theology once again redoubled and extended the effect. The CRC's forebears had felt exiled in the Netherlands for religious reasons and had been more likely to immigrate for that very reason. Yet they viewed the new land as offering more danger than hope, and concentrated more on the threats than the opportunities that lay around them. Foremost among those were religious. In the prewar generation "Modernists" and "Methodists" dominated the horizon—the first defined by their outright denial of the supernatural in Christianity, the second by their Arminian theology and focus on "feeling;" the second, therefore, being altogether too likely to slide over to the first for having neither the objective nor the subjective resources to hold against the descent into sheer unbelief. Since the Modernists, in this view, had preeminence in the high places of American church and culture, as the Methodists did among the masses, the Christian Reformed had nowhere to go in the larger society.[42] Nor was there much latitude at home, for next door stood the tents of the RCA whose lack of strictness on the fine points of the tradition, together with their open door to mainline American influences, augured only a succession of compromises that would finally end with the sacrifice of essentials as well. For six decades, then, Christian Reformed leaders turned the rank-and-file's attention inward, back into the circle of safety. Within that circle multiplied facilities and activities for all groups and interests: men's societies, ladies' societies, young people's clubs, couples' clubs, old-age homes, a tuberculosis sanitarium, two mental hospitals, and above all a complete K-12 Christian school system which extended Reformed nurture and in-group socialization through the crucial matrix of weekday education.

The behavioral tokens of this culture remain evocative to this day and signaled the key functions of its ways. The first mark of belonging was loyalty to Christian schools; by denominational norms, this was incumbent upon the vows parents made at baptism.[43] The second was a Sabbatarianism legendary for its ability to generate legalistic distinctions, but also effective in mapping time for the community on an order that distinguished them from their neighbors, that weekly recalled their attention to the sovereignty of God (on whose Sabbath one rendered him special "honor"), and that put some restraints upon the economic compulsions which were equally legendary in the group's weekday round. It is notable that only the fourth commandment rivaled the seventh in the intensity and exactness of attention deployed by the sermons on the Decalogue which the Heidelberg system regularly brought around.[44] The group's third marker, established by special Synodical decision in 1928, also regulated time—weekday leisure activities—by singling out three types of "worldly amusements" for the gravest warnings, even (per congregational option) for formal church discipline. The prohibition on playing cards for stakes touched avarice again, at the same time that it warned against trifling with divine providence. The strictures against dancing and theater-attendance aimed at lust. Modern dance, in the synod's judgment, provoked sexual desire as surely as it mirrored sexual performance; theater was a school for infidelity, a debasing arena for actor and viewer alike in "its unblushing, disgusting display of sex."[45] The late Twenties occasion of these declarations bespoke worries about the ambient culture of the time, but the prohibition on theater attendance, which also entailed movie-going, demonstrated also an acute sense of the power that outside media held to break control over group communications. Nothing could better exhibit the reinforcing cycle between theology, sociology, and everyday behavior, than the subsequent decades' worth of movie-bashing, and nothing more pointedly taught the young their elders' expectations.

Parochial as this system could appear, it bore with it a critique of American society that every soul could sense and that some leaders spelled out in a more thoroughgoing manner. The Reformed confessions figured in this critique alike by their substance, their spirit, and their systematic form. It was a commonplace of immigrant Christian Reformed commentators to characterize America as a "superficial" land, shallow, fickle, and flighty, prone to chase the latest fashion and so doomed to discontent when the fad changed and one's resources, or patience, ran out with the soul still empty.[46] This theme continued over the next generation as well. It was not just the flappers of the Twenties who exhibited this pathology, said the critics, but the whole consumer culture which that decade overheated, which the Great Depression frustrated, and which World War II finally brought into judgment. The phenomenon was worst, of course, when it corrupted religion. Cases in point were the Fundamentalist Billy Sunday, the revivalist as showman; the Modernist Harry Emerson Fosdick, with his gospel of "adjustment" to modern times; and the positive-thinking Norman Vincent Peale, vendor of mental bromides from (as Christian Reformed critics were happy to point out) the most venerable of RCA pulpits. The confessions, by contrast, provided meaty substance, tested by time and immune to fashion. Such roots nourished the soul, anchoring it against every wind of doctrine, and enabling it to grow steadily over the course of a lifetime, through weal and woe, toward the perfection of the saints.[47]

Individualism was the next point of critique. As Methodists earlier had stood for "subjectivity," so Baptists, with their congregational polity and their tests of isolate personal conversion, provided the religious referent here, and their popularity offered a sobering measure of how widespread this trait was in the United States. Theologically, the Dutch churches (for the RCA joined this chorus) explained the syndrome by pointing to the displacement of covenant by the revival, and also explained thereby the fitful results for American spiritual life. Personal decisions on the revival floor were too easily swayed by the mood of the crowd or excitement of the moment, and thus were altogether too likely to be fleeting and superficial. Such "decisions" also conveyed a false sense that salvation was of human choice; revivals were functionally Arminian. They were equally suspect ecclesiologically, for persons who took their conversion to be of their own initiative, neither derived from God nor ministered by the people of God, had neither reason to nor prospect of bonding with a larger body in any lasting way. The same syndrome, continued the critique, explained how America could lead the industrialized world in levels of religiosity *and* criminality; both were functions of the supposedly sovereign individual whose passionate ego now reached to the stars, now to the bottle or the bank safe. Until the self learned that its own pursuits, even for heaven, were part of the syndrome of sin, true salvation would go a-glimmering. But submission to a sovereign God required instruction by a Church that was itself disciplined by the lasting truth of God, systematically wrought and persistently conveyed. Concluded RCA theologian John Kuizenga: "To turn one's back on the historic creeds is therefore to turn one's back on what God has given us through the struggle of centuries, and to run the risk of trying to build up once more what has already been tried and found wanting."[48]

Amidst so pernicious a climate the Dutch churches were commended to a way of life that was at once a cycle and a pilgrimage. If believers could never

reach perfection, never be free of the gravity that pulled one back in the orbit of
sin, they could nonetheless walk faithfully on toward "the eternal and untroubled
rest" that awaited them on the eternal shore. Prewar sermons especially ampli-
fied the pilgrimage motif, declaiming on the "Character and Bliss of the Pilgrim
to God's Zion." An immigrant audience could resonate particularly well to
homilies entitled "Foreigners and Fatherland." Such messages, in fact the whole
pietist ethic, assumed, in the words of Ten Hoor, that "God's people are poor
and miserable in themselves, poor in virtue, poor in strength, poor in every respect."[49] But over time that assumption grew thin, at least as evidenced in the
community's evolving circumstances. Not all the wealth piled up by the Twenties' economic boom was lost in the Great Depression, nor was the judgment
that World War II leveled upon the passions of prosperity very long remembered
in the postwar climate. The 1950s began Dutch Americans' smart and steady
ascent in income, education, influence, and organizational aptitude that would
leave them by century's end with billionaires, national-stature journalists, world-
class academics, and representation in the halls of political, economic, and cultural power. Not accidentally, the confessionalist-pietist hegemony in the CRC
was broken by the end of that decade. Kuyperian enthusiasts and confessionally
minimalist evangelicals, alternately or in combination, have prevailed in denominational councils ever since.[50]

Already in the 1950s, the heirs of the Kuyperian heritage were calling for a
recognition that sin and poverty were not only spiritual, that the wars of industrial society could inflict the utmost damage on millions of people while its
peace left millions more under racial and colonial oppression or in dread of nuclear annihilation. Their message resonated in no small part due to the thousands
of youth who had been pulled out of the Dutch-denominational enclaves and
spun around the world in the World War II military. Meanwhile, the war itself
forced even the most insular or wary of church leaders to identify with the
American nation and sanctify its cause as never before. If the default attitude
toward government in these circles—even, or perhaps especially, during the
Great Depression—had been a suspicion of an expansive "state" that threatened
local control or personal initiative or small-business prosperity or farmer autonomy, the triumphs of "America's" global armies against fascist evil and the need
to maintain a similar watch against Communist "aggression" encouraged a sub-
conscious and sometimes forthright identification between cross and flag that
both violated confessional orthodoxy and broke with the tauter assessments of
the immigrant tradition.[51] In any case, America's industrial-imperial state grew
so large and penetrated so deeply in the post-1945 world that one could hardly
help but develop the political habit, even if one held to the dream that a confessional church properly minded its own business and not that of the world. In
fact, the Republican presidents whose pledges to "roll back" the influence of
government have become a staple of national political rhetoric since 1969 and of
political actuality since 1981 have had no more enthusiastic supporters than the
rank-and-file of CRC and RCA voters, above all those self-identified with "conservative" or "traditional" theology.[52] One might say that the cycle of confessionalist discontent has come around to endorsing a sacralized "restorationist"

regime—restored against radicals and secularists who discomfited it in America in the 1960s, just as the French had displaced it in the Netherlands a century and a half before. That the descendants of the Seceders now endorsed something of Willem I's regime is an irony matching the one on which this paper began.

Yet the confessionalist treasure house has proven any number of times in the past to be richer and not so easily despoiled as that. Behind and beneath the functions we have seen them play—as standards of orthodoxy, stabilizing roots, and channels of nurture—the confessions served, and still serve, to embody memory. They do not so much enact the "historical question" as provide a historical bed of answers. They raise for believers a lasting measure above the allegiances and insistencies of the day, pull new generations back into undiscovered depths of insight, challenge them by a comprehensive presentation of Christian truth to discover anew the mandates and the fullness of the faith amidst the crusades of the righteous, the powerful, the careless, and the merely pious. The Seceders, the immigrants, and the Mercersburg theologians all tried that, and deserve to be remembered for the attempt, whatever the imperfection of their accomplishments.

Notes

1. On the German movement, see Erich Beyreuther, *Die Erweckungsbewegung* (Göttingen: Vandenhoeck & Ruprecht, 1963); and Horst Weigelt, *Erweckungsbewegung und konfessionelles Luthertum im 19. [i.e. neunzehnten] Jahrhundert, untersucht an Karl v. Raumer* (Stuttgart: Calwer, 1968). A short overview in English is Theodore Tappert, ed., *Lutheran Confessional Theology in America, 1840-1880* (New York: Oxford University Press, 1972), 3-23. The most thorough studies of the Dutch case also give ample coverage to the larger European movement: Marie Elisabeth Kluit, *Het Protestantse Reveil in Nederland en Daarbuiten 1815-1865* (Amsterdam: Paris, 1970); and Albert J. Rasker, *De Nederlandse Hervormde Kerk vanaf 1795: haar geschiedenis en theologie in de negentiende en twintigste eeuw* (Kampen: Kok, 1974), 71-99.
2. Darryl G. Hart pleads this case in *the Lost Soul of American Protestantism* (Lanham, Md.: Rowman and Littlefield, 2002).
3. The substance and setting are well covered in Claude Welch, *Protestant Thought in the Nineteenth Century*, vol. I (New Haven: Yale University Press, 1972), 30-107; and Walter H. Conser, Jr., *Church and Confession: Conservative Theologians in Germany, England, and America, 1815-1866* (Mercer, Ga.: Mercer University Press, 1984), 13-96.
4. Rasker, *Nederlandse Hervormde Kerk*, 24-31, 37-42; and Wintle, *Pillars of Piety*, 11-20.
5. Convenient overviews are Rasker, *Nederlandse Hervormde Kerk*, 55-70, and Wintle, *Pillars of Piety*, 27-32. A brief English-language summary is James D. Bratt, *Dutch Calvinism in Modern America: A History of a Conservative Subculture* (Grand Rapids: Eerdmans, 1984), 3-10. Thorough studies are W. Bakker, *De Afscheiding van 1834 en haar Geschiedenis* (Kampen: Kok, 1984); and Lambert H. Mulder, *Revolte der Fijnen: de afscheiding van 1834 als sociaal conflict en sociale beweging* (Meppel: Boom, 1973).
6. Rasker explores this issue in *Nederlandse Hervormde Kerk*, 41-42.
7. Bratt, *Dutch Calvinism*, 7-10.
8. Bratt, *Dutch Calvinism*, 7-9, summarizes the pattern laid out in much greater detail in Robert P. Swierenga, *Faith and Family: Dutch Immigration and Settlement in the United*

States, 1820-1920 (New York: Holmes and Meier, 2000); and Pieter R. D. Stokvis, *De Nederlandse Trek naar Noord Amerika, 1846-1847* (Leiden: Universitaire Pers, 1977).

9. Outside the sometimes partisan denominational histories, see the relatively dispassionate treatments in Jacob Van Hinte, *Netherlanders in America: A Study of Emigration and Settlement in the 19th and 20th Centuries in the United States of America* (Grand Rapids: Baker, 1985 [1928]), 357-88; and Henry S. Lucas, *Netherlanders in America: Dutch Immigration to the United States and Canada, 1789-1950* (Grand Rapids: Eerdmans, 1989 [1955]), 506-14.

10. James I. Good, *History of the Reformed Church in the United States, 1725-1792* (Reading, Pa.: D. Miller, 1899); and *History of the Reformed Church in the U.S. in the Nineteenth Century* (New York: Board of Publication of the Reformed Church in America, 1911).

11. Nevin composed a detailed autobiography of his years through 1840 in, *My Own Life: The Earlier Years* (Lancaster, Pa.: Historical Society of the Evangelical and Reformed Church, 1964); quotation, 126. Theodore Appel, *The Life and Work of John Williamson Nevin* (Philadelphia: Reformed Church Publication House, 1889), covers his entire life with additional material on this period as well. Richard E. Wentz provides a national-cultural biographical interpretation in *John Williamson Nevin: American Theologian* (New York: Oxford University Press, 1997), while Darryl G. Hart, *John Williamson Nevin: High Church Calvinist* (Philipsburg, N.J.: P&R Publishing, 2005), emphasizes his persistent commitments to Reformed theology.

12. This analysis is borne out in John Williamson Nevin, *The Anxious Bench* (Chambersburg, Penn.: Printed at the office of the "Weekly messenger", 1843); and *Anti-Christ, or, the Spirit of Sect and Schism* (New York: J. S. Taylor, 1848).

13. The best single-volume introduction to the Mercersburg Theology remains James H. Nichols, *Romanticism in American Theology: Nevin and Schaff at Mercersburg* (Chicago: University of Chicago Press, 1961). Specific aspects of Nevin's contribution are taken up in Sam Hamstra and Arie J. Griffioen, eds., *Reformed Confessionalism in Nineteenth-Century America* (Lanham, Md.: Scarecrow, 1995).

14. Nevin quoted in Hamstra and Griffioen, *Reformed Confessionalism*, 70.

15. Good overviews of Nevin's theology are Nichols, *Romanticism in American Theology*, chs. 1-3, and Robert Clemmer, "Historical Transcendentalism in New England," *Journal of the History of Ideas* 30/4 (October-December 1969), 583-89. See also E. Brooks Holifield, *Theology in America: Christian Thought from the Age of the Puritans to the Civil War* (New Haven: Yale University Press, 2003), 467-81.

16. Nichols, *Romanticism in American Theology*, 194-216.

17. See Appel, *Life and Work of Nevin*, 145-56, 605-27 (quotations, 150, 152, 154). Nevin expanded his early Mercersburg lectures into *History and Genius of the Heidelberg Catechism* (Chambersburg, Penn.: German Reformed Church, 1847).

18. Appel, *Life and Work of Nevin*, 153; Nevin, *The Anxious Bench*, ch. 7.

19. Nevin's treatment of the *Apostles' Creed* is detailed in Appel, *Life and Work of Nevin*, 79-91, 551-65. His key statement, from 1849, is reproduced with critical introduction in James H. Nichols, ed., *The Mercersburg Theology* (New York: Oxford University Press, 1966), 307-17 (quotations, 308, 316).

20. Nathan O. Hatch, *The Democratization of American Christianity* (New Haven: Yale University Press, 1989).

21. This analysis is given in further detail in James D. Bratt, "Religious Anti-Revivalism in Antebellum America," *Journal of the Early Republic* 24 (Spring 2004): 65-106; and James D. Bratt, "The Reorientation of American Protestantism, 1835-1845," *Church History* 67/1 (March 1998): 52-82.

22. John Williamson Nevin, "Catholicity," originally published in the *Mercersburg Review* 3/1, January 1851, reprinted in Appel, *Life and Work of Nevin*, 369-95 (quotations, 373, 378).

23. On the larger political context, see James D. Bratt, "Nevin and the Antebellum Culture Wars," in Hamstra and Griffioen, *Reformed Confessionalism*, 1-22; and Mark A. Noll, *America's God: From Edwards to Lincoln* (New York: Oxford University Press, 2002), 409-12, 432-35.

24. The most convenient overview of Schaff's thought and life is Klaus Penzel's introduction to the edited collection, *Philip Schaff, Historian and Ambassador of the Universal Church: Selected Writings* (Mercer, Ga.: Mercer University Press, 1991), xv-lxviii. Schaff's early years at Mercersburg are further explored in Nichols, *Romanticism in American Theology*, 169-85, while Stephen R. Graham, *Cosmos in the Chaos: Philip Schaff's Interpretation of Nineteenth-Century American Religion* (Grand Rapids: Eerdmans, 1995), ties this phase to his later development. Schaff's article was "Slavery and the Bible," *Mercersburg Review* 13/2 (April 1861), 288-317; see further Noll, *America's God*, 409-12, 418-19.

25. Penzel, *Philip Schaff*, xvi-xxxvi, xlviii-li, lx-lxv.

26. Penzel, *Philip Schaff*, xxv-xxxiii; Sydney E. Ahlstrom, *Religious History of the American People* (New Haven: Yale University Press, 1972), 617-19.

27. Graham, *Cosmos in the Chaos*, 32, 89, 98.

28. Penzel, *Philip Schaff*, lxi-lxv.

29. Philip Schaff, *The History of the Creeds*, vol. I of *The Creeds of Christendom*, 4th ed. (New York and London: Harper & Brothers, 1884), 203, 8.

30. Philip Schaff, *Creed Revision in the Presbyterian Churches* (New York: Charles Scribner's Sons, 1890), 42.

31. Schaff, *Creed Revision*, vi, 40, 42; *History of the Creeds*, 795.

32. On the larger phenomenon, Graham, *Cosmos in the Chaos*, chs. 4, 5; quotations from Schaff, *History of the Creeds*, 218-19.

33. The most convenient capsule biography in English is James D. Bratt, ed., *Abraham Kuyper: A Centennial Reader* (Grand Rapids: Eerdmans, 1998), 1-16. Greater detail on his early life and formation is available in George Puchinger, *Abraham Kuyper: His Early Journey of Faith*, ed. George Harinck (Amsterdam: VU University Press, 1998).

34. Kuyper laid out his views for the American world in *Lectures on Calvinism* (Grand Rapids: Eerdmans, 1931 [1899]); see especially chapter 1, "Calvinism a Life-System." Revelatory shorter works in English translation are "Maranatha" (1891), "The Blurring of the Boundaries" (1892), and "Evolution" (1899), all in Bratt, ed., *Kuyper Reader*.

35. Kuyper's own narrative of his spiritual development is "Confidentially," in Bratt, *Kuyper Reader*, 45-61. For the "shelter" image see 57-58.

36. Abraham Kuyper, *Uit het Woord*, vol. II (Amsterdam: J. H. Kruyt, 1875), part 4 on election; *Uit het Woord*, 2nd series, vol. I (Amsterdam: J. H. Kruyt, 1884), "That Grace is Particular"; vol. II, 1885, "The Doctrine of the Covenants"; *Het Werk van de Heilige Geest* (Amsterdam: J. A. Wormser, 1888-89); *E Voto Dordraceno: Toelichting op den Heidelbergschen Catechismus*, 4 vols. (Kampen: Kok, 1892-97); *De Gemeene Gratie*, 3 vols. (Leiden: Donner, 1902); *Pro Rege, of het Koningschap van Christus*, 3 vols. (Kampen: Kok, 1911-12); *Van de Voleinding*, 4 vols. (Kampen: Kok, 1929-1931).

37. From the theological Right, Lammert J. Hulst and Gerrit K. Hemkes, *Oud- en nieuw Calvinisme: tweeledige inlichting voor ons Hollandsche volk over het oude en nieuwe Calvinisme en de kerk* (Grand Rapids: Eerdmans-Sevensma, 1913); from the Left, Bernardus D. Eerdmans, *De Theologie van Dr. A. Kuyper* (Leiden: Van Doesburgh, 1909).

38. Bratt, *Dutch Calvinism*, 40-54, 67-79.

39. Bratt, *Dutch Calvinism*, 47-50 (quotations, 49).

40. Louis Berkhof, *Reformed Dogmatics*, 3 vols. (Grand Rapids: Eerdmans, 1932); *Manual of Reformed Doctrine* (Grand Rapids: Eerdmans, 1933). On Berkhof and Kuiper's context, see Bratt, *Dutch Calvinism*, 116-26, 129-36.

41. Henry J. Kuiper, ed., *Sermons on Sin and Grace, Lord's Days I-VII* (Grand Rapids: Zondervan, 1936); *Sermons on the Apostles' Creed, Lord's Days VIII-XXIV* (Grand Rapids: Zondervan, 1937); *Sermons on Baptism and the Lord's Supper: Lord's Days XXV-XXXI* (Grand Rapids: Zondervan, 1938); *Sermons on the Ten Commandments, Lord's Days XXXIV-XLIV* (Grand Rapids: Zondervan, 1951); *Sermons on the Lord's Prayer, Lord's Days XLV-LII* (Grand Rapids: Zondervan, 1956). Henry Beets, *The Compendium Explained: A Popular Exposition of the Abridgement of the Heidelberg Catechism* (Grand Rapids: Eerdmans-Sevensma, 1915). William Goulooze, *A Young People's Study of the Heidelberg Catechism* (Grand Rapids: Eerdmans, 1936). Herman Hoeksema, *The Heidelberg Catechism, an Exposition: The Triple Knowledge,* 10 vols. (Grand Rapids: Eerdmans, 1943-56). Jan Karel Van Baalen, *The Heritage of the Fathers: A Commentary on the Heidelberg Catechism* (Grand Rapids: Eerdmans, 1948). Donald Bruggink, *Guilt, Grace, and Gratitude: a Commentary on the Heidelberg Catechism, Commemorating its 400th Anniversary* (New York: Half Moon Press, 1963). Thea B. Van Halsema, *Three Men Came to Heidelberg* (Grand Rapids: Christian Reformed Publishing House, 1963).

42. Bratt, *Dutch Calvinism*, 57-61, 127-37.

43. Donald Oppewal, *The Roots of the Calvinistic Day School Movement* (Grand Rapids: Calvin College, 1963); George Stob, "The Christian Reformed Church and Her Schools" (Th.D. thesis, Princeton Theological Seminary, 1955).

44. John Weidenaar, "The Proper Form of Worship" (on the 2nd commandment), and William Masselink, "The Meaning and Observance of the Sabbath" (on the 5th), in Kuiper, *Sermons on the Ten Commandments*, take up twenty-five percent of the volume, sometimes running twice as long as sermons devoted to the other commandments.

45. Bratt, *Dutch Calvinism*, 63-66, 115-19, 137-40 (quotation, 117).

46. Bratt, *Dutch Calvinism*, 57-61.

47. Bratt, *Dutch Calvinism*, 42-43, 58-62, 133-34, 146-55, 199.

48. The latter theme is developed in detail in James D. Bratt, "The Covenant Traditions of Dutch Americans," in Daniel J. Elazar and John Kincaid, eds., *The Covenant Connection: From Federal Theology to Modern Federalism* (Lanham, Md.: Lexington Books, 2000). For abbreviated treatment, see Bratt, *Dutch Calvinism*, 58-60, 133-34 (quotation, 134).

49. Sermon titles cited and referenced in Bratt, *Dutch Calvinism*, 42-43.

50. These trends are detailed in Bratt, *Dutch Calvinism*, 187-221.

51. Bratt, *Dutch Calvinism*, 147-56, 188-90, 199-203.

52. Information about the political behavior and orientations of CRC and RCA parishioners is given in Corwin Smidt, Donald Luidens, et al., *Divided by a Common Heritage* (forthcoming); see chapter 5, "Jesus Shall Reign? The Politics of CRC and RCA Clergy and Laity." On clergy behavior, see Corwin Smidt and James Penning, "Preachers in Politics: The Political Activities of CRC and RCA Clergy," in Sue E. S. Crawford and Laura R. Olson, eds., *Christian Clergy in American Politics* (Baltimore: Johns Hopkins University Press, 2001), 157-173.

After Establishment, What?
The Paradox of the History
of the Episcopal Church in America

Robert Bruce Mullin
The General Theological Seminary

What follows is an historical essay and some reflections on the current situation in which the Episcopal Church finds itself. The two parts may be read separately, but it is my hope that the paradox I wish to explore may not only shed light on the history of the American Episcopal Church, but also help us understand the present tension in the church.[1]

Let me begin with a truism: the Episcopal Church has been out of step with many of the Old Line Protestant church bodies from the time of its organization in the 1780s. If (as Sydney Ahlstrom claimed over forty years ago) the Puritan heritage lies at the heart of the story of religion in America, then Episcopalians are constitutionally outsiders.[2] They are (to put it provocatively) the heirs of William Laud among the children of the Puritans. Both by its tradition and its liturgy the Episcopal Church has followed a different vision from that of the rest of American Protestantism.

But this is a truism at best; the real questions are how did this tradition operate, and what effects did it have on the course of the history of the Episcopal Church? Here we must recognize that the decade of the 1780s is crucial in the story of American Anglicanism. During this decade the Episcopal Church became an anomaly in Anglicanism—a disestablished Anglican Church. The establishmentarian nature of Anglicanism was one of its central features for centuries. As Richard Hooker explained in the Lawes of Ecclesiastical Polity, "within this realm of England . . . from the pagans we differ, in that with us one society is both Church and commonwealth, which with them it was not. Also from the state of those nations which subject themselves to the bishop of Rome, in which our church hath dependency upon the chief of our commonwealth, which it hath not under him."[3] Establishment defined what the church was. It was the Church of England. It also defined the structure of the church. It was established by Parliamentary action. To be sure, there had at times existed a Convocation (or ecclesiastical governing body) as well, but this had all but disappeared by the 1780s. It was Parliament that authorized the Prayer Book, issued forth the acts of uniformity, even created parishes. The establishmentarian nature had been normative Anglicanism since the days of Henry VIII. Legal disestablishment first addressed what this new American church was not: it was no longer the Church of England, but simply the Protestant Episcopal Church in the United States of America. But furthermore, disestablishment gave to the church the freedom to define what it was to be without political interference.

But what was this new church to be? This was the paradox. Of course it wanted to be in continuity with the parent church, for as the preface to its Prayer Book stated, "This Church is far from intending to depart from the Church of England in any essential point of doctrine, discipline, or worship."[4] But nonetheless it needed a vision of what was to be its role in the new society. What one finds during this decade of the 1780s are two very different conceptual models emerging, which would continue to exert influence until the 1960s.

The first might be called the "noblesse oblige" vision. Its emphasis was on offering leadership to the nation at large. It might be true (its devotees would admit) that the church was legally disestablished and that the aristocratic hierarchy of English society (which the established church both reflected and defended) had been rejected at the time of the Revolution, but there still remained a natural aristocracy as existed in every society. There would always be persons who, because of education, resources, or social standing, would be the de facto leaders of the society. In the new nation a large portion of these persons continued to be attracted to the dignified worship and seemly propriety of the Episcopal Church. These natural aristocrats were the leaders of the society, and it was the responsibility of the Episcopal Church to minister to them and to inspire them. The fact that the first President of the new nation chose a special pew in St. Paul's Chapel in New York indicated that although establishment might be a thing of the past, the Episcopal Church still had an important if unofficial role to play in leading the new society. Particularly in those colonies where the church had been once established or where it had found special favor with colonial authorities one found presence of this noblesse oblige vision.

No one reflected better this noblesse oblige vision of the Episcopal Church than did its first Presiding Bishop, William White. Chaplain to the Continental Congress, friend of George Washington, patron of the American Philosophical Society, and first citizen (second only to Benjamin Franklin) of Philadelphia, White personified the idea of the Episcopal Church being actively involved in the larger community. One sees these attributes reflected in the well known portrait of White done by Gilbert Stuart.

White is pictured in a calm, dignified manner. He sits confidently and securely, sure of his standing. His face and manner bears a striking similarity to portraits of George Washington and other political leaders of the age. The patriarchal solidity of the founding fathers is mirrored in Stuart's rendering. Just as Washington was iconically presented as the father of the country, so too is White imaged as the father of the church.

The second alternative model is what might be called the "apostolocist" vision. It offered a very different response to disestablishment. Disestablishment rendered Episcopalians a small and comparatively unimportant religious community in the vast new nation. The larger nation neither supported nor sympathized with the principles upon which Anglicanism rested. Episcopalians found themselves to be strangers in a strange land. Where could the church turn to find a true guide to the right path? Where then could it turn to find a parallel situation to help give psychological meaning to its predicament? The new American culture could not be trusted. It operated on principles very different from those governing the church. Neither could one follow the Church of England, or any of the other Christian nations of Europe. All of them presupposed that the church was to be established. In all of Christendom throne and altar had been linked since the time of Constantine. Hence it was to the early pre-Constantinian Church that these persons turned to find guidance. The appeal to the early Church, to be sure, had been present within Anglicanism almost from the very beginning. Sixteenth and seventeenth-century divines had regularly invoked it to defend the English reformation settlement or to defend the antiquity of the office of the bishop and certain distinctive ecclesiastical practices. Now it took on a new psychological import. It gave meaning to the position in which the church now found itself. The early church saw itself as being outside of the wider world of antiquity and was always suspicious that if it drew too close to the world it would lose its purity. It needed to follow its own vision. The Church Father Tertullian put the issue most bluntly: "What did Athens have to do with Jerusalem?"[5] This was precisely the situation of American Episcopalians for apostolocists. They saw their church as in key ways out of step with the larger culture, marching to a very different religious beat. The experience of the early Church provided one final truth. In the early centuries the Christian community was not judged by its size but by its fealty to the apostolic faith and order. So too must American Episcopalians. They may be small, but they were possessors of the truth and order of the primitive church. Episcopalians might not be able to compete with Methodists and Baptists vis-à-vis numbers, but they could the claim that they better reflected the apostolic faith and order.

If William White reflected the *noblesse oblige* vision, the apostolocist vision found representation in the figure of Samuel Seabury. Apostolicism came naturally to Seabury since he was a product of the Episcopal Church in Connecticut. In Connecticut Episcopalians were a small minority, dwarfed by the established Congregational Church. A large number of its members were converts (or children of converts) abandoning Congregationalism because (as one of the early converts put it), "I am persuaded that there ought to be and originally was also an external and visible unity and that in primitive times it was very much insisted on . . . . I am no less persuaded that an external uniformity ought to be agreed on and established by the authority of the church" and that for this purpose the office of bishop was divinely ordained.[6] It is small wonder that Connecticut Episcopalians saw their church to be an alternative to the Congregational standing order and as such always on guard.

Just as portraits of White reflected the assumptions of the noblesse oblige understanding of the church, so too did images of Seabury reflect the apostolocist assumptions. In a well-known image of Seabury painted by Thomas Spence Duché, the bishop does not project the calm judicious feel of Stuart's portrait of White, but a sense of willful defiance. He is more in the spirit of Auguste Rodin's Balzac than of Gilbert Stuart's George Washington. He seems to be standing against a strong wind, which threatens but does not move him. He is rock-like in his willingness to hold his ground, undaunted by the elements. It is an image of holding fast, whatever may be the challenges.

We must be clear that both models, however useful, had telling flaws. The noblesse oblige approach operated as if the Episcopal Church were to America what the Church of England was to England. It was the location for national acts of worship, it played a role in ceremonies such as the dedication of public buildings, and it had a key place in providing religious instruction to the military elite of the nation. But all this was ultimately beside the point—there was no establishment. Episcopalians could try to place themselves in the center of things but whether other religious communities would acknowledge this claim was another matter. The flaw of the apostolocist position was the reverse. It drew its psychological vigor from the vision of the early Church. As one early bishop wrote, "I . . . have the consolation of having faithfully borne my testimony to the principles of the Apostolic and primitive Church; to principles which 'the noble army of martyrs' confessed in their writings, in their lives, in the agonies of those cruel deaths to which their persecutors hunted them, to principles which in every age have ranked among their advocates some of the brightest ornaments of science, and intrepid champions of divine truth."[7] But American Episcopalians were not an isolated and persecuted community. In the fields of economics, politics, and culture, they were key players in the social order. Apostolicism was a powerful psychological vision but it had little resonance with the actual social experience of Episcopalians.

The two attitudes I have outlined have played a very important role in the story of the Episcopal Church. The tension between them has marked key episodes in the history but I have chosen three to illustrate: issues considering the issuance of the first *Prayer Book* in the 1780s; the response of northern Episcopalians to the Civil War; and the debate over the proposed union with the Northern Presbyterians in the 1940s.

ORGANIZING A CHURCH

The creation of an American church and *Prayer Book* was an extraordinary event in the history of Anglicanism. Parliament had set both the ecclesiastical structure and the liturgy of the church in the early 1660s, and both had remained unchanged. American Episcopalians had the task of "Americanizing" both. As Episcopalians in southern and middle states began the process of organization they also addressed the issue of *Prayer Book* reform. William White's *The Case of the Episcopal Churches Considered* had offered a path forward for organization. White combined a Lockean understanding of sovereignty flowing from community, an elevation of the role of laity in governance, and a reduction of the authority of bishops, to forge a distinctively American vision of Anglican polity that was adopted by a General Convention in 1785. But what was to be done about the liturgy? A proposed liturgy was also set forth in 1785 that tried to adopt the old liturgy to the new environment. One gets a glimpse of the philosophy behind these changes in a sermon introducing the changes preached at that General Convention by William Smith. Using as his text the pericope concerning the marriage feast to which the invited guests did not come, he believed that the world would be "compelled to come in" to the new church by "the decency, devotion, fervor, and solemnity of our forms of public worship."[8] But for this to take place liturgy must reflect the age in which it was practiced, and the present was an age not of superstition but of reason. "Blessed be God we live in a 'liberal' and enlightened age, where religion, if not so generally practiced, is nevertheless generally understood; and when nothing can be considered as deserving the name of religion, which is not rational, solid, serious, charitable, and worthy of the nature and perfection of God to receive, and of free and reasonable creatures to perform."[9] An enlightened liturgy must not create roadblocks and difficulties for the people of the age. It should not be bound to the past but be concerned with the present task, which was nothing less than "the civil happiness of [the] country."[10] For this reason the proposed book jettisoned the Nicene and Athanasian creeds and doctrines such as the descent of Christ into hell. It watered down Trinitarian language and carefully eliminated many aspects of sacerdotalism that were found in the older liturgy. Just as the Revolution called for a new principle of government, it also called for a new view of liturgy.

I said southern and middle states, because a very different spirit was found in the churches in New England. Samuel Seabury put the issue most bluntly in response to the changes proposed by the southern churches: "In short, the rights of the Christian church do not arise from nature or compact, but from the institution of Christ, and we ought not to alter them, but to receive and maintain them, as the holy Apostles left them. The government, sacraments, faith and doctrines of the church are fixed and settled. We have a right to examine what they are, but must take them as they are. If we now model the government, why not the sacraments, creeds, and doctrines of the Church? But then it would not be Christ's church but our church, and would remain so, call it what we please."[11] The role of the church was not to respect the spirit of the age, but to maintain the historic legacy. This not only entailed questions about the authority of bishops (which the above quotation particularly addressed), but alterations in inherited doctrines and liturgies. William Smith might praise the virtue of elasticity so as better to serve the needs of the present age, but others saw such "elasticity" as a desire to water down the church's inheritance. It was the obligation of the Episcopal Church at present—just as it was the task of the church in every age—to be loyal to the faith as it had been received. "It is our business to hold the same faith, teach the same doctrines, inculcate the same principles, submit to the same government, recommend the same practice, enforce the same obedience, holiness and purity, and to administer the same sacraments that the Apostles and primitive Christians did."[12]

The result of the debate of the 1780s was an interesting compromise that included elements and principles from both south and north. Thus in government, popular sovereignty was affirmed by granting representation to laity, while the authority of bishops was affirmed by establishing a separate legislative house for them. Likewise in the liturgy the Athanasian Creed was removed out of modern sensibilities, yet the epiclesis (or invocation of the Holy Spirit during the eucharistic prayer) was restored to make the liturgy more apostolic in structure. Not everyone was of course pleased. Benjamin Rush, the noted physician and signer of the Declaration of Independence, abandoned the Episcopal Church for Presbyterianism upon examining the compromise book, claiming that the Episcopal Church was liturgically ruined because of the "superstitions" introduced by Seabury.[13] The advocates of noblesse oblige and apostolicism had nonetheless reached something of a compromise.

COMING TO GRIPS WITH A WAR

The second case involved the debate within the northern Episcopal Church concerning the Civil War. Throughout the antebellum period the Episcopal Church had taken a distinctive stance concerning much of the agenda of the rest of evangelical Protestantism. As is well known, the antebellum era was characterized by a great deal of popular cooperation among American Protestants as they attempted to mold the young nation. As Robert Baird proudly explained, "I hesitate not to affirm that . . . the Evangelical Churches . . . manifest a remarkable degree of mutual respect and fraternal affection. While earnest in maintaining . . . their own views of Truth and Church order, there is rarely any thing like denunciation and unchurching other orthodox communions, but every readiness, on the contrary, to offer help when needed."[14] An evangelical united front was dedicated to concerns of mission, education, and moral reform. This agenda heightened the division within the Episcopal Church that we have been tracing. Should Episcopalians take the lead in endeavors such as the American Bible Society as instruments for the common good, or oppose them as modern innovations? Likewise should Episcopalians embrace the movement away from the use of alcohol that increasingly was becoming characteristic of American Protestantism, or oppose it as modern fad? Episcopalians wrestled with such questions largely because of the division that we have noted. On the whole, while many notable Episcopalians took leading positions in these reform movements, the Episcopal Church, as a church, took no position on them.

The great debate over moral reform ineluctably led to the question of slavery. The slavery question divided many of the great American Protestant churches into southern and northern camps, but not the Episcopal Church. For a variety of reasons the Episcopal reaction to the slavery question was distinctive by it being filtered through intra-Episcopal issues. One of these was a pointed avoidance by Episcopalians of any political discussion in church settings. The church should steer clear of political involvement. It had been the church's political involvement at the time of the Revolution that had caused so much sorrow. Indeed it was a practice among Episcopal clergy, in contrast to those of other denominations, even to refrain from voting in political elections. Church squabbles also played a factor. The antebellum decades witnessed Episcopalians hotly divided over the question of churchmanship, or whether to emphasize the Protestant or Catholic part of the denomination's heritage. The high church/low church controversy regularly divided ecclesiastical gatherings. The parties involved in this debate, however, did not fit neatly into any north/south divide. Thus two of the leading centers of low church or evangelical activity were the dioceses of Virginia and Massachusetts. To raise the question of slavery would be to possibly impede cooperation on restraining the catholicizing forces in the church.

But to these general factors there were the distinctive viewpoints of advocates of *noblesse oblige* and apostolicism. For the former, the church's neutrality on slavery served as one of the few remaining sources of social unity. As other churches divided into regional sections, noblesse oblige Episcopalians clung to the spirit of unity their church offered the nation. They would have shared the sentiment of one politician, "The chords that bind the states together but various in character. . . . The strongest of those of a spiritual and ecclesiastical nature consisted in the unity of the great denominations. . . . [T]he Episcopal Church is the only one of the four great Protestant denominations which remains unbroken and entire. . . .If the agitation goes on . . . there will be nothing to hold the states together but by force."[15] Indeed in 1859 it was decided to hold the General Convention in Richmond, Virginia, rather than the customary places of New York or Philadelphia—the first time it had ever met south of the Mason-Dixon Line. The decision to meet in Richmond may indeed have been yet another sign of national unity at a time of increasing sectional strife. At the convention no mention was made of the growing national tensions, and the House of Bishops decided to issue no Pastoral Letter, since the proposed Pastoral Letter attacking national sin was feared to be a catalyst for a discussion over slavery.[16] From the *noblesse oblige* perspective, Episcopal Church unity bolstered national unity.

The issue was viewed differently by apostolocists. They had consistently argued that all modern American reform movements must be judged by the witness of the early church. There could be no new moral discoveries in the nineteenth century, particularly no such discoveries that would divide the church. To see how this logic worked let us apply it to the question of the propriety of "dis-fellowshipping" persons who either sold or partook of alcoholic beverages.

Principle one: There is no evidence in Scripture or from the apostolic age that the use of alcohol was considered in itself sinful.

Principle two: Schism or church division was always viewed as sinful.

Hence the advocacy of "dis-fellowshipping" persons because of alcohol is not a Christian principle but was derived instead from the "spirit of the age," which should always be questioned.

It was this type of reasoning that shaped apostolocist attitudes over slavery, particularly when the slavery debate became intensified in the 1830s by the claim that slavery was a *malum-in-se*, or a sin in and of itself. Such an argument was to be rejected not because slavery was not a social problem, but because to claim that it was sinful challenged a fundamental religious principle. We see this ambiguity in the diary remarks of one layperson writing in the early 1840s. Slavery he admitted was wrong, "a national sin, and the future of national curses and calamity. But the Bible and the Church are silent—and unquestionably if there were such moral guilt in slaveholding as its opponents insist on the primitive church would have entered its protest against it and overthrown it with the overt corruptions of the old world. Let it be shown that there are any indications even of such a feeling in the remains of that period and I will call myself an abolitionist most gladly. But I am suspicious of all the religious improvements of the nineteenth century."[17]

Until the 1850s both proponents of *noblesse oblige* and apostolicism could unite in a policy of a silence over slavery—for the former, out of a desire for the unity of the nation and for the latter, because it did not pass the test of apostolicity. But as the decade of the 1850s progressed, and as sectional division increased, this avoidance of the issue of slavery became more difficult. The same diarist who in 1842 could weigh the question of slavery against the apostolic rule and find it wanting, by 1856 was not so sure. There he could condemn slavery as "the greatest crime on the largest scale known in modern history . . . a blasphemy not in word, but in systematic action against the word of God." Indeed by 1860 he had become an avid Republican and campaigned for Abraham Lincoln and the restriction of slavery.[18]

The coming of the war created a real dilemma for northern Episcopalians over how to respond. Should they embrace the northern cause and risk permanently alienating the southern diocese that had separated because of secession, or should they avoid taking a position on the war and risk alienating the northern public? This was the large question but it was hashed out in sundry ways, some symbolic. One such symbolic debate was the question of the use of the American flag. Should it be flown on church buildings (as it had not been earlier) as a sign of national solidarity? The divided mind could be seen even among the Episcopalians of one city (New York). The leading parish (Trinity) broke with custom and set forth a flag upon hearing of the firing upon Fort Sumter, much to the praise of some. "The ideas of Church and State, Religion and Politics, have been practically separated so long that people are specially delighted with any manifestation of the Church's sympathy with the state and recognition of our national life on a fitting occasion."[19] But the leading theological seminary (General) pointedly refused to do so. Speaking of raising a flag, one professor protested, "The demonstration in view has not been required of us by any law, or by any constituted authority . . . . [Furthermore] I do not think that an institution purely religious in its character, intended for all sections of the country and all parties, and all the members of which are by their calling non-combatants, has any business with political and military demonstrations."[20] Still another symbolic issue was the question of how the church should tell its own story. Thus the early 1860s witnessed a debate within Episcopal publications over who was the actual patriarch of the Episcopal Church: William White or Samuel Seabury?[21]

All this lay as background for the General Convention that convened in New York during October of 1862. The Civil War was then at a crucial point. The Union army's advances of earlier that year had been reversed, and the momentum of the war seemed to shift to the Confederacy. Leading journals from the Church of England were pointed in their sympathy for the Southern cause as reflective of true religion, and they proudly noted that earlier that year as Federal forces neared Richmond, the President of the Confederacy, Jefferson Davis, had publicly received the rite of confirmation, thus showing his commitment to the Church.[22]

As scholars have noted, during the early months of the Civil War the northern Protestant churches, and particularly the clergy, had enthusiastically pledged themselves to the cause of union.[23] Episcopalians, however, during this period had been (on the whole) silent. No official statements had been made concerning the war. Such silence was viewed as disloyalty. "Unless we can admit that the Convention now sitting at St. John's Chapel," warned the *New York Times*, "includes among it a majority of sympathizers with secession, or partisans of their Northern allies, it is difficult to understand how a church with such historic memories and traditions . . . should hesitate to declare in this hour of trial its unaltered devotion to the American Constitution."[24]

The debate over the war lasted a number of days and involved both the House of Bishops and the House of Deputies. In the debate one saw the clash of two very different visions of the church. One delegate having just returned "from the battlefield near Sharpsburg" (i.e., Antietam) called for a condemnation of the "rebellion." Others rose to quickly attack the harshness of the language and of the introduction of "political" issues into the church's tribunal. Another delegate claimed that the moderation of the church's language over the years leading up to the war had been a source of peace. "If evil must come, the Church can at least say 'Thou canst not say I did it' . . . and if all religious denominations had followed our example, there would have been no war, and we should now have been one country." The debate then turned to the question of whether the southern dioceses that had departed to form a separate church were guilty of the act of schism. Likewise the question was raised whether southern clergy who had altered the liturgy so as no longer to pray for the President of the United States had violated their vow at ordination and should be censured. Others called for charity and noted that Roman Catholics did not censure each other though similarly divided by war. Such were the categories into which the war was rendered through Episcopal spectacles. After much debate the Deputies agreed to encourage the formal prayer for President and Congress already present in the liturgy, to pray for the restoration of peace, and to recognize that citizens had a duty to sustain and defend their country. But they rejected any formal condemnation of southern Episcopalians.[25]

Even greater turmoil was taking place among the House of Bishops. There the outcome was different. Very early in the war President Lincoln had asked Charles P. McIlvaine, Bishop of Ohio, to visit England as one of a select group of religious figures to present the northern side of the struggle to a nation strong in its southern sympathies. Upon his return, McIlvaine continued to be a strong advocate of Lincoln and the northern cause. In the House of Bishops he accomplished something near to an ecclesiastical coup d'état. The acting Presiding Bishop at the time was John Henry Hopkins of Vermont. He had penned a pastoral letter that referred to the present political crisis of union in only an oblique way, or as one of many social challenges the nation and the church confronted. McIlvaine convinced his fellow bishops to reject Hopkins' letter for one of his own composition, which unabashedly supported the Union and opposed the rebellion. In McIlvaine's letter the Anglican tradition was invoked through long passages taken from the Elizabethan homily "Against Willful Rebellion" and loyalty to the nation was pledged. It "grieved" over those southern church persons who not only participated in ecclesiastical disunion but "to a sad extent sympath[ized] with the movement [and gave] it their active cooperation." The bishops now spoke out, he continued, because "our communion is nobly represented wherever the nation's has dangers to brave, difficulties to be surmounted, sacrifices to be made, or sufferings to be borne."[26] And these loyal citizens and church persons needed to be instructed and encouraged. It was claimed at the time that McIlvaine's letter of support for the Union and the war effort had been championed behind the scenes by Episcopalians William Seward and Salmon P. Chase, both serving in Lincoln's cabinet. Others denied this, but clearly in the actions of the House of Bishops *noblesse oblige* had at least temporarily triumphed over apostolicism.[27] In all of this debate, however, the General Convention was strangely operating in a world of its own. Even though the convention was held less than a month after the Emancipation Proclamation had been announced, slavery had no place in the debate. Many national sins were evoked as the reason for God's judgment upon the country, but slavery was not one of them. Neither *noblesse oblige* nor apostolocist Episcopalians were able to grasp the centrality of slavery. The oddity of the Episcopal debate was noted by two visiting Methodist clergy who witnessed it. "They are a set of stupid asses: of moral imbeciles; they are living in an age, when oppressed humanity calls on them for relief, and yet though they have discussed this question for a week they haven't said one word about *Slavery*."[28]

THE ISSUE OF CHURCH UNITY

The last issue concerned the question of church unity. No other issue so fully illuminated the different visions of the *noblesse oblige* and apostolocist proponents. For the former, church unity was a perennial concern. A united church could fill a crucial void in American public life, by providing a true religious center to influence civil life. Furthermore the Episcopal Church could and should take a lead in this regard. During the 1850s some Episcopalians began noting that there was something wrong with the Episcopal Church at present. Clearly if every person were rational and reasonable, the attractiveness of the church would have quickly made it the preeminent Protestant communion. But somehow this did not occur. Hence, if the American religious public would not enter into The Episcopal Church, the Episcopal Church must share its gifts with others. The Muhlenberg Memorial of 1854, proposed by William A. Muhlenberg and a number of other clergy, called for the Episcopal Church to share the charism of Episcopal ordination to other religious communities without asking them to submit to other peculiarities of Episcopal polity and worship.

Muhlenberg's plan for church unity with the Episcopal Church at the center came to naught. Less than two decades later, however, William Reed Huntington provided another schema for church unity in *The Church-Idea* (1870). Huntington argued for a united national Protestant church based upon the essence of Anglicanism, which he reduced to four points: the authority of the Bible as the word of God, the primitive creeds (i.e., the *Apostles'* and *Nicene*) as the rule of faith, the two sacraments ordained by Christ himself, and the episcopate as the keystone of governmental unity. Huntington's *Church-Idea* became the foundation of the Chicago-Lambeth Quadrilateral that continues to be the principle ecumenical statement of the Anglican Communion. But in its original form we can see that *The Church-Idea* had other agendas: one sociological and one theological. On the sociological level it worked toward the creation of a great national Protestant church that could offer a counterweight to an increasing Roman Catholic presence in the United States. Indeed, one cannot truly understand pre-Vatican II Protestant ecumenical efforts without seeing them at least in part as a response to Roman Catholicism. Roman Catholics, although a minority in the population, exercised influence because they were the largest single church, and spoke in a common voice. Protestants dissipated their numerical strength because they spoke out of division. Hence unity was necessary and Huntington was clear, church unity could only be on either an Anglican or a Roman basis. "Two religious systems and only two offer to the Christian people of this country an historical basis of unity. These are respectively the Anglican and the Roman Churches . . . one of Anglo-Saxon, and the other of Italian stock, each maintaining . . . that it can offer to the American people an historical basis of unity. . . .The truth is that Anglicanism is the only form of Christianity of which Rome is seriously and thoroughly afraid. In the national church of the Anglo-Saxon she sees a plant of hardy growth, and one which all her blasts do not suffice to wither."[29] On the theological level, church unity allowed churches to clean house vis-à-vis their inherited doctrines, and determine which were relevant to the present age, and which had become obsolete. Huntington, for example, saw his quadrilateral as in fact replacing the *Thirty-nine Articles* as the theological essence of Anglicanism. It is not surprising that this agenda appealed particularly to those who occupied what might be described as the liberal or broad church wing of the Episcopal Church. For more Roman Catholic-leaning Episcopalians, such an agenda was wrought with problems. A pan-Protestant ecumenical movement with Episcopalians at the center could only weaken the catholic inheritance of the church. Likewise what some saw as ecclesiastical house cleaning, the catholic-minded persons saw as threatening inherited doctrines that linked Episcopalians to other catholic churches. It was *noblesse oblige* versus apostolicism all over again.

The simmering disagreement came to a head when plans began in the 1930s to explore the union of Presbyterians and Episcopalians. On one level such a union was obvious. Both were the heirs of the established churches of the British Isles, where there had been periodic talk over the centuries of also mending this rupture from the Reformation. In America the two churches occupied the same socio-economic niche. They were powerful insiders in the Protestant establishment. Their communicants were educated in places like Princeton, Smith and Yale, and, as the saying went, they belonged to the same country clubs. In 1931 the Episcopal General Convention authorized a commission to confer with Presbyterian representatives to explore the possibility of church union. In 1936 a "Proposed Concordat" with the Presbyterian Church was issued and this in turn was approved by the General Convention of 1937. In the Concordat the Presbyterian Church was invited to begin a process to achieve organic union between the two churches. It looked as if church unity was in the offing.

Almost immediately this plan was viewed quite differently from our two points of view. For those we have been calling the *noblesse oblige* the plan was attractive on a number of grounds. On the theological level it placed the Episcopal Church in the forefront of the ecumenical movement. Few theological movements captured the imagination of the time as did ecumenism. Individuals wrote of the excitement of moving from the great ecumenical meetings of the spring and summer of 1937 in Oxford and Edinburgh, at which a vision of Christian unity was posited, to the Episcopal General Convention of that fall at which this vision began to be actuated. The American accomplishment could also serve as a first fruit of a much larger phenomenon. "Should the Union of the Protestant Episcopal Church in the United States of America and the Presbyterian Church U.S.A. be realized," one commentator wrote, "it would prepare the way for a possible union of the Presbyterian Communion and the Anglican Communion throughout the world. This would mean the birth of a new church, probably greater in size, and, we believe, in vitality, than any non-Roman Church the world has ever known."[30] Furthermore it seemed to flow also from the revival of Protestant theology associated with the movement of Neo-Orthodoxy. Neo-Orthodoxy lifted up again the great message of the Reformation against both liberalism and Catholicism (whether it be Roman or Anglo). The theological trends all pointed towards church unity. On the social level it would provide a strong counter-balance to a growing Roman Catholic influence. It was an idea whose time had come. As one commentator noted, it could only be opposed within the Presbyterian Church by those who clung to "Fundamentalist Protestantism" and in the Episcopal Church by those who preferred to be stuck in a "Fundamentalist Catholicism."[31]

For those whom we have been calling the apostolocists, union with Presbyterians was not an issue of "Fundamentalism" but rather of a betrayal of fundamentals. A series of tracts with titles such as "Shall the Episcopal Church Repudiate the New Testament?" claimed that the proposed plan repudiated the witness of the ancient church in the abandonment of the three-fold ministry of bishop, priest and deacon, in its de-emphasis upon the sacrament of confirmation, and in other particulars.[32] The proposed basis of union for them threatened the fundamental nature of the Episcopal Church. "If these 'Basic Principles' be accepted," wrote William Manning, bishop of New York, "the Episcopal Church would no longer be the Church for which Seabury . . . and our fathers in the faith who stood with [him], made such sacrifices and endured such great trials to secure the Apostolic Ministry, and to which John Henry Hobart gave his great watchword—'Evangelical Truth and Apostolic Order.'"[33] Such intensity of opposition surprised the proponents of merger, particularly since the 1937 action of General Convention authorizing the seeking of a plan of union had passed both houses so easily. But by the early 1940s many grass root Episcopalians, for whom the new theological movements meant little or nothing, believed that key principles were being threatened. It was a case of the phenomenon that John Henry Newman had noted a century earlier concerning the Arian controversy—

that in many ways the laity were far more conservative and appreciative of inherited belief than were clerical theologians.[34] In the debate over church union, many of the most sophisticated voices called for merger. They often cited current scholarship that raised questions about traditional Anglican doctrines such as apostolic succession. The opposition was far less sophisticated, but passionate as reflected by the title of one of the more strident tracts: *Bishops? A Defense and an Appeal by A Fool. Possibly a Damned Fool. God Knows.*

When the proposal came to a vote at General Convention in 1946 General Convention it was defeated. This was viewed with great displeasure by the Presbyterians who had earlier passed the measure. Presbyterians rightly noted that it was the Episcopal Church and not they who had inaugurated the discussion, yet now they were recipients of the Episcopal desire to stop the action. As one Presbyterian noted, "I felt like a man who had been invited to dinner and had the door slammed in his face."[35] Presbyterians were able (regrettably) to witness at fist hand the tension between noblesse oblige and apostolical Episcopalians.

THE MODERN PREDICAMENT

What we have seen is that these two understandings of the role of the Episcopal Church in American society—which I have designated the *noblesse oblige* and apostolical—were a decisive influence in the denomination from its founding through the 1940s. In many ways we have seen them balancing each other off, as one strove to draw the church closer to the society while the other worked to create a critical distance. Over the past fifty years the balance seems to have shifted in favor of the former, and I want to make a few tentative suggestions as to why this has been the case.

The first is that both views were tempered over the period we have looked at by the hegemonic role of the Church of England and of English precedent. Not only was the Church of England the unquestionable center of worldwide Anglicanism, but also English cultural, social, and intellectual attitudes were largely normative within the Anglican communion. Manifestations of this phenomenon can be seen in as varied examples as the fondness for English gothic as the preferred architectural style for church buildings, to the wide-scale adaptation of the English custom of "muddling through" or the avoidance of sharp issues of disagreement. But after 1945 this world began to change. In the political realm the capital of the world no longer was London but somewhere along the NewYork-Washington corridor (some might say the New York/Washington/Los Angeles triad, but I do not think that things have sunk that low). In the realm of education, by the 1970s, America, and not England, became the place where bright young students wanted to study. Although this shift was much less apparent ecclesiastically, the shift can be seen here as well. Simply to take my institution: In the 1960s six of eighteen faculty members had degrees from either Oxford or Cambridge. By 2005 the number was down to one. Although difficult to gauge, there also seems to have been something of a decline in Anglophilism in the Episcopal Church during this period. This has perhaps been helped by a sociological shift in the make-up of the American Episcopal Church. The large numbers of Roman Catholics who have been attracted to the Episcopal Church in the last twenty-five years have been drawn more by the church's perceived combination of social liberalism and Catholic liturgy than by its identification with English culture. The decline of English hegemony has had the effect of making American Episcopal actions more autonomous.

A second factor has been what the historian Robert Handy has called the "Second Disestablishment."[36] Until the early part of the previous century, Handy argued, the old line Protestant churches did serve as an unofficial establishment in providing a religious vision for the nation. The period after 1945 has seen a gradual erosion of the privileged position the historic Anglo-Saxon Protestant churches have played in American culture. Protestants were no longer seen to be at the very center of American culture.

These two factors have led to a morphing of what we have called the *noblesse oblige* tradition. Those holding to this tradition, one recalls, had believed that the Episcopal Church played an important role in shaping and directing the larger society. For most of the period we have been looking at, this responsibility was understood in quasi-establishment ways. The Episcopal Church should function as a key insider in the larger culture, educating its elites, providing a location for acts of public piety, and upholding key religious values. The struggles of the 1960s led to a reexamination of this role. With the large scale questioning of the concept of civil religion and quasi-establishment, it came to be argued that the proper model for the church was not an establishmentarian stance but a prophetic stance. It was only as a prophetic community that the church could make its influence on the larger world. The paradigmatic experiences here were the civil rights and anti-war movements. Here individuals confronted a complaisant world and a complacent church for the sake of justice and peace. But although this call to action was now cast in prophetic language rather than establishment language, there is still the sense that it was the particular role of Episcopalians to witness to the larger society, by giving to it a sense of moral direction. Thus at the General Convention of 1967, when the Presiding Bishop, John Hines, called for the Episcopal Church to redirect its resources to address the problems of the inner city, he said that it was the role of the church to offer "healing for our national life."[37] There are still intriguing elements of *noblesse oblige* but now cast in a fundamentally different idiom. To what degree there is continuity between the earlier and the latter idioms is of course open for debate, but the impulse remains.[38]

The shift from establishmentarian rhetoric to prophetic rhetoric has served to strengthen the old *noblesse oblige* position over the past forty years. And what has happened, we may ask, of the old apostolocist position? This view has weakened over these years. The apostolocist position had always argued that the church must cling fast to the essentials of the faith as they were found in the early church. But what exactly did the early church teach and believe? The picture of the faith and practice of the early church was far more complicated in 1960 than it was in 1860 and was even more complicated by century's end. The scholarly view of doctrine, liturgy, ecclesiology, even what constituted the authorities to which one was to seek, was far less certain now than when apostolocists could rally supporters against the plan of Presbyterian union with the cry "Shall the Episcopal Church Repudiate the New Testament?" Even in the 1940s, we noted that new scholarly studies were being used to challenge traditional apostolocist doctrines. We began by noting that the apostolocist position contained a fundamental falsehood: for all the talk of separation, the Episcopal Church was not socially or culturally at odds with the larger society, but rather deeply involved in it. One could hear echoes of Tertullian's famous query, "what has Jerusalem to do with Athens?" but it was more for effect than anything else. By the middle of the twentieth century it also became apparent that the church was not separated intellectually. Ecumenical theology had called into question many of the theological claims apostolocists had long held dear. Hence as Athens (i.e., the academy) changed, the apostolocist position became less and less tenable.

In some ways the last hurrah of the apostolocist position came during the debate over the ordination of women in the 1970s.[39] The continuation of an all-male priesthood was seen as being in continuity with the universal experience of catholic Christianity. A "Committee for the Apostolic Ministry" was established to defend the traditional practice, but in actuality there was little if any appeal to the practice of the apostolic church. Other arguments made up the arsenal of the opponents to women's ordination. The approval of the ordination of women by the General Convention of 1976, and the gradual, overwhelming acceptance by Episcopalians of a female priestly ministry (despite the absence of apostolic sanction), gravely weakened the old apostolocist position.

If this analysis is true, then one might see the present debate in the Episcopal Church as a re-shifting of the apostolocist position, resting it now upon a new foundation. Scripturalism and an appeal to an international Anglican witness (particularly found in the witness of African Anglicanism) now are beginning to function in the way that the appeal to the apostolic witness had traditionally done. In this sense the apostolocist position has become more evangelical than it had traditionally been, but although the theological presuppositions have changed, the cultural principle (at least in its own self-perception) has not. There continues to be a concern that the church would lose its distinctiveness if it draws too close to the spirit of the age. Scripturalism and international Anglicanism, it is believed, can provide that foundation by which to judge an ever changing society. They can function as the fixed point to navigate the Episcopal Church through the always tricky sees of American culture. And there are even some elements of continuity. Writing in 1973, John L. Scott, chair of the Committee for the Apostolic Ministry, challenged the authority of General Conventions by asking "Whether General Convention can give a bishop power to make female priests. Is there not in these Watergate days room to question limitations of power? Could General Convention for instance declare that homosexual marriage is possible?"[40]

This final section is merely the reflection of a person who observes the culture of the Episcopal Church. It may be wrong in analysis (i.e., seeing a continuity between the establishmentarian *nobles oblige* tendency and the more recent prophetic tendency, and also continuity between the new conservatism and the older apostolocist tendency). It may be that the shifts of the past forty plus years are creating a fundamentally new church and that the dichotomy we have been tracing is of mere historic interest. But what this exercise has attempted to demonstrate is that within a given religious tradition there exist inner tensions that the outsider (and all too often the insider) does not perceive. A focus upon these tensions may help both to understand why the community has acted in the way that is has done.

Notes

1. This essay is an outgrowth of themes I have treated in an earlier work, "Denominations as Bilingual Communities," in Robert Bruce Mullin and Russell E. Richey, ed., *Reimagining Denominationalism: Interpretive Essays* (New York: Oxford University Press, 1994).
2. Sydney Ahlstrom, *A Religious History of the American People* (New Haven: Yale University Press, 1972), 1079 ff.
3. Richard Hooker, *On the Lawes of Ecclesiastical Polity,* Book VIII, 1:7.
4. "Preface to the Book of Common Prayer" (1789).
5. Tertullian, *De praescriptione haereticorum,* vii, 9.
6. Samuel Johnson, "My Present Thoughts of Episcopacy," in *Samuel Johnson . . . His Career and Writings,* ed. Herbert and Carol Schneider, 4 vols. (New York: Columbia University Press, 1929), 3:3-4.
7. John Henry Hobart, *An Apology for Apostolic Order and its Advocates . . . .,* 2d ed. (New York: Stanford and Swords, 1844), 16.
8. William Smith, *A Sermon Preached in Christ Church Philadelphia . . .*(Philadelphia: Robert Aiken, 1785), 21.
9. Ibid., 23.
10. Ibid., 31.
11. Letter from Samuel Seabury to Dr. Smith, reprinted in Francis L. Hawks and William Stevens Perry, eds., *Documentary History of the Protestant Episcopal Church . . .,* 2 vols. (New York: J. Pott, 1863-64), 2:280.
12. *Bishop Seabury's Second Charge, to the Clergy of his Diocess*[sic] (New Haven: Thomas and Samuel Green, 1786), 12.
13. Paul V, Marshall, *One, Catholic, and Apostolic: Samuel Seabury and the Early Episcopal Church* (New York: Church Pub., 2004), 22.
14. Robert Baird, *Religion in America* (New York: Harper and Brothers, 1856), 537.
15. John C. Calhoun, quoted in Chester Forrester Dunham, *The Attitude of the Northern Clergy Toward the South, 1860-1865* (Toledo, Oh.: The Gray Company, 1942), 1-2. Calhoun himself worshipped in the Episcopal Church, as did also Henry Clay.
16. Thomas M. Clark, *Reminiscences* (New York: Thomas Whittaker, 1895), 136.
17. *The Diary of George Templeton Strong,* ed. Allan Nevins and Milton Halsey Thomas, 4 vols. (New York: Macmillan, 1952), 1: 195.
18. Ibid., 2: 278, 304-05.
19. Ibid., 3: 124-26.
20. Milo Mahan to William L. Johnson, 20 April 1861, Deans Papers, The General Theological Seminary.
21. See, "The First Bishop of Connecticut and the *Episcopal Recorder,"* *The American Quarterly Church Review* 15 (1863): 30-76.
22. See the citations in "The American Church in the Disruption," *Christian Remembrancer* 45 (1863): 162-84.

23. See, in particular, James H. Moorhead, *American Apocalypse: Yankee Protestants and the Civil War, 1860-1869* (New Haven: Yale University Press, 1978).

24. The *New York Times* October 9, 1862, 4.

25. Speeches in the debate can be found in the *Church Journal*, October 8, 1862.

26. *A Pastoral Letter of the House of Bishops of the Protestant Episcopal Church . . .* (New York: Baker & Goodwin, 1862), 4, 8.

27. Contrast the editorial "Government Pressure," *Church Journal*, November 16, 1862, 348-49, which claimed strong government intrigue, with the citations found in Diana H Butler, *Standing Against the Whirlwind: Evangelical Episcopalians in Nineteenth Century America* (New York: Oxford University Press, 1995), 177, n. 162.

28. "General Convention of 1862," *American Church Quarterly Review* 15 (1863): 118.

29. William Reed Huntington, *The Church-Idea: An Essay Towards Unity* (Harrisburg, Penn.: Morehouse Publishing, 2002), 111-13.

30. Gardiner M. Day, *Why Unite With the Presbyterians?* (Cambridge, Mass.: Episcopal Evangelical Fellowship, 1945), 8.

31. Theodre O. Wedel, "Fundamentalist Catholicism: An Open Letter to an Anglo-Catholic," *Anglican Theological Review* 25 (1943): 161-81.

32. This was the title of one of a series of tracts published by Joint Committee to Maintain Prayer Book Principles.

33. William T. Manning, *The Proposed Basic Principles for Merging the Episcopal Church with the Presbyterian Church* (New York: n.p., 1945), 9.

34. John Henry Newman, *On Consulting the Faithful on Matters of Doctrine*, ed. John Coulson (London: Collins, 1961).

35. Quoted in George E. DeMille, *The Episcopal Church Since 1900: A Brief History* (New York: Morehouse-Gorham, 1955), 160.

36. Robert T. Handy, *A Christian America: Protestant Hopes and Historical Realities*, 2d ed. (New York: Oxford University Press, 1984). Whereas most scholars accept Handy's assessment, many place it chronologically later than does Handy (who puts it in the decades 1920-1940).

37. See Kenneth Kesselus, *John E. Hines: Granite on Fire* (Austin: Episcopal Theological Seminary of the Southwest, 1995), 261 ff. As Kesselus makes clear, one sees this morphing yet the continuing idea of Episcopal leadership in many aspects of the career of John Hines.

38. For an example of how a non-Episcopalian has argued that the current Episcopal debate over sexuality serves the larger community, see Harvey Cox's op-ed essay, "A Schism Averted?," *The Wall Street Journal* (August 12, 2003).

39. The standard study on the debate over the ordination of women in the Episcopal Church is Pamela W. Darling, *New Wine: The Story of Women Transforming Leadership and Power in the Episcopal Church* (Cambridge, Mass.: Cowley Publications, 1994).

40. Letter printed in *The Living Church*, September 23, 1973.

Who's Got the Spirit in the Episcopal Church? A Case Study of the "Connecticut Six"

Kathryn Greene-McCreight
St. John's Episcopal Church
Albertus Magnus College

I would like to approach my contribution to the investigation of American confessional churches from the point of view of a case study. The particular case study I would like to present is from the contemporary scene in the Episcopal Church, USA, my own church tradition. That situation, I will suggest, is one where the Holy Spirit, traditionally linked in prayer to the Father and the Son, and systematically to the interpretation of Scripture, is now being understood in many Episcopal parishes and dioceses across America, as in the apostolic era, as the root and ground of prophecy. That is, the work of the Holy Spirit has been severed from its presence in Scripture and in the doctrine of the Trinity, and the proponents of such a practice place themselves in apostolic authority. But there has been a backlash against this appropriation of the Holy Spirit, both in theology and liturgics, which anchors again the Holy Spirit to the biblical witness and opposes outright the new shining forth of the Holy Spirit in the way it is being presented. In short, my question will ultimately be this: who has the Spirit in the Episcopal Church, and how do we know this?

Others would certainly approach my case study differently than I will. Questions might be brought to bear regarding the nature of the body; the nature of marital love; the nature of justice? And these would all be theological ways into the case study. Still others might choose an historical-descriptive framework, researching the roots of the present controversies. I will choose, however, a theological-systematic approach. I think most fundamentally the matter of my case study is of the Holy Spirit, and how it has become conventionally linked to Christian experience throughout the Episcopal Church, USA (ECUSA), in particular in the American scene, Canada and the United States. *Ecclesia semper reformanda* now in the Episcopal Church USA entails the "Hurricane Spirit, Toppling Taboos."[1]

Of course, the main point to make here before I start on the case is to admit up front that the Episcopal Church is not precisely a confessional church, although these chapters suggested a broader approach to confessional traditions. This does not mean that it has no clear faith to confess, but that it has no *Augsburg*, no *Dordt*, no *Heidelberg*. There is no historic document that defines its faith over against other denominations in this manner. Of course, there are many resources which do point to the regulation of doctrine and practice in the

Episcopal Church, which we will see later. But for now, while our topic is on confessional traditions, it must be said, as Bruce Mullin has also articulated, that the ECUSA is not properly a confessional tradition.

BACKGROUND TO THE CASE STUDY: GC 2003

The case study of the "Connecticut Six" (CT6), as they have been come to be called, cannot be understood apart from the General Convention of the ECUSA and the proceeding discussions about General Convention 2003 (GC2003). The CT6, six parishes of Connecticut who have united as a single voice, are among the many across the country who formally have objected to one of the decisions of GC2003, which allowed for the consecration of an "openly gay" bishop for the Diocese of New Hampshire, V. (Vicky) (Imo)Gene Robinson (Robinson's Kentucky parents thought he was going to die as an infant and thus did not think the gender of the name mattered and thus named him "Vicky Imogene"; the birth certificate was never changed). Bishop Robinson was elected by his Diocese, and his case was forwarded to the Convention for confirmation in order that he be consecrated. The case went to convention because of its own particular timing; not all bishops need to be voted on at GC. It has been commented by those who disapprove that this was a "conspiracy" to force the issue to Convention, where a vote would solidify the practice.

Gene Robinson had been married to a woman, fathered two children, divorced his wife and has been openly living with his male partner for many years since then. He had been active in his diocese with youth who are experiencing homosexual tendencies and desires, and Robinson considers encouraging and supporting them in this journey to be a vital part of his ministry.

Evangelical Catholics and orthodox among ECUSA, who are committed to the authority of Scripture and therefore also to a traditional understanding of the purposes of sexuality, have been shocked by this vote.[2] Most of the two-thirds world rejects the revisionist vote and most of the prospective policies linked to it which have been suggested.[3] The vote openly overturned the collective position of the Communion, which had been made clear in the 1998 Lambeth Conference resolution.[4] Proposals which would follow the GC2003 convention decision are the development of liturgies for the binding in covenant of marriage consenting adults of the same sex.[5] Many parishes and priests among the evangelical Catholics and orthodox have organized groups of like-minded in order to move the denomination to change its stated views on sexuality, or as they say, to "repent." Such groups go by the names of the American Anglican Council, the Anglican Communion Institute, and the Network.

Even the Archbishop of Canterbury and the Anglican Consultative Council (ACC) have tried to exert some form of discipline on the ECUSA, stating that it has "broken the bonds of affection in Communion." They had invited ECUSA to absent itself from the Nottingham meeting of the ACC in the summer of 2005, but ECUSA sent a larger (unofficial) delegation than usual in order to explain its vote. The stated explanation given by ECUSA was that their vote at GC2003 to consecrate Gene Robinson (which was 60% pro, 40% con) had been on the basis and authority of the Holy Spirit, and was a prophetic utterance on the part of the "winners." The exegetical biblical basis given for the vote was the story of Acts 10, where Peter's vision of the picnic blanket shows him that all foods are clean.[6] Likewise, say those who claim the authority of the Holy Spirit, they have received the message that gay and lesbian sex is no longer prohibited by God, and gay and lesbian people are to be included in all ranks of church lay and ordained leadership. The next question to be pushed will be gay marriage.[7]

After GC2003, many parishes, priests and parishioners gathered under the auspices of the newly formed reactionary groups, such as the Anglican Communion Institute (ACI) and the Anglican American Council (AAC). There are and have been many such splinter groups throughout the Episcopal Church, even long before the Convention of 2003, but these two seem to have the loudest voices among them at present writing regarding this particular issue.

The CT6, after GC2003, banded together out of a sense of solidarity in the light of conscientious objection and inquired about the possibility of applying for DEPO (Delegated Episcopal Pastoral Oversight),[8] which is a provision recommended by the Archbishop of Canterbury and the Anglican Consultative Council in its Windsor Report of 2004 and acknowledged as necessary by the Primates at Dromantine.[9] The provision of DEPO allows for a parish disagreeing in good conscience with their bishop to apply for another bishop from another Diocese of the Episcopal Church to serve them as a "flying bishop." Bishop Smith of Connecticut, however, changed this suggested policy for his Diocese, stating that if parishes choose this, the Bishop would still like to make his Episcopal visitations to the parishes and still to be the ultimate authority over them, receiving still their tithes and submission. This, of course, basically defeated the purposes of DEPO, which was meant to distance the parish from the Bishop's lately announced heterodoxy and place them under an orthodox bishop or, if a revisionist parish under an orthodox Bishop, to place them under a revisionist Bishop. At the time of this writing, it is believed that one parish in the Diocese of Connecticut (not a member of the CT6) has applied for DEPO.

The CT6 report feeling betrayed by the Bishop's GC2003 vote. The Bishop "changed his mind"[10] at Convention by voting (previously he had promised not to acknowledge homosexuality as normalized) for the consecration of Gene Robinson as Suffragan Bishop of New Hampshire. The CT6 found this to be an abandonment of historic Christian confession about the nature and purposes of sexuality and marriage, and an unlacing of the ties to the former doctrine of the ECUSA. Now Bishop Smith, along with approximately 60 percent of the House of Bishops, was seen as creating his own provisions, other than those agreed upon by the primates at Windsor and the Primates' Communiqué of February 2005.

Relations between the Diocesan Bishop of Connecticut, Andrew Smith, and the CT6 parishes became brittle. The Bishop rejected any pleas coming from the CT6 in phalanx against him, and chose to focus canonically on one parish at a time. The CT6 chose to offer to meet with the Bishop as a group, rather than one by one. This the Bishop apparently perceived as threatening, and indicated that he did not want to deal with them as a little diocese within his own Diocese. One parish in particular was singled out for his attention, one which was coincidentally having trouble repaying a diocesan loan on its new building.

St. John's, Bristol, is a mid-sized congregation of about 300 parishioners which had recently built a new church, having taken out a loan from the diocese, a large sum which it was apparently unable to repay. The Convention decision over Gene Robinson had caused turmoil in the parish, and some parishioners had left because they could not countenance this decision. They felt that remaining in ECUSA amounted to blasphemy. Others had left because of the priest's orthodox stance and rejection of the Bishop's vote. This left the parish weakened financially as of the end of 2003 and the beginning of 2004.[11]

The priest, the Rev. Mark Hansen, apparently chose to take a sabbatical during the spring and summer of 2005 according to his contracted policy at his hiring twelve years earlier. While the Bishop states that Fr. Hansen did not notify him of his wanting to take a sabbatical, Fr. Hansen insists that he did notify one of the Suffragan Bishops. Fr. Hansen took a job outside the parish while on sabbatical, but has not communicated why. The Bishop took issue with this also. In addition, the Bishop accused Fr. Hansen of leaving his parish without adequate pastoral care during his sabbatical, when according to Fr. Hansen, two other priests were left in charge of the parish. For over two months, they had been preaching, celebrating the sacraments and providing pastoral care. Bishop Smith seemed to be threatening with inhibition on the basis of going on an uncommunicated sabbatical, of leaving the parish without pastoral care, of not paying their assessments to the Diocese, and of not paying on a Diocesan loan of some $70,000.[12] In actual fact, the Bishop registered the inhibition claiming the application of Title IV Canon 10 which has nothing to do with sabbaticals, defaulting on loans, or writing fiery letters to the Bishop, which Mark Hansen had apparently done.[13] Instead, Title IV Canon 10 points to the abandonment of the Anglican Communion on the part of the priest.

Advised by his Standing Committee, Bishop Smith then threatened the priest of this parish with inhibition, but was assuaged at a meeting of all the clergy in the Connecticut diocese and encouraged to "slow down" and "back up." This stay of execution lasted approximately two or three months.

The Bishop then formally accused Fr. Hansen of abandoning communion. He used a canon which is normally intended for the Episcopal priest entering another Communion, such as if he or she were to become Roman Catholic. This canon is meant to be used when a priest or deacon either renounces the doctrine, discipline or worship of the Episcopal Church or makes a formal admission into a religious body not in communion with the Anglican Communion. That would be "abandoning the Communion" according to this canon. But for the first time this canon was used to inhibit an Episcopal priest for disagreeing with the Bishop over the matter of homosexuality in the church, and for financial breach of responsibility.[14]

The inhibition took place like this, according to members of the parish. Bishop Smith arrived unannounced at the church one morning with twelve other associates while Father Hansen was at his second job.[15] With Bishop Smith was a locksmith who changed the locks to the building and to the office so that no one would be able to get into the church except the new priest whom he was installing in Fr. Hansen's place. She was at his side. She is known in the Diocese for having been a brilliant lawyer in her former career. She is also known for a public comment to the effect that the Episcopal Church should split rather than compromise with traditionalists on the issue of homosexuality in Holy Orders and Holy Matrimony. With the Bishop also came a computer technician who pulled down the web page and rerouted it to the Diocesan home page. The technician also apparently pulled the financial and parish files for the Bishop's use.

At this point the parish treasurer was no longer allowed to access the accounts. According to the then-vestry of the parish, the treasurer had been planning to pay the bills the next day. The Bishop turned this fact into another damning detail, claiming that the parish electricity was about to be turned off and that he hastily had the account paid off, saving the church from lack of electrical power. Guards were posted at the doors of the church, and no one was allowed to enter, not even the vestry. The church secretary was asked to stay and help with the takeover, but said she could not do that in good conscience. She wept when the Bishop's entourage demanded keys to the offices and insisted she give them the password to the computer, and began threatening her with violation of canon law. It has been reported that she said "But I am not even an Episcopalian!"

There was then galvanized against Bishop Smith a group of nine bishops from across ECUSA who were furious at his activities with this parish, and who threatened to bring charges against him, accusing him in his turn of abandoning the Anglican Communion for his misuse of Canon Law. The Presiding Bishop had apparently notified Bishop Smith in mid-April that the use of this Canon for the purpose the Bishop used it was indeed deemed invalid.

The next step in this unfolding drama is that formal ecclesiastical charges were filed against Bishop Smith.[16] Nineteen Episcopal lay leaders and priests in Connecticut from the parishes of the CT6 (Christ Church, Watertown; Bishop Seabury, Groton; Trinity, Bristol; St. Paul's, Darien; Christ and the Epiphany, East Haven; and St. John's, Bristol) have brought charges against Bishop Smith to Frank Griswold, Presiding Bishop of ECUSA. These charges accuse Bishop Smith of violating the Constitution and Canons of ECUSA and laws of the State of Connecticut. According to the then-vestry, they address Bishop Smith's actions to freeze bank accounts, custodial funds and securities of Bishop Seabury Church, Groton; Christ Church, Watertown; Christ and the Epiphany, East Haven; and St. John's, Bristol. Under Title 4 of the disciplinary canons of the General Convention, the Presiding Bishop is required to communicate the charge to Bishop Smith and to forward the charge to a Review Committee no later than 90 days after it is received. The Review Committee and an attorney representing ECUSA will then determine whether the charges constitute a formal presentment, or a call for adjudication. The case would then proceed to ecclesiastical trial, involving confidential proceedings.

Then, in addition, the CT6 filed charges with the state of Connecticut, claiming that Bishop Smith had violated the statutes and constitution of the state. The results from both of these cases, the ecclesiastical and the civil, remain pending at the time of this writing. However, what is certain is that Bishop Andrew Smith won the day with the inhibition. A new vestry was chosen, and the parish has relinquished all ties to the AAC and the ACI.

BIBLICAL INTERPRETATION AMONG THE ORTHODOX AND THE REVISIONISTS

I would like at this point to share the contents of a document which was prepared by the Ekklesia Organization[17] at the commissioning of three non-ECUSA Anglican bishops, the Most Rev. Drexel W. Gomez, The Most Rev. Gregory Venables, and the Most Rev. Bernard Malango.[18] In this document they attempted to lay out Anglican biblical interpretation in preparation for the meeting of the Anglican Communion Council (ACC) in Nottingham, England, from June 18-25, 2005. The debate which sparked the document was, as in the case above, the status of homosexuality within the Anglican Communion. Two of the 38 provinces of the Anglican Communion, the United States and Canada, have suggested that traditional teaching on sexuality needs to be revised, on the basis of what is claimed to be the prophetic inspiration of the Holy Spirit, such that homosexual erotic activity is to be seen as holy as is heterosexual marriage when practiced between two consenting, committed adults (non-related, presumably). Archbishops Gomez, Venables, and Malango are on the orthodox side of the discussion.

In their missive they say that, while the revisionists of the United States and Canada declare the debate to be a matter of the interpretation of Scripture—suggesting that everyone has his or her own interpretation of Scripture—the Archbishops would say that it is a matter of the *method* of Scripture's interpretation. They then seek to outline the method by appeal to Thomas Cranmer (1489-1556) and Richard Hooker (1554-1600). They offer "Anglican Principles of Biblical Interpretation" drawn from Hooker and Cranmer. Certainly their mention of Hooker's "three legged stool" of theological method, that is, Scripture, Tradition, and Reason as the overriding authorities for Anglican Theology, is helpful, but it is often misunderstood and misused in the contemporary debate. It should be not seen as a three legged stool, with equal "lengths" of legs and therefore of the equal authorities of Scripture, Tradition and Reason. Hooker would have been appalled at such a suggestion. Rather, I would say that the three legs of the "stool" function in Hooker more like the three wheels of a Tricycle, with the grand front wheel of Scripture supported by the two smaller wheels of Tradition and Reason.[19] That is, for Hooker the "three legged stool" assumed the primacy of Scripture over the other two authorities.

I therefore do not agree with Archbishops Gomez, Venables, and Malango when it comes to the way in which they open their missive on the interpretation of Scripture. I do not understand the proper reading of Scripture to be about the search for a correct method, but in emulating the proper postures, attitudes and presuppositions adequate for reading the Holy Writings which we learned from the Fathers, especially in the *Rule of Faith*. And I do believe that Cranmer and Hooker would agree with me, and not with the Archbishops. Why did these Bishops appeal to Anglican Reformation Tradition rather than going squarely for the Church Fathers, not to mention to the biblical texts themselves? The primacy of Scripture had always been a distinctive teaching of Anglican Doctrine, even where theologians have disagreed with it.

THE RULE OF FAITH

At this point I should say something about the *Rule of Faith*. This, to me, is or should be the crux of the matter for the Anglican Communion's addressing of biblical interpretation. The *Rule of Faith* is an ancient "take" on the whole narrative of Scripture, such that the Old and New Testaments must be held together in dialectical tension, both as the Word of God, with the central stories of Jesus' life, death, and resurrection at the core. The *Rule of Faith* itself can be found among the Church Fathers from the second century, but its roots are within the biblical texts themselves.[20] "Their strong center, strong enough to be recognizable in works as diverse as those of Jude and Ignatius, James and Justin Martyr, was not a theory or a new ethic, not an abstract dogma or rote-learned teaching, but a particular story told and lived."[21]

We can find early kernels of the *Rule of Faith* which expand upon New Testament statements about Jesus and his relation to the Father in Ignatius' *Letter to the Ephesians* and *Letter to the Trallians* and in Polycarp's *Letter to the Philippians*. References to and longer summaries of the *Rule of Faith* can be found in Tertullian (160-225), *Veiling of the Virgins*, 1, where we see the similarities between the *Rule of Faith* and the creeds:

> The *Rule of Faith*, indeed, is altogether one, alone immoveable and irreformable, the rule, to wit, of believing in one only God omnipotent, Creator of the Universe, and His Son Jesus Christ, born of the Virgin Mary, crucified under Pontius Pilate, raised again the third day from the dead, received in the heavens, sitting now at the right of the Father, destined to come to judge the quick and the dead through resurrection of the flesh as well [as of the Spirit]. The law of faith being constant, the other succeeding points of discipline and conversation admit the novelty of correction.[22]

We also find similar material in Irenaeus, who as early as 180 C.E. in his treatise *Against the Heretics* expresses the Church's understanding of the faith. This understanding can be expressed in different words, but the content remains the same: a Trinitarian creedal affirmation which later develops into the fixed forms of creeds like the *Apostles' Creed* and the *Nicene Creed*. The *Rule of Faith*, says Irenaeus, is like a rich man who puts his money in a bank: so the Apostles deposited in the Church their faith by bequeathing to the Church the *Rule of Faith* and the Scriptures (*AH* 3.4.1). Irenaeus illustrates the relationship between the *Rule of Faith* and Scripture by using the metaphor of a mosaic (*AH* 1.8.1) which can be arranged to form the portrait of a king or that of a dog. In the ancient world, mosaics were shipped unassembled with the plan or key (*hypothesis*) according to which they were to be arranged. The *Rule of Faith* is like the key, he says, which explains how the Scriptures (mosaics) are to be arranged, to render the portrait of the King, whereas the heretics arrange the Scriptures wrongly to form the picture of a dog or fox. Thus, the *Rule of Faith* assures a correct reading of Scripture, indeed a Christological reading (in accordance with the "King").

In a subsequent passage, Irenaeus points out how the heretics are like the readers of Homer's poetry who take bits and pieces of text and string them together in their own fashion, taking them out of context such that they now form a new narrative (*AH* 1.9.4). This is exactly what the heretics do with Scripture. (Tertullian also refers to these Homeric textual distortions, *Presc.* 39.)

> So the person who holds to himself unswervingly the Canon of Truth he received in baptism, will recognise the names and terms and parables as being from the scripture, but will not recognise this blasphemous *hypothesis* of theirs. Though he will detect the mosaic pieces, he will not accept the fox instead of the king's image. Restoring each of the expressions to it own rank, and accommodating it to the body of truth, he will expose as naked and unsubstantiated their fiction (Irenaeus *AH* 1.9.4).

The *hypothesis* is characterized implicitly as the "king's face," or the Christological referent. The "plan" is Christological. We can see that in Irenaeus' *Demonstration of the Apostolic Preaching* (*Dem.* 6), which links the Father and the Son, insisting that the Word is active in creation, that the Creator God is the God of both Old and New Testaments. This is precisely what the heretics do not acknowledge. The *Rule of Faith*, then, forms a hermeneutical circle, on the inside of which are many possible, not overdetermined, readings of Scripture, while outside are the readings of the heretics. "The law of faith being constant, the other succeeding points of discipline and conversation admit the novelty of correction" (Tertullian, *Veiling*, 1). The *Rule of Faith* thus functions hermeneutically to hold together theologically the confessions of God the Creator and Jesus Christ the Son and the Holy Spirit, and thus also to bring together in a dialectical relation the two Testaments.

The *Rule of Faith*, I would say, is being violated in the decisions over sexuality in the Episcopal Church. The mosaic pieces are being rearranged such that a picture of a dog rather than the King is being formed. The Old Testament is being disregarded as witness to Christ. Even though the matter at hand, the life of gays and lesbians within the church, is a crucial matter for our deliberation, the deliberations themselves are being conducted on a faulty basis.

RESOURCES FOR ADDRESSING THE DEBATE IN ECUSA

There are indeed resources for addressing the opening divide in the Episcopal Church. There are Scripture and the *Rule of Faith*, as I have shown. There are many other resources as well. As we saw above, some of the archbishops and primates would like to appeal to the founding "fathers of the Anglican Communion," such as Cranmer. Others would like to hold up the historical documents of the church. These are now found in the back of the *Book of Common Prayer* (*BCP*, 864-878). Indeed, in addition to the Scriptures and the

Rule of Faith, the *Prayer Book* itself is a source of authority vital for this discussion.

The historical documents of the Church include the *Definition of Chalcedon* (A.D. 451), the *Quicunque Vult* or Creed of St. Athanasius, the *Preface* to the first *Book of Common Prayer* (1549), the *Articles of Religion*, also known as the *Thirty-nine Articles*, and the *Chicago-Lambeth Quadrilateral* of 1886, 1888. The *Thirty-nine Articles* are particularly important to this debate. Even though, as "historical documents," they are not specifically authoritative for the Communion, they do communicate doctrine and practice important for this debate. In the *Thirty-nine Articles* stands Article VI, "Of the Sufficiency of the Holy Scriptures for Salvation": "whatsoever is not read therein, nor may be proved thereby, is not to be required of any[one]." Certainly blessing of homosexual erotic activity is not within the Scriptures. How then can the denomination require this perspective of its priests, except by political (not theological) pressure?

In addition, the *Book of Common Prayer* itself includes in its service of Holy Matrimony a theology of marriage which holds that marriage is between one man and one woman. In the rubrics we find that "Christian marriage is a solemn and public covenant between a man and a woman in the presence of God" (*BCP 422)*. In the service itself, the opening states "Dearly beloved, we have come together in the presence of God to witness and bless the joining together of this man and this woman in Holy Matrimony. The bond and covenant of marriage was established by God in creation, and our Lord Jesus Christ adorned this manner of life by his presence and first miracle at a wedding in Cana of Galilee. It signifies to us the mystery of the union between Christ and his Church, and Holy Scripture commends it to be honored among all people" (*BCP* 423).

This last statement, that marriage signifies the union between Christ and his Church, is probably the most important, for Christ is always depicted as a man (Chalcedon, 451) and the church as the female Bride of Christ in the Scriptures. To suggest that gay unions can be celebrated like marriage is a fundamental misunderstanding not only of Scripture but also of the *Prayer Book*. Pushing for gay marriages and the production of such liturgies was declared by Bishop Smith to be the "mind of the diocese" at the Diocesan Convention (CT, 2005) even though some 1/3 voted against it. No numbers were counted on this vote, unlike many of the others.

Still others would like to appeal to the Instruments of Unity. These are the Lambeth conference, which meets every 10 years, for bishops; the Primates' Meetings, which are regular meetings for the senior archbishops and bishops of the 38 Provinces, the ACC (Anglican Consultative Council), meeting every three years or so (this includes laity, bishops, priests and deacons); and the Archbishop of Canterbury in his international role as *primus inter pares*, first among equals. However, none of these instruments are binding on the Provinces, as would be the case in Roman Catholicism regarding the *Magisterium* on Church Teaching. This ECUSA has repeatedly reminded Canterbury.

Others would like to appeal to Canon Law. Canon Law itself has been appealed to in the matter of the Bishop of Connecticut's inhibition of Fr. Mark Hansen of St John's Bristol, as I pointed out earlier. This would certainly be a place to turn, although as I have said in my understanding the Bishop misapplied the Canon in this case. The group of bishops who are appealing to this same Canon to bring to trial Bishop Smith because of his seizure of the parish of St. John's Bristol without consulting the vestry show the use of this canon to be ambiguous or multivalent, or even contradictory. This is simply to say that canon law can cut both ways, and is indeed presently doing so. Some also point out that since the Bishop may have taken HPPA documents or other confidential files from the parish, this could be also a federal legal matter.[23] Indeed, one of the charges brought by the nineteen priests and lay people is that the Bishop has interfered with parish mails, having the mailbox reassigned without the parish's approval, which would also be a federal offense. Of course, this could be understood to be the Bishop's right and responsibility.

Still others, especially the revisionists, would like to appeal to ethical notions and concepts such as justice and love. The problem here is that no one on either side of the divide can agree on the content of such concepts. What is justice? Is it a notion birthed by Enlightenment Rationalism? Is it a concept shaped by the biblical narrative and the God of Israel presented there? These two are usually mutually exclusive.

Back to Scripture. Others would say that the most highly valued authority is Scripture. Even the revisionists will appeal to Holy Scripture, in particular to Acts 10 and 15. These they turn into proof-texts for the inclusivity of the gospel. The surface intent of the stories in Acts is to include the Gentiles as they are, without becoming Jews first, into the people of God. According to the revisionist reading this now extends to homosexuals as they are, that they should be welcomed into the sacramental life of the church as clergy and married couples.

The orthodox, on the other hand, will appeal to Leviticus 18:20-23 and 20:13, Romans 1, 1 Timothy 3:1-7, Titus 3:9-11, Genesis 1-2, Ephesians 5, etc., for a biblical Christian understanding of sexual purity and holy matrimony. They would rather read the surface meaning of the texts here than turn the Scriptures into allegories as do the revisionists. The revisionists complain bitterly that the orthodox and evangelical Catholics are literal Fundamentalists, while the orthodox claim that the revisionists turn the Scriptures, as did the Roman Church according to its Reformation detractors, into a wax nose.[24] The interesting thing in this comparison is that the revisionists are more like the "traditional" Roman readers of Scripture and the "traditionalists" or orthodox are more like the Reformers in hermeneutics. That is, while the revisionists want to claim a Holy Spirit inspired, prophetic Reformation of the church's hermeneutic, in fact they are reading allegorically like the Romans often did.[25] And the orthodox are more like the Reformers, in reading according to the literal or surface meaning of the text and following the ancient hermeneutical traditions of the Fathers and their *Rule of Faith*.

Ultimately the appeal to Holy Scripture is an appeal to the Holy Spirit for both sides in this matter. The traditionalists or orthodox understand the Scriptures to be inspired by God. This points to no necessarily theory-laden notion of inspiration, but would embrace many different possible theories of inspiration. The revisionists understand themselves to be inspired by the Holy Spirit and therefore the readings of Scripture which they offer are inspired. The term they use here is "prophetic." Can such a prophetic reading be proved by Scripture according to the way the words and stories go? The judge of the movement of the Holy Spirit has always been Scripture itself, and doctrine and practice are never understood to be based on allegory.

TWO CHURCHES IN ONE COMMUNION: WHERE IS THE SPIRIT?

Each side, then, claims to know the mind of the Holy Spirit on this issue: the orthodox on the basis of the witness of Scripture and the revisionists on the basis of what they would call "prophetic experi-ence." Who has the Spirit in the Episcopal Church? We could adjudicate this according to any or all of the above resources. But the fact of the matter is that the revisionists, or spiritualists as may be a better term for them in these matters, do not seem to want to appeal to any of the Instruments of Unity (for this would destroy their argument) except Canon Law against their detractors. The orthodox can appeal to the Instruments of Unity, but it will not get them very far, since neither Lambeth nor the Primates nor the ACC nor the Archbishop of Canterbury have binding power to convince ECUSA to "repent."

Ultimately, how does the fact that ECUSA is a church with such doctrinal resources, albeit not a confessional church per se, give it an "edge" over non-structured churches in addressing such controversy and dissension? While it has many resources to tie it to the past and to Scripture, ultimately the case of the CT6 shows how a "prophetic" hermeneutic sweeps this all aside. In the end, there are (at least) two ecclesial bodies within ECUSA: they have very different understandings of the doctrine of the Trinity, and in particular, of the person of the Holy Spirit, and they operate with very different *Rules of Faith*. Only derivatively do they then have different understandings of human sexuality. How this controversy will bear itself out will probably be more a matter of carefully-wrought political rhetoric than theological understanding in the end. Will we have to make a Solomonic choice as to who gets ECUSA, its name, its buildings, its traditions?[26] The irony here is that it is being decided vote by vote, as if the Holy Spirit now were reduced to a tool of democracy. Who has the Spirit in the Episcopal Church? The Spirit blows where it wills. Who is justified in their claim to where the Spirit is blowing these days?

Notes

1. Marilyn McCord Adams, "Hurricane Spirit, Toppling Taboos," in *Our Selves, Our Souls, Our Bodies*, ed. Charles Heffling (Boston: Cowley, 1996), 129–41.
2. The term evangelical-catholic is associated with the Mercersburg movement in Pennsylvania during the second half of the nineteenth century and the names Philip

Schaff and John Nevin. Today the term is also used among Roman Catholics and Lutherans. In general it refers to a common belief in biblical authority and the sacramentality of worship. Today in its Lutheran-Roman Catholic usage, the term points to a hoped-for ecumenism of the orthodox among the many different communions. For example, see the Center for Catholic and Evangelical Theology. I am using the term here to bring together both "sides" of the Anglican Communion, those which are evangelical and/or orthodox, and those which are catholic. The Anglican Communion has been termed a "via media" or middle way between these two. Both of these sides of the via media tend to object to the ordination and marriage of "practicing" homosexuals, although there are many more Anglo-Catholic than evangelicals who do indeed applaud the decisions of GC2003.

3. See for example the Primates' Communiqué from Dromantine, February 24, 2005, which may be found at www.anglicancommunion.org : "Many primates have been deeply alarmed that the standard of Christian teaching on matters of human sexuality expressed in the 1998 Lambeth Resolution 1.10, which should command respect as the position overwhelmingly adopted by the bishops of the Anglican Communion, has been seriously undermined by the recent developments in North America. . . . [Even so], we continue unreservedly committed to the pastoral support and care of homosexual people. The victimization or diminishment of human beings whose affections happen to be ordered towards people of the same sex is anathema to us. We assure homosexual people that they are children of God, loved and valued by him, and deserving of the best we can give of pastoral care and friendship" (Par. 6). For the Lambeth Resolution, see www.Lambethconference.org.

4. See the Lambeth Conference 1998, Resolution 1.10, reproduced in the Appendix, Three/6, of the Windsor Report. The covenanted position was against ordaining those who are involved in same-gender unions. "By electing and confirming such a candidate in the face of the concerns expressed by the wider Communion, the Episcopal Church (USA) has caused deep offence to many faithful Anglican Christians both in its own church and in other parts of the Communion." Windsor Report, 52, 127. See also Lambeth Conference 1998: Resolution I.10 Human Sexuality, in the Windsor Report, 77, 2, 4-5: "In view of the teaching of Scripture, [the Church] upholds faithfulness in marriage between a man and a woman in lifelong union, and believes that abstinence is right for those who are not called to marriage . . . while rejecting homosexual practice as incompatible with Scripture, calls on all our people to minister pastorally and sensitively to all irrespective of sexual orientation and to condemn irrational fear of homosexuals, violence within marriage and any trivialization and commercialization of sex . . . cannot advise the legitimizing or blessing of same sex unions nor ordaining those involved in same gender unions." This, then, was the official position of the Anglican Communion on sexuality when the General Convention of 2003 voted to consecrate Vicky Gene Robinson.

5. This was voted on and won the day at the Annual Convention of the Diocese of Connecticut on October 22, 2005.

6. Jeffrey Siker, "How to Decide: Homosexual Christians, the Bible, and Gentile Inclusion," *Theology Today* 51 (1994): 219–34.

7. E.g., at the Convention of the Diocese of Connecticut, October 22, 2005.

8. For DEPO, see the Windsor Report 2004, 85, under section 11, "Caring for all the Churches: A response of the House of Bishops of the Episcopal Church to an expressed need of the Church, March 2004": "if reconciliation does not occur, then the rector and two-thirds of the vestry, or in the absence of a rector, two-thirds of the canonically designated lay leadership, after fully engaging the congregation, may seek from their diocesan bishop, (or the diocesan bishop may suggest) a conference regarding the

appropriateness and conditions for Delegated Episcopal Pastoral Oversight. . . . After such a conference the bishop may appoint another bishop to provide pastoral oversight."

9. At the Dromantine meeting in 2005, the Primates stated that "In order to protect the integrity and legitimate needs of groups in serious theological dispute with their Diocesan Bishop, or dioceses in dispute with their Provinces, we recommend that the Archbishop of Canterbury appoint, as a matter of urgency, a panel of reference to supervise the adequacy of pastoral provisions made by any church for such members in line with the recommendation in the Primates' Statement of October 2003. Equally, during this period we commit ourselves neither to encourage nor to initiate cross-boundary interventions" (Par. 15).

10. When ordained, Bishop Smith had said that he affirmed same-sex unions, but promised not to act on this until ECUSA changed its teaching.

11. The rumor mill has run wild with this unfortunate parish and its Bishop, and it is at the time of this writing a game of "he said, she said" between the Bishop and the parish. Somehow, the truth must lie in the middle, or someone is not being forthcoming. In any event, I approach this case study not to claim the right for one side or the other, but to explore the resources which ECUSA has for dealing with the crisis and how a confessional church approaches differences of theological and ethical matters.

12. According to the Vestry, the parish had consulted with the Diocese and all decided that to pay month-to-month expenses was more important than paying on the loan. The Diocese never communicated to the parish that it was in arrears, nor in default.

13. IV.10: "Of the Abandonment of Communion of this Church by a Priest or Deacon." This was an unfortunate choice on the part of Bishop Smith. The circumstances surrounding the case of Father Hansen seem to have warranted Canon IV, 11, not Canon IV, 10: "Of a Priest or Deacon Engaging in Secular Employment without Consent, Being Absent from the Diocese, or Abandoning the Work of the Ministry."

14. To be sure, there had been tension in the Diocese with this parish prior to its priest being inhibited, and there were clear reasons for the bishop to become involved in the parish's well being. However, one finds it hard to imagine that the priest would have been inhibited if he had not so vociferously disagreed theologically with the bishop.

15. Fr. Hansen has not been forthcoming with the reason for taking another job. This is a legal matter and he has been advised not to communicate with the parish. The vestry had not therefore been notified.

16. Here I am relying on a press release by the American Anglican Council of August 24, 2005. I am not certain if all the facts here are correct, since it is so new and I have heard no counter-reports yet.

17. Ekklesia is an "international society committed to making disciples of Jesus Christ affirming: the authority of the Scriptures, the faith of the historic creeds, the Sacraments as instituted by Jesus, historic, apostolic ministry." See website, www.ekk.org. Ekklesia is composed of primates and bishops from the two-thirds world and the ECUSA. It is affiliated with the Anglican American Council.

18. The Most Rev. Drexel W. Gomez, the Most Rev. Gregory Venables, *Biblical Interpretation and Preparing for the Anglican Communion Council* (Www.ekk.org: Ekklesia, 2005).

19. Thanks to the Rev. Dr. George Sumner for this insight.

20. I will here only be able to do short shrift of the *Rule of Faith*, but have written about it elsewhere. See also Paul M. Blowers, "The *Regula Fidei* and the Narrative Character of Early Christian Faith," *Pro Ecclesia* 6 (1997): 199-228; L.William Countryman, "Tertullian and the Regula Fidei," *Second Century* 2 (1982): 208–27; Bryan Litfin, "The Rule of Faith in Augustine," *Pro Ecclesia* 14 (2005): 85–101; Dieter Lührmann, "Confesser Sa Foi à l'Epoque Apostolique," *Revue de Théologie et de Philosophie* 117

(1985): 93–110; Timothy F. Merill, "Tertullian: The Hermeneutical Vision of *De Praescriptione Haereticorum* and Pentateuchal Exegesis," *Patristic and Byzantine Review* 6 (1987): 153–65; Jaroslav Pelikan, *Credo: Historical and Theological Guide to Creeds and Confessions of Faith in the Christian Tradition* (New Haven and London: Oxford University Press, 2003); Robert W. Wall, "Reading the Bible from Within Our Traditions: The 'Rule of Faith' in Theological Hermeneutics," in *Between Two Horizons: Spanning New Testament Studies and Systematic Theology*, ed. Joel B. Green and Max Turner (Grand Rapids: Eerdmans, 2000), 88–107.

21. Blowers, "Regula Fidei," 203; N. T. Wright, *The New Testament and the People of God, Vol. 1*, in *Christian Origins and the Question of God* (Minneapolis: Fortress, 1992), 456; Blowers, "Regula Fidei," 203.

22. Tertullian, *The Veiling of the Virgins*, 1:4.

23. This has been speculated about on the internet, but there is no firm evidence for this. Certainly Fr. Hansen had confidential files in his office, which was broken into. Only Fr. Hansen knows what was taken, and he is not allowed to communicate with the parish.

24. This phrase, traceable to Geiler of Kaiserburg in the fifteenth century, was much used by the Reformers to speak of Roman exegesis. "What! So the Church's decrees are to be reduced to nothing, are they? The Scripture is a wax nose; it has nothing sure or consistent; it can be twisted in any direction, and hypocrites always abuse the Word of God." *Corpus Reformatorum* 38, 311. Kathryn Greene-McCreight, *Ad Litteram: How Augustine, Calvin and Barth Read the 'Plain Sense' of Genesis 1–3* (New York: Peter Lang, 1999), 154, n. 51.

25. At the same time, if you consider their claim to spiritual exegesis, the revisionists of ECUSA may be closer to the hermeneutics of the Radical Reformation where the Spirit was accounted responsible for the views of many phissiparous sects.

26. Already the civil courts have judged against the Diocese of L.A., which wanted to take over the property of a dissenting parish leaving the denomination.

Mennonites and Democracy:
Shaped by War and Rumors of War

James C. Juhnke
Bethel College

PACIFISTS AND EMPIRE

In 1745, the second year of King George's War, Mennonite leaders on the periphery of the British Empire at Skippack, in the Quaker province of Pennsylvania, took action to assure "steadfast constancy in our faith" in case "cross and tribulation may . . . fall to the lot of the nonresistant Christian."[1] They arranged for the translation from Dutch to German, and the printing of, the *Martyrs Mirror,* a book of martyr stories from the crucifixion of Jesus through the torturing and killing of Anabaptists into the seventeenth century. Prefacing the martyr stories in the big book were a brief Church history, the *Apostles' Creed,* and three Dutch Anabaptist confessions of faith. With 1,512 pages, the *Martyrs Mirror* was the largest book published by any group in the British colonies. The pacifist Mennonites expected the martyr stories to steel the will of their people to resist conscription into the Pennsylvania militia.

From the 1740s into the twenty-first century, first under the British Empire and then under the American republic, pacifist Mennonite communities in America defended themselves against the ideology and practice of militarism —the myth of redemptive violence and the dominion of war.[2] The new republic, though it was born in violent conflict, saw itself as anti-imperialist and anti-militarist. In its early years it was biased against "standing armies." Americans never overcame the conviction that warfare, torture and terrorism were alien phenomena that originated beyond their own borders. Nevertheless, American democracy was relentlessly expansionist and prone to violence, especially on its outer boundaries. From the War for Independence through the occupation of Iraq, America has been imperialistic in ways similar to that of other great powers of world history. That is, the United States progressively extended its "dominion over the lands or lives of others, as a means of imposing what the builders of empires understand as order and peace on dangerous or unstable peripheral regions."[3] America became an empire of freedom, committed to extending its form of democracy and freedom to others. The symbiosis of the nation's quasi-pacifist self-image and the reality of a militant expansionist democracy provided a critical context for the distinctive Mennonite development from European sect to American denomination.

Between wars, the American empire of freedom produced political stability, economic growth, and generally peaceable social development. Mennonites benefited immensely from religious toleration and economic prosperity. But in

wartime the United States, like all modern expansionist nation states, demanded
military contributions from all citizens. America was particularly prone to popular wartime fits of patriotic intolerance. Between the wars, Mennonites remembered past struggles and prepared for future ones. While they were significantly
shaped by the four aspects of the American religious environment identified by
Mark Noll in *The Old Religions in a New World* (space, race and ethnicity, pluralism, and the absence of confessional conservatism), Mennonite old world
religion was distinctively transformed by the context of democratic expansionist
militarism in the new world.[4]

MENNONITE CONFESSIONALISM

Compared to Roman Catholics with their *Confession of Trent* (1556), Lutherans with their *Augsburg Confession* (1530), and other religious bodies with
centrally defined and authoritatively enforced statements of faith, the Anabaptists and Mennonites barely met the definition of a "confessional tradition."[5] The
Anabaptists were the *victims* of magisterial confessions. The *Augsburg Confession* sought unity with Catholics in part through condemnations of alleged Anabaptist heresies that Lutherans and Catholics could denounce in common.

The Anabaptists wrote their confessions on the run, a step ahead of the
Anabaptist hunters, the *Taueferjaeger*. Michael Sattler, an ex-Benedictine prior,
wrote the *Schleitheim Confession* of 1527 in haste. Within a few months the
Catholic authorities arrested Sattler, tore out his tongue, burned him at the stake,
and drowned his wife, Elizabetha, in the Neckar River. The *Schleitheim Confession* set forth only a limited number of doctrines of Christian belief. It focused
upon the distinctive beliefs and practices of the Swiss brethren. It had a Benedic-
tine-influenced dualistic theme of separation from the world. The church was "to
go out from Babylon and from the earthly Egypt." The state was ordained of
God to maintain secular order, "an ordering of God outside the perfection of
Christ." God's people were not to carry the sword, take oaths, or serve as magistrates. Published and circulated by the enemies of the Anabaptists, the *Schleitheim Confession* helped give a fragile identity to the fledgling movement in
Switzerland and South Germany, but it was never formally adopted by any general body in the Anabaptist family—Hutterites, Amish, or Mennonites.[6]

Although Old World Mennonites were too scattered, divided, and non-
scholarly to produce comprehensive and authoritative confessions, they did
write dozens of occasional local and regional confessional documents to instruct
their youth, to witness to the world, or to resolve controversy among Mennonite
groups.[7] These confessions were orthodox and evangelical. They began with
God, the Word of God, Jesus Christ, and the Holy Spirit. They included distinctive Anabaptist/Mennonite understandings of church discipline, Christian life
and nonconformity, integrity and oaths, and nonresistance and revenge.[8] The
Dortrecht Confession of 1632 came to be the most widely accepted of Mennonite confessions. In 1727 the Pennsylvania Mennonites published an English version of the *Dortrecht Confession*, the first Mennonite book printed in North
America.

Well into the modern era Mennonites maintained identity more by the practice of traditional folkways than by written confessions. Historian Beulah Hostetler observed that the expressions of belief that counted for communal survival among Franconia Mennonites north of Philadelphia were "embedded in patterns of life and were largely non-verbal in character." Hostetler argued that the effective Mennonite "charter" of values corresponded more closely to the Swiss-South German *Schleitheim Confession* of 1527 than to the Dutch *Dortrecht Confession* of 1632—even though the verbal form of *Schleitheim* was not available to new world Mennonites.[9]

PENNSYLVANIA AND THE PARADOXES OF PACIFIST EMPIRE

The first successful Mennonite settlers in the new world came at the invitation of William Penn, a Quaker pacifist who planned a new community of social harmony and liberty of conscience. From the 1680s to the 1750s the Quaker experiment in Pennsylvania was a remarkable success, with far less violence between European settlers and Indians than occurred in New England and Virginia. Penn believed that Indians possessed the light of God. He learned the Delaware language, paid generous prices for Indian land, and sold the Indians trade goods, arms and ammunition, while forbidding his colony to have its own militia. Nevertheless, Penn's experiment was an outpost of an expansionist empire. His European settlers, including the nonresistant Mennonites, were beneficiaries of favorable military alliances and arrangements. At first the friendly Delaware Indians served as a buffer against more hostile tribes to the west and north. Later the Scotch-Irish, welcomed to Penn's frontier despite their militancy, provided a buffer against Indians who resisted the European settlers' westward advance.

There was no better place than Penn's colony for a sectarian religious group such as the Mennonites, with their history of persecution and exclusion, gradually to give up the sharp edges of their sectarian identity and to take a place alongside other ethnic/religious groups in a more pluralistic social and religious system. The Pennsylvania German groups—including Lutherans, Reformed, Moravians, Mennonites, Dunkers, the Ephrata Society and the Schwenkfelders—all came to the American frontier with confident and exclusive visions of divine truth. They slowly learned mutual toleration and respect as they became more secure in their separate identities. Former outsiders became comfortable insiders within a pluralistic Pennsylvania system that allowed them to preserve and develop their separate identities. Pennsylvania was the original hearth of the American invention of denominationalism—and the first experiment in a new system of stable political parties that defined and promoted the broad public interest.[10]

The Mennonites too became insiders in colonial Pennsylvania.[11] They adapted to, and thrived in, this new world in ways that belied their doctrine of separation from the world. They settled on individual farmsteads, not in communitarian collectives. They sent their children to private schools that were bridges to social relationships with different religious groups. Many self-supporting Mennonite preachers also became local community leaders. Their

successful farmers, millers, weavers, or blacksmiths earned community respect
in secular as well as religious matters. Mennonites voted in elections, providing
key support for the dominant Quaker party. Some of them held political offices.
While they became active participants in the newly formed Pennsylvania German subculture, colonial-era Mennonites did not have a modern outlook of taking responsibility for the public order. They were still subjects more than citizens. In political elections they "seem rather to have been trading votes for
pacifist privileges." In the process they established themselves in a Mennonite
heartland that was to thrive longer at one place than Mennonite settlements
anywhere else in the world.[12]

Both in Europe and in America, Mennonites absorbed influences from the
Pietist renewal. They shifted from their traditional austere martyr hymns of the
Ausbund to Pietist hymns of greater joy and consolation. Their devotional literature became more Pietist than Anabaptist. This transition was possible because
Anabaptism and Pietism shared a common biblicism, practical holiness, and
concern for inward transformation. But Pietists began with individual justification, while Mennonites aimed to bring the reign of Christ through the example
of an obedient church. Pietists prayed to be embraced by a "sweet Jesus" of personal salvation. Mennonites followed a "bitter Jesus" whose suffering led to the
cross.[13] The attractions of Pietist and revivalist ways sometimes led to controversy and division. In 1781 Mennonite minister Martin Boehm was influenced
by a dramatic Methodist revival. He eventually was excommunicated by the
Mennonites and became a co-founder of a new "United Brethren" denomination.

Mennonites did set some limits to ecumenical cooperation. In the 1740s,
Nicholas von Zinzendorf, founder of the Moravians, a radical Pietist group, vis-
ited Pennsylvania and initiated conversations designed to bring religious groups
together. The Mennonites, along with the Schwenkfelders, withdrew from the
discussions.[14]

The Mennonite situation in the Pennsylvania German subculture was paradoxical in more than one sense. They were pacifists whose hold on the land was
made secure by military force. If they agonized about this apparent contradiction, they left no record of it in any of their writings. In addition, they faced an
increasing disparity between their inherited European traditional piety, which
was oriented to suffering and martyrdom, and the realities of social acceptability
and economic prosperity in America. One theological adjustment toward the end
of the colonial era was to shift emphasis from the theme of suffering to the
theme of humility. Heinrich Funck, a wealthy and socially prominent Franconia-
area Mennonite leader marked the beginning of this transition in a posthumously
published book (1763), *Eine Restitution*. Why were Mennonites no longer suffering? Funck answered, "The ways of the world are adopted in a life of pride
and ambition for worldly honor and wealth in order to be like the world, and
thereby avoid being despised by the world."[15] Funck thought that the rejection of
pride and the embrace of humility might lead once again to suffering. In the
nineteenth century Mennonites shifted to humility as the central Christian value
in its own right.

A WAR FOR INDEPENDENCE AND A PEOPLE APART

In the French and Indian War, Mennonites and other peace groups refused direct participation in the volunteer militia, although Mennonites provided wagons, teams, and drivers for Major General Edward Braddock's military expedition to the Ohio Valley.[16] In the independence agitation of the1770s, most Mennonites were neutral, inclined to wait for the outcome of events they could not control. The religious freedom guaranteed in William Penn's Charter was endangered when anti-British local committees began to function as alternative governing bodies and to harass those who refused to volunteer for the militia, to pay a war tax in lieu of military service, or to take the test oath of allegiance to the free and independent state of Pennsylvania. The *Dortrecht Confession* had called Mennonites to "honor and acknowledge" secular authorities "as ministers of God, and be subject and obedient unto them." But which claimants to sovereignty in a revolutionary civil war were to be considered the authorities ordained by God? Some Mennonites who wanted to stay under the British flag migrated to Ontario, although their motives may have been more economic than political.

The war resulted in one Mennonite schism over the war tax issue. Christian Funk, a Mennonite bishop over congregations in Bucks and Montgomery counties, led those who were willing to pay taxes to the new government. "Were Christ here," Funk said, "He would say, 'Give to Congress that which belongs to Congress and to God that which belongs to God.'" The Franconia conference excommunicated Funk in 1778, together with a few of his followers. Nevertheless, in the assessment of historian Richard MacMaster, "virtually all" of the Mennonites privately and reluctantly paid what the state demanded to meet war needs and the cost of the Continental Congress.[17]

During the war the new American political leaders imprisoned and confiscated the property of some Mennonites who balked at militia service and test oaths. In Northampton County, patriotic public officials spent more time tyrannizing their pacifist neighbors than in fending off the British.[18] The pattern of popular, patriotic, out-of-control, local militancy was to be repeated in the nation's subsequent wars for democratic freedom. Nationalistic militancy became a characteristic sign of the modern nation state. In the words of Mennonite historian Richard MacMaster, the enthusiastic patriots were "modernizers who were trying to get people to take on identity as national citizens in contrast to older identities based on village, clan, or faith."[19] In the face of such pressures, a few Mennonites left their faith and joined the new nation on its own terms. But most of them resisted and became, more than they had become in the colonial era, "a people apart." Their experience in the American War for Independence enhanced Mennonite separate identity over against American democracy.

THE ETHOS OF HUMILITY AS ACCOMMODATION AND RESISTANCE

In the intervals between times of war hysteria, the forces of American democratic toleration and pluralism proved to be a powerful solvent. The War for Independence may have reminded Mennonites of their Anabaptist roots, but in the nineteenth century they continued to adapt to their American social and religious environment, rather than engage in a radical separation. Many of them joined the American westward movement in quest of free land, benefiting without protest from the violent removal of Indians on the frontier. Often settling in places some five to ten years after Indian removal, Mennonites spread in many directions, but their primary route of internal migration extended in an arc to western Pennsylvania, Ohio, Indiana, Iowa, and down toward Missouri and Kansas. In the 1870s a substantial immigration of Mennonites of Dutch and Low German background from Eastern Europe added to their ethnic diversity and variation in religious outlook and practice. The Low German immigrants, who had their own markers of separation from the world, were not tuned into the Pennsylvania German Mennonite gospel of humility.[20]

Two nineteenth-century adaptations by the Swiss and South German Pennsylvania German Mennonites illustrate the ways they adapted to the American democratic environment without giving up their ethnic and religious identity. One adaptation was the consolidation of the gospel of humility. While the War for Independence had strengthened Mennonite sense of separateness, it was not followed by a return to the Anabaptist themes of suffering and martyrdom. Until the latter nineteenth century, Mennonites increasingly expressed and lived out a humility theology that was, in the words of Mennonite historian Theron Schlabach, "quite at odds with the mood and emphasis of revivalism. More broadly but less directly it was at odds also with a youthful, boastful, expansionist U.S. nation."[21]

The classical statement of Mennonite humility theology was a pamphlet in 1867 by John M. Brenneman, *Pride and Humility: A Discourse setting Forth the Characteristics of the Proud and Humble*. Brenneman traced his theme through the Scriptures, noting particularly the humility of Jesus who washed his disciples' feet and humbly accepted death. Brenneman advocated humble manners in conversation, clothing, carriages, furniture, eating, and learning. He did not separate salvation, the receiving of God's grace, from the outward marks of humility.[22] "All such penitent and humble sinners, seeking grace, shall obtain it of God through Jesus Christ. . . . But bear in mind, this grace is given only to the *humble.*"[23]

For Brenneman and Mennonite church leaders generally, the gospel of humility was an instrument of church discipline and control. It helped them to rein in members who were tempted by fancy clothing or personal photographs— "clear evidence that pride is still lurking in your hearts." Brenneman quoted Paul's admonition in Romans 13, "Obey them that have the rule over you, and submit yourselves," not in reference to political authorities but to church leaders who tried to keep their flock from "the silly fashions of the world."[24] Mennonite leaders called their people to avoid the prideful ways of revivalist preachers, ecumenical gatherings, and institutions of higher learning. Even as Brenneman wrote his pamphlet, a group of more progressive Mennonites, including recent immigrants from Europe, was building the first American Mennonite seminary in Wadsworth, Ohio—a project fraught with dangers of worldly pride.

Mennonites expressed a demeanor of humility and deference in social relationships—holding their heads down and averting their eyes in the face of worldly authorities. But they also stubbornly resisted government powers that called them to military service against their Christian conscience. In 1862, in the face of a civil war military draft, John M. Brenneman drafted a petition to President Abraham Lincoln, clothed with deferential language of humility, but making it crystal clear that Mennonites would refuse to fight—even though they would be willing to pay a wartime tax.[25]

The Civil War marked America's transition from pre-modern limited war to modern total war aimed at annihilation of, and unconditional surrender by, the enemy.[26] Although Mennonites did not make a prophetic protest against aggressive militarism, either during the Mexican-American War (1846-48) or the Civil War (1861-65), they, for the most part, steadfastly maintained their refusal to participate directly in the killing. As the war took its astonishingly excessive toll, both the Union and the Confederacy resorted to military conscription. Some Mennonites escaped the battlefield by paying a fee or hiring a substitute. Those living in the burned over battlegrounds of the Shenandoah Valley in Virginia suffered the most destruction and dislocation. Perhaps the most famous Mennonite story from the Civil War was that of Christian Good, a Virginian who was conscripted into the Confederate army. When the captain reprimanded Good for failing to shoot at the Yankees, Good allegedly replied, "They're people. We don't shoot people."[27] The stories Mennonites told of their war experiences, including the story of Christian Krehbiel's friendship with the man he hired as a substitute for military service, helped sustain their identity as a separate people.[28]

At the end of the nineteenth century, the largest branch of Mennonites (that is, the "old" Mennonites, who were less traditionalist than Old Order Mennonites and Amish, more conservative than the "new" Mennonites, and culturally different from the Dutch-Russian immigrant Mennonites) made a momentous adaptation to American revivalism. But they did it cautiously, in ways that preserved their separate identity. The first and most influential broker of this change was John S. Coffman, a gifted editor and evangelist of Elkhart, Indiana. In 1881 he initiated "protracted meetings," which were until then generally prohibited in "old" Mennonite churches, and called people to conversion and changed lives. Coffman spoke in a humble and modest voice, unlike the bombastic revivalists or the sing-song recitations of traditional Mennonite preachers. He wore the plain coat and affirmed the traditional rules of Mennonite nonconformity. The resulting revivals across the church brought a widespread revitalization of the "old" Mennonite church on distinctively Mennonite terms. A new generation of young people joined the church with new spiritual energy along with new commitment to teach and enforce the marks of Mennonite separation from the world. Meanwhile, Mennonites of the Dutch-Russian migration stream had their own trajectory, influenced by revivalism in somewhat different ways.

In the long run the Mennonite adaptation to revivalism had consequences unintended by Coffman and the movement's early leaders. Mennonite revivalist preachers soon appeared who adopted the more aggressive and individualistic styles of American revivalism, and who proudly kept records of the numbers of people converted under their preaching. Mennonite young people were converted and joined the church at an earlier age. The average age of baptism dropped dramatically. The high point in believers' personal narratives shifted from life in the congregation to a specific experiential moment of individual conversion. Thus the old European religious practices of Mennonites were significantly Americanized in a democratic environment. Acceptance of revivalism opened the door to other changes—interest in Sunday Schools, overseas missions, new singing styles, and more. The changes brought new divisions between progressives and traditionalists. Moreover the traditionalists who resisted the Mennonite version of revivalism in one generation became vulnerable to new waves of the movement in subsequent generations. Many great- grandchildren of conservative Mennonites who had rejected John Coffman's "protracted meetings" were converted in a new wave of Mennonite revivals after World War II.[29]

In the decades before World War I, progressive Mennonites initiated a new era of denominational organization and institution building. They organized conferences, sent missionaries overseas, built colleges and hospitals, in general taking on the shape and style of the larger Protestant denominations. Mennonite historian Theron Schlabach has outlined some of the costs and benefits of this transition. He summarized the changes at the end of the nineteenth century under four rubrics: "A more outward looking vision," "More Protestant, more American kinds of structures," "Separation of salvation from Christian practice," and "From humility to aggressive action."[30]

MENNONITES AND THE CENTURY OF TOTAL WAR

The World Wars of 1914-1918 and 1939-1945 were the central events in a century of total war that forced Mennonites into a new balance between civic alienation and civic respectability. Presidents Woodrow Wilson and Franklin Delano Roosevelt deliberately conducted the great wars of the twentieth century as popular democratic crusades—holy wars that mobilized all the nation's energies in behalf of freedom and democracy. Because Germany was the primary enemy in both wars, crusading patriots in American communities with Mennonite populations directed their zeal against the available pacifists of German background. Protestant churches were in the forefront of the attacks.[31]

In the First World War, official government policy vagueness with regard to military conscription and the means of financing the war contributed to the Mennonite dilemma. Mennonites were clear that they must refuse military service. Nevertheless when the government said the conscripts' consciences would be respected, Mennonites sent their drafted young men to military camps. In the camps the men suffered hazing and humiliation. Some two hundred Mennonites were court-martialed and imprisoned at Fort Leavenworth. Meanwhile in the home communities, some Mennonites bore the consequences of resisting community pressures to buy war bonds. The government's decision to finance the war largely through voluntary bond collections, rather than taxation, complicated the issue for Mennonites who were ready to pay taxes but hesitated before contributing voluntarily. Local patriots terrorized Mennonites in Michigan and Oklahoma by burning to the ground two churches (and one barn to which Mennonites had resorted for worship); elsewhere they smeared many Mennonite churches with yellow paint or otherwise defaced them. There were several dozen cases of mob violence directed against Mennonites who refused to buy war bonds or who otherwise offended local sensibilities.[32] Hundreds of Mennonites and Hutterites escaped the persecution by fleeing to Canada.[33]

The First World War was a turning point in Mennonite civic identity, especially for the denominational progressives who wanted to find an acceptable place in American society. Stung by accusations that they were not worthy American citizens, Mennonites in the post-war era developed new strategies and institutions—above all the Mennonite Central Committee—to engage in ministries of benevolence that served as a moral equivalent for military service and warfare. They explained and promoted their outpouring of benevolence in biblical and historical terms rooted in their Anabaptist tradition. In the wider context of American democratic philanthropy, however, the dramatic growth of Mennonite benevolent institutions after World Wars I and II was another accommodation to American democracy. Mennonites came to be known not only for their refusal to participate in war, but also for their work in cleaning up after tornados and hurricanes, for their world-wide relief and development ministries under Mennonite Central Committee, and for their celebrative fund-raising relief sales and thrift shops. They became a people of both peace and service.[34]

In World War II the government instituted a Civilian Public Service (CPS) program for conscripted conscientious objectors. The young men worked without pay in separated civilian work camps for service "in the national interest"—including forestry, conservation, public health, and mental hospitals. The historic peace churches ran the camps and paid the administrative costs. As a form of unpaid conscript labor this was a punitive system, but it was far more satisfactory and productive than the confrontation of World War I. The historic peace churches turned the CPS camps into worshipping communities and leadership training grounds for a new generation of church leaders. Mennonite horizons for Christian service were immensely broadened by the war. In the words of historian Paul Toews, "CPS helped link orthodoxy to social compassion. Now the church could be more socially active while remaining theologically conservative."[35]

Meanwhile in the home communities the patriotic pressures upon Mennonites were less intense and violent than in World War I, but strong enough to confront Mennonites with the argument that they owed their freedom to American soldiers who were fighting and dying overseas. The thriving American economy during and after the war helped enable Mennonites to finance new missionary and benevolent programs. On the whole, both world wars helped to revitalize (and, in some cases, to fragment) Mennonite communities. Even though about half of drafted Mennonites in World War II entered the military forces, the church remained strongly committed to its traditional peace position. The total warfare of the twentieth century left most Mennonites with a stronger separate identity and with a new appreciation for America as a home for nonconforming pacifists.

FROM NONRESISTANCE TO PEACEMAKING

For the nation, the myth of democratic victory proved inadequate to explain the real consequences of twentieth-century warfare. American victory in World War I did not make the world safe for democracy. It led to even more destructive war. Victory in World War II did not produce peace but rather led to Cold War militarization, to proxy wars on the periphery of the Soviet and American empires, and to a nuclear arms race that late in the century swept into a new and more dangerous phase of proliferation. Mennonites increasingly sensed that their doctrines and practices of peace and nonresistance were relevant to government policy.

In the latter half of the twentieth century, the progressive denominational Mennonite mainstream underwent a great transition away from their traditional patterns of separation, humility, and nonresistance toward new patterns of engagement, assertive witness, and proactive peacemaking. The transition was advanced by accelerating modernization among Mennonites—urbanization, occupational diversity, higher education, and geographical mobility.[36] There was a transformation, in the words of historian Perry Bush, in "the entire Mennonite landscape."[37]

The issue of military conscription was critical in this transition. In 1948 Congress enacted the first peacetime draft in American history. The Selective Service System, put on a permanent basis in 1951, continued to conscript men until it fell apart in 1973 late in the Vietnam War. The system was generous to conscripted religious conscientious objectors, but it led to a great diffusion of Mennonite forces. The I-W program, as it was called, typically placed drafted men in individual assignments away from oversight by their home congregations or denominational agencies.

The Vietnam War and the simultaneous counter-cultural revolution wrought agony and change among Mennonites, as in American culture more broadly. The military draft remained a flashpoint, as suggested by two transforming developments. One was a challenge from a small but articulate group of young Mennonite men who refused to register for the draft, saying the church had compromised its prophetic peace tradition by allowing the Selective Service System to domesticate and silence the pacifists. The major Mennonite bodies had long endorsed alternatives to military service (CPS and I-W) as the favored official church position. Now they adopted two official responses as authentically Christian: alternative service and draft resistance.

The end of the military draft in 1973 revealed the extent of Mennonite acculturation. They had come to depend upon conscription as a model and impetus for Christian service. The church's standard two-year term of voluntary service had been modeled on the Selective Service requirement. With the end of the draft came a drastic decline in the number of Mennonites who volunteered for church programs. The end of the Vietnam War diminished the need for Mennonites to provide a moral equivalent for war. Mennonite interest in social reform causes such as race relations, women's rights, peace studies programs, homosexuality, and abortion—vigorous and creative as that interest was in the late twentieth and early twenty-first centuries—took their cues and their timing from larger society.[38] And yet it can be said that in the late twentieth century Mennonites exercised an influence far greater than their small numbers on the cutting edge of the peace movement—especially with programs such as Christian Peacemaker Teams, and Conflict Transformation Programs at Mennonite Colleges, and creative efforts to orient liberal arts disciplines around the idea of peacemaking.

Late twentieth-century Mennonite confessional statements continued to reject war and to ground that rejection in the teaching and ministry, the life and death, of Jesus. In 1995 the Mennonite Church and the General Conference Mennonite Church jointly adopted an updated confession that served as one basis for the merger of those groups in 2001. Article 22 of that confession, "Peace, Justice, and Nonresistance," said, "As followers of Jesus, we participate in his ministry of peace and justice. . . . As disciples of Christ, we do not prepare for war, or participate in war or military service."[39] Mennonites expected confessional statements to be periodically updated and revised to reflect new language and new concerns.

In the late twentieth century Mennonites, quite belatedly in comparison to the larger confessional traditions, began to develop a tradition of their own theological reflection and biblical studies. Mennonite theology has had a strong historical cast, expressed in the mid-twentieth century by the influential "Goshen school of Anabaptist historiography."[40] The most important statements from the Goshen school were Harold S. Bender's essay, "The Anabaptist Vision," and Guy F. Hershberger's book, *War, Peace and Nonresistance.* Later in the century two prominent Mennonite theologians, Gordon Kaufman of Harvard University and John Howard Yoder of Notre Dame, restated the Anabaptist/Mennonite theme of peace from quite different perspectives. Kaufman addressed the doctrine of God in a modern rational idiom. Yoder's focus was more on Christology. His master work, *The Politics of Jesus,* found an audience among American evangelicals.[41] Other significant Mennonite theologians included C. Norman Krause, Thomas N. Finger, J. Denny Weaver, and James E. Reimer. The journal *Conrad Grebel Review* became an important forum for Mennonite theological dialogue and debate.[42]

REFLECTING PROTESTANT POLARITIES

Two historical polarities have been foundational in the American Mennonite experience. One was the ethnic/cultural difference between Mennonites of Swiss and South German background on one hand, and Mennonites of the Dutch Prussian Russian stream on the other.[43] Another polarity was the difference between traditionalists and progressives—actually a complex spectrum of groups ranging from rural Old Order Mennonites and Amish on the right to highly acculturated urban congregations on the left. The social dynamic of the Mennonite experience in America has had to do with relationships of these groups to each other, and movement of individuals and groups across the spectrum. Even though Mennonites often lamented the scandal of their many church divisions, the process of division was often energizing to both the traditionalist and progressive sides of a given split. The migration of people on the Old Order or conservative side up the ladder of acculturation has been a significant source of members and leaders for the more liberal groups. Despite their occasional losses, the conservative groups, with large families and ability to hold most of their members, have sustained surprising growth and vitality. On the progressive side, inter-Mennonite ecumenical cooperation has often been a major source of denominational energy.[44]

One way to read American Mennonite history is the gradual displacement of old polarities indigenous to Mennonite life with new polarities from the American Protestant environment. Thus the cultural and doctrinal peculiarities of Mennonite traditionalists and progressives, as well as of Mennonite Swiss and Dutch, have receded in importance as all of them have taken on new identities of America's polarized religious and political culture wars. The attractions of American versions of Pietism, revivalism, and evangelicalism have especially eroded old Mennonite identities.[45]

Mennonite progressives, including a strong majority of leaders in denominational offices, were the first to engage in prophetic political involvements. They tended to identify with the anti-war wing of the Democrat party, to listen to National Public Radio, and more recently to read messages from "Move-On" on their computers. Meanwhile Mennonite traditionalists and conservatives had long held to a time-honored Anabaptist separation from the political order. But by 2004 significant numbers of traditionalists and conservatives had been attracted to right-wing evangelicalism and its pro-family, anti-abortion, and traditional-values agenda. These folk tended to make alliance with President George Bush and the Republicans, and to absorb attitudes and language they heard on Fox News and such radio shows as "Focus on the Family" or conservative talk shows.[46] Mennonite conservatives became increasingly politicized.

Would the old Anabaptist/Mennonite commitment to biblical nonresistance and peacemaking be able to survive this new Americanized polarization? During the highly contentious Bush vs. Kerry blue-state vs. red-state political campaign of 2004, Mennonite historian John Roth observed that members of many Mennonite congregations were arguing and insulting each other with language and styles taken from the political world. Roth proposed a quasi-separationist Anabaptist solution to what he considered a crisis of denominational discord: All Mennonites should take a five-year sabbatical from political involvement.[47]

CONCLUSION

Historians Fred Anderson and Andrew Cayton in *The Dominion of War* alleged that the wars in American history were not exceptions to an otherwise pacific history, but rather were the definitive moments for American political culture and nationhood as the nation expanded and strove toward ultimate global hegemony.[48] Hidden behind the triumphalist national master narrative of American history was a tragic reality that would have the last word in case of a future nuclear holocaust or even in case of perpetually escalating violence and terrorism on the periphery of America's global militarized empire. Whether or not the Anderson-Cayton thesis is valid for the national story, America's wars have exercised substantial influence over the identity and life of religious communities in the Mennonite story. To be sure, a balanced view of Mennonite accommodation to American democracy would need to take into account many other dimensions of social and religious life. Nevertheless, Mennonite identity in American democracy has been foundationally shaped by the dominion of war.

On the whole, democracy's popular warfare has helped to guarantee Mennonite identity, even while it meant that pacifist Mennonites would never experience dramatic church growth. Unlike their cousins in the Ukraine, whose subculture was destroyed by World Wars I and II and by Communist terror, American Mennonites generally prospered economically in wartime. They became the objects of popular scorn and persecution, sufficient to remind them of the first principles of the New Testament and Anabaptist heritage. The apparently triumphant democratic war crusades generated resources and energy for Mennonites to build programs of benevolence that served as a moral equivalent for war. American toleration and pluralism made a comfortable place for Mennonites in the national denominational mosaic, while American warfare helped make the themes of peace and service central to Mennonite denominational identity.

At the same time, the allure of evangelical religious ways in American democracy deeply threatened the future of Mennonites. Mennonites are in any case a very fragmented and small denomination, compared to the major confessional traditions. On the one hand, progressive Mennonites may be drawn toward a wider national secularized anti-war movement that separates their pacifism from Scripture and from the cross of Christ. On the other hand, the more conservative Mennonites may be attracted to an American evangelicalism that seems to have an inviting theology and an alluring worship style, but that has largely sold its soul to American nationalism and militarism while "spiritualizing into irrelevance ethical issues other than those of personal morality."[49] Meanwhile the nation has embarked upon paths of imperialism and militarism that do not require the military conscription that once forced the issue for Mennonites. The United States fights its wars with the assent and support of evangelicals, but without making overt sacrificial demands upon all citizens. How can the central principles of Anabaptism survive where there is no focused confrontation with the world? The new world's democratic environment continues to have ambiguous effect—both energizing and enervating—on the Old World confessional tradition of European Anabaptist Mennonites.

Notes

1. "Letters to the Dutch Mennonite Church, October 19, 1745," in Richard K. MacMaster, et. al., *Conscience in Crisis: Mennonites and Other Peace Churches in America, 1739-1789* (Scottdale, Penn.: Herald Press, 1979), 85.
2. On the myth of redemptive violence see Walter Wink, *Engaging the Powers: Discernment and Resistance in a World of Domination* (Minneapolis: Fortress Press, 1992), 13-31. The term "dominion of war" is from Fred Anderson and Andrew Cayton, *The Dominion of War: Empire and Liberty in North America, 1500-2000* (New York: Viking, 2005). For a peace-minded revisionist interpretation of main themes in American history,

see James C. Juhnke and Carol Hunter, *The Missing Peace: The Search for Alternatives to Violence in American History,* 2d ed. (Waterloo, Ont: Pandora Press, 2004).

3. Anderson and Cayton, *The Dominion of War,* xiv.

4. Mark A. Noll, *The Old Religion in a New World, The History of North American Christianity* (Grand Rapids: William B. Eerdmans, 2002).

5. The role of creeds and confessions in the Anabaptist/Mennonite tradition is a disputed topic among Mennonite scholars today. See the essays by Ben Ollenburger, Duane Friesen, J. Denny Weaver, Gerald Biesecker-Mast and Brett Dewey in the September 2005 issue of *Mennonite Life.* <http://www.bethelks.edu/mennonitelife/2005Sept/>

6. Translation by John H. Yoder, *The Schleitheim Confession* (Scottdale, Penn.: Herald Press, 1973).

7. *The Mennonite Encyclopedia* (1969), *s. v.* "Confessions of Faith," by Christian Neff, J. C. Wenger, and Harold S. Bender, 679.

8. *The Mennonite Encyclopedia,* (1990), s. v. "Confessions, Doctrinal," by Howard Loewen, 185.

9. Beulah Hostetler, *American Mennonites and Protestant Movements* (Scottdale, Penn.: Herald Press, 1987), 18.

10. Alan Tully, *Forming American Politics: Ideals, Interests, and Institutions in Colonial New York and Pennsylvania* (Baltimore: Johns Hopkins University Press, 1994), 429.

11. On the paradox of outsiders becoming insiders while enhancing separate identity in the American democratic environment, see R. Laurence Moore, *Religious Outsiders and the Making of Americans* (New York: Oxford University Press, 1986).

12. Richard K. MacMaster, *Land, Piety, Peoplehood, The Establishment of Mennonite Communities in America 1683-1790* (Scottdale, Penn.: Herald Press, 1985), 148-9, 198-9, 230.

13. Theron Schlabach, *Peace, Faith, Nation, Mennonites and Amish in Nineteenth-Century America* (Scottdale, Penn.: Herald Press, 1988), 88.

14. MacMaster, *Land, Piety, Peoplehood,* 141-3.

15. Heinrich Funck, *Ein Spiegel der Tauffe, mit Geist mit Wasser und mit Blut* (Germantown, Penn.: Christoph Saur, 1744), cited in MacMaster, *Land, Piety, Peoplehood,* 180.

16. MacMaster, *Conscience in Crisis,* 72-83.

17. MacMaster, *Land, Piety, Peoplehood,* 266.

18. Mark Noll, "Ordinary People, Extraordinary Times: The Moral Complexity of the American Revolution," *Books and Culture* (July/August 2001): 29, in a review of Francis S. Fox, *Sweet Land of Liberty: The Ordeal of the American Revolution in Northampton County, Pennsylvania* (University Park: Pennsylvania State University Press, 2000).

19. MacMaster, *Land, Piety, Peoplehood,* 205.

20. The Mennonites were a small denomination, numbering only 54,523 in the United States in 1906. United States Department of Commerce Bureau of the Census. *Religious Bodies: 1936* (Washington D.C.: Government Printing Office, 1941).

21. Schlabach, *Peace, Faith, Nation,* 29.

22. Schlabach, *Peace, Faith, Nation,* 102.

23. John M. Brenneman, *Pride and Humility: A Discourse setting Forth the Characteristics of the Proud and Humble,* 3d ed. (Elkhart, Ind.: J. F. Funk & Bro., 1873), 39, 41.

24. Brenneman, *Pride and Humility,* 28.

25. Schlabach, *Peace, Faith, Nation,* 182-5.

26. Russell Weigley, *The American Way of War* (New York: Macmillan, 1973).

27. Samuel Horst, *Mennonites in the Confederacy: A Study in Civil War Pacifism* (Scottdale, Penn.: Herald Press, 1967), 23-27.

28. Christian Krehbiel, *Prairie Pioneer* (Newton, Ks.: Faith and Life Press, 1961), 43-4.

29. Paul Toews, *Mennonites in American Society, 1930-1970, Modernity and the Persistence of Religious Community* (Scottdale, Penn.: Herald Press, 1996), 294.

30. Schlabach, *Peace, Faith, Nation,* 301-321.

31. Ray H. Abrams, *Preachers Present Arms* (New York: Round Table Press, 1933).

32. On the Mennonite experience in World War I see Gerlof Homan, *American Mennonites and the Great War, 1914-1918* (Scottdale, Penn.: Herald Press, 1994), and James C. Juhnke, *Vision, Doctrine, War, Mennonite Identity and Organization in America 1890-1930* (Scottdale, Penn.: Herald Press, 1989), 208-42.

33. Allan Teichroew, "World War I and the Mennonite Migration to Canada to Avoid the Draft," *Mennonite Quarterly Review* 45 (July 1971): 219-149.

34. Juhnke, *Vision, Doctrine, War,* 246-53.

35. Paul Toews, *Mennonites in American Society,* 182. On the Mennonite experience during World War II see also Perry Bush, *Two Kingdoms, Two Loyalties, Mennonite Pacifism in Modern America* (Baltimore: Johns Hopkins University Press, 1998), 90-128.

36. The transition has been chronicled by Mennonite sociological studies, especially two church-wide surveys published in 1975 and 1991 (and another currently in progress): Leland Harder and J. Howard Kauffman, *Anabaptists Four Centuries Later* (Scottdale, Penn.: Herald Press, 1975), and J. Howard Kauffman and Leo Driedger, *The Mennonite Mosaic: Identity and Modernization* (Scottdale, Penn.: Herald Press, 1991). Leo Driedger and Donald B. Kraybill, *Mennonite Peacemaking, From Quietism to Activism* (Scottdale, Penn.: Herald Press, 1994).

37. Bush, *Two Kingdoms,* 257.

38. Bush, *Two Kingdoms,* 259-62.

39. *Confession of Faith in a Mennonite Perspective* (Scottdale, Penn.: Herald Press, 2005), 81-82.

40. Rodney James Sawatsky, *History and Ideology, American Mennonite Identity Definition through History* (Kitchener, Ont.: Pandora Press, 2005).

41. John Howard Yoder, *The Politics of Jesus* (Grand Rapids: William B. Eerdmans, 1972). Gordon D. Kaufman, *Theology for a Nuclear Age* (Manchester: University of Manchester, 1985). Gordon D. Kaufman, *In Face of Mystery, A Constructive Theology* (Cambridge: Harvard University Press, 1993).

42. C. Norman Kraus, *Jesus Christ Our Lord, Christology From a Disciple's Perspective* (Scottdale, Penn.: Herald Press, 1987); Thomas N. Finger, *A Contemporary Anabaptist Theology, Biblical, Historical, Constructive* (Downers Grove: InterVarsity Press, 2004); J. Denny Weaver, *The Nonviolent Atonement* (Grand Rapids: Eerdmans, 2001); A. James Reimer, *Mennonites and Classical Theology, Dogmatic Foundations for Christian Ethics* (Kitchener, Ont: Pandora Press, 2001).

43. James C. Juhnke, "Mennonite History and Self Understanding: North American Mennonitism as a Bipolar Mosaic," in Calvin Wall Redekop and Samuel J. Steiner, eds., *Mennonite Identity, Historical and Contemporary Perspectives* (Lanham, Md.: University Press of America, 1988), 83-99.

44. Paul Toews, "Dissolving the Boundaries and Strengthening the Nuclei," *Christian Leader* 45 (1982): 6-8.

45. Two sociological studies that have documented this dynamic are: J. Howard Kauffman and Leland Harder, *Anabaptists Four Centuries Later,* and J. Howard Kauffman and Leo Driedger, *Mennonite Mosaic.*

46. The recent politicization of Mennonite conservatives and traditionalists parallels the politicization of American fundamentalists and evangelicals analyzed by George M. Marsden, *Fundamentalism and American Culture,* 2d ed. (New York: Oxford University Press, 2006).

47. For Roth's analysis and responses by commentators, see the June 2005 issue of the online journal, *Mennonite Life:* http"://www.bethelks.edu/mennonitelife/ current_issue_toc.php.
48. Fred Anderson and Andrew Cayton, *The Dominion of War: Empire and Liberty in North America, 1500-2000* (New York: Penguin, 2005).
49. Bush, *Two Kingdoms, Two Loyalties,* 271.

Rome in America: Transnational Allegiances and Adjustments[1]

Peter R. D'Agostino
University of Illinois—Chicago

On 14 November 2002, John Paul II entered the Palazzo di Montecitorio in Rome and became the first pope in history to address the Italian parliament. In his forty-five minute speech, he asked authorities to show clemency for prisoners through reduced sentences, and he urged Italians to have more children to reverse a declining birthrate, one of the lowest in the world. The *papa polacca* was keenly aware of the tortuous (and torturous) relationship between modern Italy and St. Peter's successors. "Truly deep is the bond that exists between the Holy See and Italy! We all know that this association has gone through widely different phases and circumstances, subject to the vicissitudes and contradictions of history. But at the same time we should recognize that precisely in the sometimes turbulent sequence of events that bond has had highly positive results, both for the Church of Rome, and therefore for the Catholic Church, and for the beloved Italian Nation." John Paul reminded parliament, "Italy's social and cultural identity, and the civilizing mission it has exercised and continues to exercise in Europe and the world, would be most difficult to understand without reference to Christianity, its lifeblood." In conclusion, he implored "the Redeemer of man to grant that the beloved Italian Nation will continue, now and in the future, to live in a way worthy of its radiant tradition, and to draw from that tradition new and abundant fruits of civilization, for the material and spiritual progress of the whole world. God bless Italy!" John Paul's appearance in the Palazzo di Montecitorio inspired little comment in the United States. It was an Italian event of little import to Americans.[2]

However, American indifference to the Holy Father's relationship to modern Italy is relatively novel, a luxury of the last fifty years. In John Paul's words, the "association" between Italy and the Holy See that "has gone through widely different phases and circumstances, subject to the vicissitudes and contradictions of history," has had profound importance for modern Catholicism and for social relations among American Catholics and their neighbors. The "turbulent sequence of events" from 1848 to 1940, in particular, was not merely an Italian or even a strictly European matter. It shaped American Catholic identity and conditioned how Protestants, Jews, and liberals understood Roman Catholics in the United States. I will examine this turbulent century below.

WHOSE ROME? WHOSE ITALY?

In 1848 Rome erupted in revolt. Liberal nationalists throughout the politically fragmented Italian peninsula rose up to topple oppressive rulers and expel

Austrian overlords. Frightened and bewildered, Pope Pius IX fled his Eternal City and went into exile. Although French arms restored the pope-king's rule over his Papal States in central Italy, liberals soon realized their dream of Italian unity and in 1861 proclaimed a constitutional monarchy. On the twentieth of September 1870 the young kingdom conquered Rome itself, and the Papal States disappeared from the map of Europe. This time Pius chose an internal exile. For the next sixty years, he and his successors on Peter's throne cloistered themselves in the Vatican and hailed themselves "prisoners" of the evil Kingdom of Italy. Catholics throughout the world made these papal protests their own. They embraced popular devotions that cultivated heartfelt affections for their embattled Holy Father. Liberal barbarians, a new breed of pagans, vandalized the Eternal City and crucified Christ's Vicar, humanity's suffering servant, on a Calvary called the Vatican. Deceitful proponents of modern civilization peddling illusions of false liberty were in revolt against God. Apocalyptic broodings rattled the lost remnants of papal Rome.[3]

The Kingdom of Italy, conventionally called "Liberal Italy" from 1861 to 1922, insisted Rome's status had been settled after the conquest of 1870. The prisoner popes, however, never acquiesced to the loss of the temporal power. Christ's Vicar broadcast dramatic lamentations of this "Roman Question," the abnormal status of the pope as a prisoner of Liberal Italy without a territorial sovereignty to guarantee his spiritual autonomy. The Holy Father called upon Catholic states and his faithful children in non-Catholic states to participate in his incessant rituals of protest. Liberal Italy, on the other hand, had the backing of liberals, Protestants, and Jews the world over. It denied the existence of a Roman Question and contended the pope was a spiritual leader who did not need to rule land in order to carry out his religious mission. The temporal power of the pope was a medieval anachronism in a world of progress. Liberal Italy assured the pope a secure place in the new liberal world order that granted his church freedom from state interference, even if it denied his legitimacy as a territorial prince. Wisdom dictated that he halt his violent denunciations.

This conflict between Catholic and liberal conceptions of papal sovereignty was not an abstract debate. It was inseparably linked to the contest over the meaning of Italy as a nation and a state. Catholics throughout the world contended Italy was a Catholic nation whose greatest individuals were saints, whose most beautiful monuments were Catholic in inspiration, and whose center was the Holy Father in papal Rome. Village festivals to patron saints that marked the many *patrie*, or homelands, on the peninsula and its islands fused family, village, and municipality into Catholic Italy, the *patria*, the land of the popes. In the Catholic understanding of history, St. Peter's successors in Rome had always protected this beloved nation from foreign domination. Through God's Providence, the Roman Empire had fallen, and the bishop of Rome had become an Italian ruler and the moral arbiter of Europe. From papal Rome all civilization emanated. It assimilated barbarians and taught natural and divine law to the nations. God had chosen Italians to be the pope's champions and agents of civilization.

Before 1848 Catholics had proposed a variety of formulas to expel Austrian power and unite Italy into a confederation that honored the pope as its head and preserved his Papal States. The European revolutions of 1848 shattered this dream. When the Kingdom of Italy became a reality in 1861, Pius IX intransigently condemned the new state as an evil invention of bloodthirsty radicals, Freemasons, secret societies, and pseudoliberals who used nationalism as a pretext to attack the pope, the Church, and God. Awaiting the collapse of this demonic monarchy, Pius IX forbade Catholic participation in the political system of this degenerate state. A masterful manipulator of public opinion, he cultivated the affective loyalties of Catholics throughout the world to support his intransigence.

This high drama became a lens through which Catholics perceived the modern world, and through which Protestants perceived Catholics. The meaning and status of Rome, the Italian nation, and the Italian state became the focal point of an international contest. Catholics fought liberalism and its unrelenting rejection of the papal claim to temporal sovereignty. Throughout Europe and America, journalists, scholars, and politicians debated the significance of the Roman Question. Thousands of American Catholics took to the streets in snowy frontier towns and genteel eastern cities to march against the symbols and holidays of Liberal Italy, to communicate solidarity with their Holy Father, and to keep the Roman Question alive. Their activism marked Catholic identity and inspired among their Anglo-Protestant foes a great love of Italian liberal nationalism.

The Roman Question never disappeared from public discourse, much to Liberal Italy's disgust. It persisted as a theological, cultural, and political rupture from 1848 until 1929, when the pope attained a small temporal sovereignty, the State of the Vatican City. During the interim, the Roman Question conditioned European and American Catholic life on the diplomatic plane right down to the parish level and helped shape how Protestants understood their own ecclesiopolitical positions.[4] Catholics responded to the Risorgimento—the movement to unify Italy—and the concomitant loss of the Papal States, by creating what I call the *ideology of the Roman Question*, a constituent element of Catholic culture that, in the United States, generated boundaries separating Catholics from other Americans.

The ideology of the Roman Question had two parts. First, it argued that the pope required the temporal power for spiritual independence and for the health of civilization itself. Thus, it condemned the liberal legislation the Italian state unilaterally imposed upon the pope, the Law of Guarantees (1871), which acknowledged his spiritual, but denied his temporal, sovereignty. Second, the ideology of the Roman Question ferociously cudgeled Liberal Italy as an illegitimate polity. The "movement" of these two parts of the ideology in relationship to one another, in particular their uncoupling in the twentieth century, constitutes *the transformation of the ideology of the Roman Question*. Although the intensity of the Catholic condemnation of the Italian state diminished in the early decades of the twentieth century, the popes still rejected the Law of Guarantees and called for the restoration of the temporal power. Finally, in 1929 dec-

ades of Catholic perseverance paid off in *the realization of the ideology of the
Roman Question.* Fascist Italy and the Holy See signed the Lateran Pacts, which
established the State of the Vatican City. At each stage the Roman Question
shaped the American Church and the social relations between Catholics and
others.

The problematic historical relationship of Catholicism and modern liberalism in the United States and Europe cannot be understood when it is manicured
too neatly, abstracted out of the Italian and Roman contexts where conflicts
broke out most vociferously and colored how the papacy reacted to tensions
elsewhere. In light of that conviction, I tell the story of the creation, transformation, and realization of the ideology of the Roman Question in a narrative that is
largely a contest over the status of Italy as a nation and a state.[5]

TRANSNATIONAL PERSPECTIVES ON AMERICAN RELIGIOUS HISTORY

Students of religion in the United States are not accustomed to a story
whose center pivots around myths and symbols of Rome. We know that Israel
has a potent place in the life of American Jews and Protestant premillennialists
and that Ethiopia triggers deep associations in the African American religious
imagination. However, the symbolic significance of the pope, Rome, and Italy
after 1848 remains conspicuously unexplored.

The Vatican before the pontificate of John XXIII (1958-63) usually appears in American historiography as a prosaic gathering site of deteriorating
Italian men. They intrude, discipline, misunderstand "American life," and stifle
the creativity of "American Catholicism." This trope, for lack of a better word,
has undermined historical understanding. In fact, most American Catholics
stumbled over each other trying to display loyalty and love for their Holy Father,
and they consistently invited the authority of the Vatican into U.S. affairs to
adjudicate conflicts and discipline opponents. This may sound strange to American ears today. But the story told here demonstrates how a three-generation battle between the Kingdom of Italy—a second-rate power—and five aged occu-
pants of the papal throne, an anomalous ecclesiastical office in a southern
European city, preoccupied millions of Catholic Americans, inflamed their passions, mobilized their resources, and deeply troubled their Protestant, liberal,
and Jewish neighbors.

Rome, not Jerusalem, Washington, Baltimore, or Dublin, was the center of
the American Catholic world from 1848 to 1940. There were, of course, lesser
centers, from home altars to statues in parish churches, from lay societies to the
many Episcopal cathedrals that jutted across the skyline of dreary industrial ci-
tyscapes. However, papal Rome—the source of juridical and dogmatic authority
and a rich reservoir of history and symbolism—made possible whatever unity
existed among disparate American Catholic classes, ethnic groups, and regions.
Rome and the pope also defined Catholics in the imagination of other Americans. Furthermore, to invoke the Holy Father or papal Rome after 1848 was tan-
tamount to inviting a discussion of the Roman Question and the meaning of Lib-

eral Italy, and if non-Catholic Americans joined the conversation, a brawl inevitably ensued.

Historians have erroneously assumed that the Roman Question was an irrelevant diversion in a distant Europe about which Americans remained indifferent.[6] However, U.S. newspapers, sermons, books, lectures, devotional practices, public rituals, and diplomatic activities tell a very different story. Vague references to the French Revolution and the apostasy of Father Felicité de Lamennais usually stand in among American historians for an explanation of why the papacy turned against liberalism. But when Americans actually debated the Vatican's troubled relationship to liberalism after 1848, they discussed the status of Rome and the Vatican within Liberal Italy. I have followed this lead in my research.

This essay finds a comfortable place in the scholarship on American religion. Historians have identified three periods of American religious pluralism. In the colonial and early national era, Protestants maintained denominational distinctions through confessional commitments and symbolic activity. As denominational boundaries weakened, a pan-Protestant cultural consensus emerged in the mid-nineteenth century. By the 1840s this Protestant "righteous empire" contended with growing communities of Jews and Catholics who resisted assimilation into the Protestant majority. It was not until after World War II that cultural divisions separating "Protestant-Catholic-Jew" began to wane. This "restructuring of American religion" created new social cleavages. Conservative and liberal axes within Judaism, Protestantism, and Catholicism increasingly structured religion in America. The new lines of conflict, liberal against conservative, cut through the historic faith traditions and, in the most aggressive (and simplistic) formulation, generated contemporary "culture wars." Although social historians could poke holes in, and enumerate exceptions to, this grand model, it provides a helpful starting point to our story, which falls squarely within the second period.[7]

The creation, transformation, and realization of the ideology of the Roman Question fortified the considerable ramparts that separated Catholics from other Americans. This is not to say that the status of the pope in Rome was the only marker of Catholic identity, but it was pervasive and provocative, a recurring source of tension between Catholics and others. For three generations it contributed to Catholic distinctiveness, boundary maintenance, and survival in Protestant America. Protestants, liberals, and Jews, in turn, helped to strengthen the ideology of the Roman Question as they condemned it and tendered their own beliefs about Rome and Italy.

American Catholic scholarship is often frustratingly internalist. It frequently deploys history as ammunition in contemporary intra-Catholic debates about Church governance—the Church should be more democratic, the Church should not tolerate so much dissent, and so on. This internalist scholarship emphasizes public sparring among a minority of U.S. bishops from 1880 to 1900 and suggests these conflicts hardened into a "liberal" versus "conservative" divide that anticipated today's Catholic culture wars. Historian R. Laurence Moore, outside of this intra-Catholic fray, has dissected this story line of good-guy "liberals" versus bad-guy "conservatives." His deconstruction of this inter-nalist narrative has gone largely ignored. So has his call to bring "American Catholics to the center of American religious history where they belong" and to demonstrate how the massive Catholic presence in the United States shaped Protestant understandings of the role of religion in society.[8]

If an internalist narrative driven by a presentist agenda obfuscates the rele-vance of American Catholic history for nonspecialists, it also engages in an un-productive polemic with "European Catholicism," a straw man that serves as a monolithic, static symbol of ecclesiastical absolutism and a foil to an imagined democratic "American Catholicism." For instance, a recent volume explores how "minority faiths" such as Judaism and Catholicism adopted "strategies for survival" to maintain their identities in the face of a hegemonic "American Prot-estant mainstream." The essay on Catholicism insists that true American Catho-lics in the nineteenth century wished to create an "American Catholicism" that was "modern and democratic," the opposite of "European Catholicism," which was "feudal and monarchical." This simplistic and awkward nod toward a com-parative history that never actually investigates Europe ignores the many Catho-lics in European society who have fought and suffered for democratic and liberal values. Likewise, this reading of the past ignores the intense affection American Catholics harbored for the monarchical nineteenth-century papacy and its indis-criminate condemnations of every variety of European liberalism.[9]

Most students of American religion rarely tread upon this treacherous Catholic turf. They accept a story line churned out by "Americanist" Church historians and use it to whitewash Catholicism in the United States of its dis-tinctiveness. In so doing, they assimilate the Church in a way that Catholics themselves struggled so passionately and successfully to avoid. American histo-rians and sociologists make aggressive claims for uniformity across religious traditions. Catholic parishes in America are "de facto" Protestant congregations; Counter-Reformation parish missions mimicked Protestant revivals; Catholic immigrants understood their migration to the United States within a biblical Exodus paradigm, like the Puritans; the engagement of American Catholics, like Protestants, with biblical criticism and Darwinism inspired a "modernist im-pulse"; "American Catholicism" is just another "denomination." Notwithstand-ing the insights offered in these analogical studies of Catholics, a selective ren-dering of the national context inevitably takes an unexplained priority over the transnational one. Catholicism appears as a quirky Protestantism, divorced from its international matrix, the original and enduring context that preserved its dis-tinctiveness and ensured its survival as a minority faith in the United States. The exercise of papal power among American Catholics appears as a vindictive bolt of lightning from an unenlightened foreign despot for mysterious Latin reasons, a "holy siege."[10]

This quest for uniformity of organizational forms across religious tradi-tions has distorted our understanding of institutions such as parishes and made distinctively Catholic institutions invisible altogether. Religious orders, mission-ary societies, Catholic juridical and financial structures, episcopal diplomatic activities, the Vatican's apostolic delegation in Washington, and the papacy—

Catholic institutions without obvious Protestant correlates—rarely appear in the indexes of works culminating in "models" and "paradigms" of "American religion." The Methodist Church simply does not have a Secretary of State. This study hopes to recover the particular nature of Catholicism in the United States through attention to transnational factors and its dialectical relationships to Protestantism and liberalism.[11]

AMERICAN HISTORY IN A GLOBAL AGE

It has become popular in the last decade to declare that U.S. history is an aspect of "international history" and to proclaim the value of placing U.S. history within a global or transnational context.[12] This contemporary interest in transnationalism has arisen at a time when observers claim the nation-state grows weaker. But even during the heyday of the nation-state system, modern Catholics within states forged an "imagined community" with myths, shared symbols, and a calendar of prescribed rituals. The Holy See in the Eternal City was the center of this community. The Holy Father communicated his suffering, frequently through disapproval of events in Italy, a Catholic nation within a state established against his will. He won the unprecedented affection of Catholics everywhere, including the United States, with significant consequences for American social relations. The international frame of reference to this story makes it no less a part of U.S. history. It is a study akin to what historian Akira Iriye calls "cultural internationalism," but the focus is upon the implications of this particular papal internationalism for U.S. history.[13]

The ideology of the Roman Question, in all of its stages, was an international structure, but one that cannot be understood without special consideration of events in nineteenth and twentieth-century Italy. The conquest of the Papal States created an anomaly within the concert of nations—a national capital with two legitimate sovereigns. Both had active diplomatic corps, denied the other's claims to temporal sovereignty, and deployed their resources to undermine the other's prestige. U.S. historians, however, have adopted liberal premises in their confrontation with (or avoidance of) this odd Roman phenomenon. They have considered the papacy an Italian domestic matter, and since the Kingdom of Italy was never a "great power," the Holy See rarely appears in their accounts of Euro-American diplomatic relations.

But European and American Catholics did not abandon their Holy Father to the Kingdom of Italy, and they never accepted the liberal solution to the Roman Question imposed upon the papacy. Although reactions varied by nation, region, and class, the Roman Question preoccupied Catholics everywhere, generating conflicts between Catholics and other citizens (or subjects) and provoking anxiety among nation building statesmen. During international crises, foreign offices and state departments, with good reason, wondered whether their Catholic populations or those of their allies could be trusted. This was surely the case during the Great War when President Woodrow Wilson, his advisers, and his allies, tracked papal diplomacy with angst and wondered whether the American Catholic population—not merely Irish or German Americans—was all aboard for the war to end all wars. "Nativism" was an international phenomenon, and Catholic ghettos emerged within many modern states, even those that were ostensibly Catholic.[14] During the Fascist period (1922-43), American Catholics qua Catholics were perceived to be aligned with Fascist Italy or at least to support many of its illiberal policies. I set this international Catholic factor in relief in the hope that specialists in politics and foreign relations might begin to pay greater attention to Catholicism as a form of internationalism. Still, I maintain an American focus in this study in order to explore the political, cultural, and social implications of this international story for the United States.

SOCIAL THEORY AND IDEOLOGY

In this discussion of theory and method, I hope it becomes clear that the dichotomy between Europe and America, applied with normative implications to matters in Catholic history, can be artificial and misleading. This is a historical study of ideology. It is neither a church history in the theological sense nor a community study of a Catholic social group. I track neither an institution nor a cohort of people through time. Instead, I have chosen to narrate the rise, transformation, and realization of an ideology and how it worked in American society.[15]

In the stories they tell, historians find a balance between impersonal structures that facilitate and limit human behavior and the agency of people who create their own lives. Structures, however, are also human creations, made and remade through social action. With each re-creation of these patterns of symbols in social life, with each reproduction of cultural schemas that generate human action, resources are mobilized and new situations arise in which structures are remade once again. Each application of inherited rules of behavior leaves room for innovation, that is, for human agency. Social theorist Anthony Giddens captures this dialectical quality: "Social structures are both constituted by human agency, and yet at the same time are the very medium of this constitution." As one of his interpreters puts it, structures "are both the medium and the outcome of the practices which constitute social systems."[16]

Structures are not all alike. Language, for example, is a particularly deep structure, one that is persistent and pervasive over time and space. Deep structures cannot be easily changed or eliminated. They set the foundation for enduring institutions because they can organize human behavior into a social system. The capacity of structures to mobilize resources determines their power. A dictatorship, with its ubiquitous police force and repressive mechanisms, exemplifies a powerful (but not very deep) structure. Needless to say, structures do not necessarily respect political borders. Catholic juridical codes and capitalism, for example, are both deep structures and relatively immune to national borders.

Ideologies, as sociologist Gene Burns has explained, "are actually special types of social structures." They comprise verbal or written utterances capable of communicating beliefs and duties. According to Robert Wuthnow, an ideology "may also include visual representations (objects such as flags or pictures), symbolic acts (salutes and genuflections), and events (sets of related acts such as a parade or religious service). In this sense ideology obviously blends with and subsumes much of what is usually referred to as ritual." As a structure that both facilitates communication and behavior as well as limits and directs thought and action, ideology requires constant social interaction to preserve its structure, which can change as historical agents transpose cultural schemas or symbolic patterns to new cases or contexts.[17]

The ideology of the Roman Question took a plurality of forms. Variations resulted from its replication on different social levels. Not every ideology appears as a propositional statement that coheres into a totalistic, all-encompassing worldview. Theorists draw helpful distinctions between "lived" and "intellectual" ideological forms. Unstable and incomplete, lived ideologies are likely to communicate assumptions or emotions, not reasoned argument. Popular forms of media—newspapers, parish bulletins, sermons, devotional tracts, letters to editors—most effectively communicated the ideology of the Roman Question. Group exegesis of these media in churches, offices, barbershops, and taverns further generated popular expressions of ideology.[18]

Changes in the political and social environment tend to transform existing ideologies or generate new ones. This often happens quite rapidly. The conquest of the Papal States and the establishment of Liberal Italy gave rise to the ideology of the Roman Question. It restructured preexisting cultural forms to challenge the existence of the Kingdom of Italy and the liberal understanding of religion as a purely "spiritual" affair. A transformation in this ideology resulted from the rise of socialism and the massive upheaval brought about by World War I. The collapse of Liberal Italy after the Great War frightened Catholics, many of whom feared a socialist revolution, but it also created an opportunity for ideological change. In this new environment, tension with Liberal Italy was relaxed and disengaged from the enduring quest for the restoration of the temporal power. After 1922, Catholics both facilitated and exploited the rise of Fascist Italy, accelerating this ideological transformation.

Ideologies have modes of operation. Popular modes analyzed in this study were the deployment of symbols, artful gestures of protest, and implicit threats of retaliation. Repeated to the point of tedium, they constructed an interpretation of the past. Within a generation after 1848, the ideology of the Roman Question had become integrated into Catholic processes of socialization, securing broad dissemination. The expansion of print media, increased literacy, and technological developments in communication and transportation enhanced the power and depth of the ideology of the Roman Question. A voluminous transatlantic Catholic correspondence and the establishment of the Vatican's apostolic delegation in the United States in 1893 did the same. As this work shows, American Catholics participated in an international "imagined community"—the Church—of Catholic peoples in a world dominated by nation-states suspicious of all forms of internationalism.[19]

Ritual is a powerful medium to communicate ideology. Wuthnow explains that a ritual is "a symbolic-expressive aspect of behavior that communicates something about social relations, often in a relatively dramatic or formal manner." It is not a special type of activity set apart from others but the expressive dimension of all social activity. It need not be a face-to-face event; mass media also facilitate ritual. Our story describes a variety of Catholic rituals: marches and sermons of protest; tedious reiterations of key words and phrases that triggered affective associations; parliamentary speeches, public letters, and papal allocutions to cardinals. The back-and-forth polemics between American Protestants and Catholics, or between the pope and Italian statesmen, over the meaning of Italian symbols had a dramatic and formal character—they too were rituals.[20]

Competition is an important element of ideological analysis. The Roman Question instigated intra-Catholic competition. Many Catholics were committed to mixing liberalism and Catholicism. But the "intransigents"—Catholics committed to the restoration of the Papal States, the necessity of the temporal power, and an unequivocal condemnation of Liberal Italy—had the backing of the papacy, a powerful resource. Commitment to intransigence became a marker of loyalty to the Church during the nineteenth century and had a profound impact on Catholics in the United States, even those who absorbed other values from liberalism.[21]

Some historians use "ideology" to designate illusory ideas or collectively shared values that facilitate state domination. As I have defined it, the ideology of the Roman Question means something else. It is what impassioned Catholics to struggle toward a goal and mobilized resources in that struggle. Catholic cultural producers employed the ideology of the Roman Question to heighten Catholic consciousness, preserve collective memories, and act to regain the temporal power. Notwithstanding failures along the path from 1848 to 1929, the Holy Father did in the end acquire sovereignty over an autonomous and theocratic state. The State of the Vatican City exists today for all to see. It serves as an effective launching pad for papal intervention in international affairs. Before 1929, the papacy lacked that political legitimacy.

The ideology of the Roman Question affected Catholics in different ways. Bishops, editors, and priests, for example, exercised greater power than others. As cultural producers in the public sphere, they had the power to communicate their ideas. On the other hand, they had little autonomy to deviate from prescribed Catholic positions. While a bishop could author a circular letter read to thousands of Catholics at Sunday mass, this very power assured that ideological deviation in the content of that circular letter would trigger punishment from the Vatican. Conversely, lay people had less power (as Catholics). They did not fill a recognized office in the Church, and they lacked easy access to Catholic communication media to broadcast their ideas. This absence of power, however, was also a form of "negative autonomy." If a lay woman could not publicize her views, she nevertheless did have autonomy in her home, or corner grocer, or reading circle, to voice heterodoxy safely. In addition, she could more easily avoid active participation in Catholic ideology. Thus, the ideology of the Roman Question, like all ideologies, embodied mechanisms of power and discipline.[22]

CHRONOLOGY AND OVERVIEW

The ideology of the Roman Question falls into three periods: intransigence (1848-1914), transformation (1914-29), and realization (1929-40).

My examination of the period of intransigence describes how the *Risorgimento*—the movement to unify Italy—led to international Catholic condemnations of Liberal Italy as a "usurper" state controlled by evil forces who used nationalism as a pretext to attack the pope, the Church, and the Catholic nation of Italy. Catholics adopted an alternative, Catholic idea of the Italian nation that was at odds with the state's promotion of a liberal national identity. Catholics rejected Liberal Italy's unilaterally imposed legislation—the Law of Guarantees—to regulate the position of the Holy See within the Italian kingdom and expressed solidarity with their suffering Holy Father, a Christ figure redeeming the world on a crucifix constructed by plundering revolutionaries.

This study demonstrates how American Catholics, particularly of Irish and German descent, participated in the intransigent expressions of the ideology of the Roman Question. They protested the Risorgimento and communicated solidarity with their Holy Father through public rituals that separated Catholics from their American neighbors. By contrast, American liberals and Protestants celebrated the unification of Italy as the progressive realization of liberal and millennial hopes. Garibaldi, Cavour, and Mazzini, who were marauding degenerates from the Catholic point of view, in the Protestant mind, were latter-day Washingtons, Jeffersons, and Franklins who liberated the Italian nation from papal tyranny.

In the generation after the Risorgimento, almost all Catholics in the United States—those dubbed both "liberal" and "conservative" in Catholic scholarship—supported intransigent expressions of the ideology of the Roman Question. They condemned Liberal Italy and demonized its leaders. They insisted that the liberalism behind the U.S. political order was radically different from Europe's pseudoliberalism that had imprisoned the pope. American liberalism, they insisted, was in perfect harmony with the restoration of the temporal power. Put another way, the Roman Question inspired an American Catholic version of "American exceptionalism."[23]

Immigration created an Italian diaspora in America. Representatives of the Italian state (the embassy and consulates) and the Italian Church (the clergy) followed migrants to the United States. The presence of Italian Americans forced Catholics from all national groups to confront the symbols and rituals of both Catholic and Liberal Italy with great frequency. Catholics, Protestants, and liberals from all national backgrounds participated in the ideological contest that erupted within and about this Italian diaspora. Catholics turned to the Vatican for instructions, welcoming its authority into U.S. affairs to adjudicate the proper behavior in this contest. Protestant home missionary societies, settlement houses, and liberal activists compelled Catholics to mobilize their resources. Migration thus intensified the ideology of the Roman Question and forced Catholics in the United States to participate in it.

The Great War initiated a transformation of the ideology of the Roman Question. A cataclysm that rocked the foundations of civilization, World War I reawakened Catholic hopes to regain the temporal power. The Holy See sought to arbitrate a treaty during the war, gain entrance into the peace conference, and compel the European Powers to resolve the Roman Question on Catholic terms. The United States and American Catholics had an important role in papal diplomacy during the Great War. Their potential influence on President Woodrow

Wilson, the Democratic Party, and the Allied states was central to the Holy See's strategy to resolve the Roman Question.

A change within the structure of the ideology of the Roman Question marked this period of transformation. The Holy Father continued to condemn the usurpation of the Papal States, decry his loss of temporal power, and withhold formal recognition of Liberal Italy. However, the Vatican for the first time permitted unrestricted Catholic political participation within Liberal Italy. The pope instructed clergy to act as Italian war chaplains and did not censure Catholic politicians actively supporting the war effort. Furthermore, in 1919 the papacy allowed Italian Catholics to create a nonconfessional but Catholic political party.

This rejection of intransigence also transformed the relationship between Italian Americans' liberal nationalist organizations and the Church. Intense intra-Catholic ideological competition broke out among Italian priests in the United States during the Great War regarding the significance of ethnic organizations within the Italian diaspora. Just as the Holy See eased opposition to Liberal Italy, the Vatican and American bishops eased intransigent resistance to the Order Sons of Italy in America, a powerful fraternal organization. The Vatican permitted Catholic institutional links with the Order and similar organizations that had previously been prohibited.

The collapse of Liberal Italy after the Great War and the rise of Benito Mussolini's Fascist dictatorship in the 1920s intensified the transformation of the ideology of the Roman Question. Important strands of Catholicism and Fascism shared notable affinities, particularly a disdain for liberalism, socialism, and political democracy. Fascist Italy, in contrast to Liberal Italy, acknowledged the Catholic character of the Italian nation and held out promise that the Kingdom of Italy could finally become a legitimate home for the Catholic nation. Mussolini celebrated Italy's Catholic heritage and awarded privileges to the Church. The Vatican applauded and rewarded these developments.

American Catholics participated in this ideological transformation. As the world watched Pope Pius XI (1922-39) and Mussolini perform unprecedented gestures of reconciliation, American Catholics reiterated the Vatican's position, embraced the symbols of Fascist Italy, and accepted the legitimacy of Italy's official state representatives. American Catholics supported the U.S. government's financial policy of stabilizing Fascist Italy during its vulnerable years while Mussolini consolidated his dictatorship. When debates over the religious policies of Fascist Italy surfaced, Catholics clashed with liberals and Protestants, who feared the religious liberties Italians had known under Liberal Italy were at risk. Debates about the nature of Fascism were central to religious tensions in the 1920s, when Mussolini became a protean American icon with different meanings for Catholics and Protestants. American Catholics participated in important ways in the reconciliation leading up to the Lateran Pacts of 1929, when the Holy See and Fascist Italy resolved the Roman Question and formally recognized one another. The pope became the temporal ruler of the State of the Vatican City, what G. K. Chesterton called "The Holy Island." Catholic ideology had demanded nothing less.[24]

The realization of the ideology of the Roman Question had implications for American life. Most significantly, the establishment of the Vatican City instigated polemics and apologias in the United States. The American Catholic defense of the Lateran Pacts in the face of liberal and Protestant critiques intensified preexisting hostilities toward Catholics that had surfaced during Al Smith's 1928 presidential campaign. Some Catholic thinkers stubbornly insisted the Lateran Pacts created in Fascist Italy an environment of religious liberty analogous to that in the United States. Others claimed that a Catholic confessional state was appropriate for the Italian people, a Catholic nation.

American Catholics, like their Holy Father, participated in rituals legitimating Fascist Italy's religious policies and, in many instances, the Fascist regime itself. The Italian embassy and consulates promoted Fascist propaganda within U.S. society. They forged excellent relations with American Catholics and received cooperation from the apostolic delegation, U.S. bishops, clergy, and both English-speaking and Italian-speaking laity. The same consulates, however, now representatives of a Catholic confessional state, found the Lateran Pacts a liability in their encounters with Protestant Americans who had committed resources to evangelizing Italians.

Among American Catholics, there was never an anti-Fascist movement. The experience of two stubborn and lonely Catholic anti-Fascists demonstrates the transnational networks of authority and discipline that linked Fascist Italy and the Holy See after the Lateran Pacts. No less a figure than the Vatican Secretary of State, Cardinal Eugenio Pacelli, the future Pius XII (1939-58), and his office disciplined Fathers James Gillis and Giuseppe Ciarrocchi for their anti-Fascist journalism.

After the Lateran Pacts, the links forged among American bishops, Fascist consulates, and the Holy See facilitated cultural activism to improve the image of Italian Americans during a period in U.S. history when popular movies and fiction smeared their character. American Catholics also entered into polemics with liberals and Protestants over the fate of postwar Italy. Catholics staunchly defended their anti-Fascist credentials against accusations that the papacy and the American Church had no moral authority to participate in Italian reconstruction. Catholic elite argued (unsuccessfully) that the Italian monarchy that had supported the Fascist regime for twenty years ought to be maintained and that Italian republicans were untrustworthy red revolutionaries. I suggest that the American Catholic relationship to Fascism between the wars helps explain why mid-century liberals looked upon Catholicism as an authoritarian culture with affinities to reactionary politics.

In 1948, one century after Pius IX fled papal Rome and condemned the *Risorgimento*, the Christian Democrats, essentially a Catholic party, took the mantle of the new Italian republic and claimed the heritage of the *Risorgimento* as their own. The Church in America mobilized resources to bring the Christian Democrats to power against its competitor, the Communist Party. These efforts, however, no longer clearly distinguished Catholics from other Americans. American Catholic and Vatican policies toward republican Italy during the Cold War did not generate clear social boundaries between Catholics and other

Americans. The Roman Question ceased to exist in the new environment. This is not to say that the pope has not remained an important symbol to Americans, but his status is no longer linked to debates about the nature of the Italian nation and state. Furthermore, while the debate about Catholicism and liberalism continues, Italy has no privileged place in these reflections.

Notes

1. This chapter has been adapted from the preface and introduction to Peter R. D'Agostino, *Rome in America: Transnational Catholic Ideology from the Risorgimento to Fascism* (Chapel Hill: University of North Carolina Press, 2004), by permission of the University of North Carolina Press.
2. For the text of the speech, see the Vatican office's Web site at <http://www.vatican.va /holy_father/john_paulii/speeches/2002/november/documents>.
3. Giacomo Martina, "La fine del potere temporale nella coscienza religiosa e nella cultura dell'epoca in Italia," *Archivum Historiae Pontificiae* 9 (1971): 309-76.
4. Pier Giorgio Camaiani, "Motivi e riflessi religiosi della questione romana," in *Chiesa e religiosità in Italia dopo l'unità (1861-1878)* (Milan: Vita e Pensiero, 1973), 65-128.
5. See Peter Steinfels, "The Failed Encounter: The Catholic Church and Liberalism in the Nineteenth Century," in R. Bruce Douglass and David Hollennback, eds., *Catholicism and Liberalism: Contributions to American Public Philosophy* (New York: Cambridge University Press, 1994), 19-44; Philip Gleason, "American Catholics and Liberalism, 1789-1960," in Douglass and Hollennback, eds., *Catholicism and Liberalism*, 45-75; and John T. McGreevy, "Thinking on One's Own: Catholicism in the American Intellectual Imagination," *Journal of American History* 84 (June 1997): 97-131. These rich essays on liberalism and Catholicism more or less ignore the Italy-Vatican contest.
6. There has been no systematic study of the topic, which is usually ignored. Marvin R. O'Connell, in *John Ireland and the American Catholic Church* (St. Paul: Minnesota Historical Society, 1988), 276, and James Hennesey, S.J., in "Papacy and Episcopacy in Eighteenth and Nineteenth Century American Catholic Thought," *Records of the American Catholic Historical Society of Philadelphia* 77 (September 1966): 184, dismiss the topic as irrelevant.
7. See Martin E. Marty, *Righteous Empire: The Protestant Experience in America* (New York: Dial, 1970); Will Herberg, *Protestant-Catholic-Jew: An Essay in American Religious Sociology* (New York: Doubleday, 1955); Robert Wuthnow, *The Restructuring of American Religion: Society and Faith since World War II* (Princeton: Princeton University Press, 1988); and James Davidson Hunter, *Culture Wars: The Struggle to Define America* (New York: Basic Books, 1991), 67-106.
8. R. Laurence Moore, *Religious Outsiders and the Making of Americans* (New York: Oxford University Press, 1986), 48-71 (quote on 71). On presentist uses of Catholic history, see R. Scott Appleby, "The Triumph of Americanism: Common Ground for U.S. Catholics in the Twentieth Century," in Mary Jo Weaver and R. Scott Appleby, eds., *Being Right: Conservative Catholics in America* (Bloomington: Indiana University Press, 1995), 37-62; and Philip Gleason, "The New Americanism in Catholic Historiography," *U.S. Catholic Historian* 11 (Summer 1993): 1-18.
9. Jay P. Dolan, "Catholicism and American Culture: Strategies for Survival," in Jonathan D. Sarna, ed., *Minority Faiths and the American Protestant Mainstream* (Urbana and Chicago: University of Illinois Press, 1998), 63. See Patricia Byrne, C.S.J., "American Ultramontanism," *Theological Studies* 56 (1995): 301-26.

10. See R. Steven Warner, "The Place of the Congregation in the Contemporary American Religious Configuration," in James P. Wind and James W. Lewis, eds., *New Perspectives in the Study of American Religious Congregations*, vol. 2 of *American Congregations* (Chicago: University of Chicago Press, 1994), 54 (on parishes); Jay P. Dolan, *Catholic Revivalism: The American Experience, 1830-1900* (Notre Dame: University of Notre Dame Press, 1978) (on parish missions); Timothy L. Smith, "Religion and Ethnicity in America," *American Historical Review* 83 (December 1978): 1155-85 (on the Exodus paradigm); R. Scott Appleby, *"Church and Age Unite!" The Modernist Impulse in American Catholicism* (Notre Dame: University of Notre Dame Press, 1992) (on the Catholic modernist impulse); William R. Hutchison, *The Modernist Impulse in American Protestantism* (New York: Oxford University Press, 1976); Gertrud Kim, O.S.B., "Roman Catholic Organization since Vatican II," in Ross P. Scherer, ed., *American Denominational Organization: A Sociological View* (Pasadena, Calif.: William Carey Library, 1980), 84-129 (on Catholicism as a denomination); and Kenneth A. Briggs, *Holy Siege: The Year That Shook Catholic America* (San Francisco: Harper San Francisco, 1992).

11. For recent works that capture Catholic distinctiveness, see Thomas A. Tweed, *Our Lady of theExile: Diasporic Religion at a Cuban Catholic Shrine in Miami* (New York: Oxford University Press, 1997); Robert A. Orsi, *Thank You, St. Jude: Women's Devotion to the Patron Saint of Hopeless Causes* (New Haven: Yale University Press,1996); and John T. McGreevy, *Parish Boundaries: The Catholic Encounter with Race in the Twentieth-Century Urban North* (Chicago: University of Chicago Press, 1996). Tweed as well as Deirdre M. Molony, in *American Catholic Lay Groups and Transatlantic Social Reform in the Progressive Era* (Chapel Hill: University of North Carolina Press, 2002), and Patrick Allitt, in *Catholic Converts: British and American Intellectuals Turn to Rome* (Ithaca, N.Y.: Cornell University Press, 1997), also deal with transnational Catholic issues.

12. See Thomas Bender, ed., *Rethinking American History in a Global Age* (Berkeley and Los Angeles: University of California Press, 2002); and Akira Iriye, "Internationalization of History," *American Historical Review* 94 (February 1989): 1-10. For exemplary works, see James T. Kloppenberg, *Uncertain Victory: Social Democracy and Progressivism in European and American Thought, 1870-1920* (New York: Oxford University Press, 1986); and Daniel T. Rodgers, *Atlantic Crossings: Social Politics in a Progressive Age* (Cambridge, Mass.: Belknap Press of Harvard University Press, 1998).

13. See the special issue of the *Journal of American History* 86 (December 1999) titled "The Nation and Beyond: Transnational Perspectives on United States History." "Imagined community" is from Benedict Anderson, *Imagined Communities: Reflections on the Origins and Spread of Nationalism* (New York: Verso, 1983, 1991). See also Akira Iriye, *Cultural Internationalism and World Order* (Baltimore: Johns Hopkins University Press, 1997).

14. Oded Heilbronner, "From Ghetto to Ghetto: The Place of German Catholic Society in Recent Historiography," *Journal of Modern History* 72 (June 2000): 453-95.

15. I draw upon Anthony Giddens, *Central Problems in Social Theory: Action, Structure, and Contradiction in Social Analysis* (Berkeley and Los Angeles: University of California Press, 1979), and idem, *The Constitution of Society: Outline of the Theory of Structuration* (Berkeley and Los Angeles: University of California Press, 1984); William H. Sewell, Jr., "Theory of Structure: Duality, Agency, and Transformation," *American Journal of Sociology* 98 (July 1992): 1-29; John B. Thompson, *Studies in the Theory of Ideology* (Berkeley and Los Angeles: University of California Press, 1984), 148-72, and idem, *Ideology and Modern Culture: Critical Social Theory in the Era of Mass Communication* (Stanford: Stanford University Press, 1990); David Held and John B. Thompson, eds.,

Social Theory of Modern Societies: Anthony Giddens and His Critics (New York: Cambridge University Press, 1989); Robert Wuthnow, *Meaning and Moral Order: Explorations in Cultural Analysis* (Berkeley and Los Angeles: University of California Press, 1987), idem, *Restructuring of American Religion,* and idem, *Communities of Discourse: Ideology and Social Structure in the Reformation, the Enlightenment, and European Socialism* (Cambridge, Mass.: Harvard University Press, 1989); Gene Burns, *The Frontiers of Catholicism: The Politics of Ideology in a Liberal World* (Berkeley and Los Angeles: University of California Press, 1992); and Göran Therborn, *Ideology of Power and the Power of Ideology* (New York: Verso, 1980).

16. Anthony Giddens, *New Rules of Sociological Method: A Positive Critique of Interpretive Sociologies* (New York: Basic Books, 1976), 121; Sewell, "Theory of Structure," 6.

17. Burns, *Frontiers of Catholicism,* 9; Wuthnow, *Meaning and Moral Order,* 145.

18. Alan Cassels, *Ideology and International Relations in the Modern World* (New York: Routledge, 1996), 1-8; Thompson, *Ideology and Modern Culture.*

19. Thompson, *Ideology and Modern Culture,* 59-67, 163-271. On the importance of repetition in Catholic ideology, see Michele Dillon, *Catholic Identity: Balancing Reason, Faith, and Power* (New York: Cambridge University Press, 1999), 74; and Anderson, *Imagined Communities.*

20. Wuthnow, *Meaning and Moral Order,* 97-109 (quote on 109).

21. On ideological competition, see Wuthnow, *Meaning and Moral Order,* 148-49, 159-61.

22. On "negative autonomy," see Burns, *Frontiers of Catholicism,* 8-12.

23. Scholars have incorrectly assumed that Catholics, because they supported the First Amendment of the U.S. Constitution or liberal political parties, did not support the pope's temporal power. See, e.g., Burns, *Frontiers of Catholicism,* 79-80; and Jeffrey von Arx, S.J., "Cardinal Henry Edward Manning," in Jeffrey von Arx, S.J., ed., *Varieties of Ultramontanism* (Washington, D.C.: Catholic University of America Press, 1998), 8, 92, 96.

24. See G. K. Chesterton, *The Resurrection of Rome* (New York: Dodd, Mead and Co., 1930), 263.

Tammany Catholicism:
The Semi-Established Church
in the Immigrant City

Christopher Shannon
Christendom College

At a dinner celebrating the dedication of New York City's St. Patrick's Cathedral, "Honest John" Kelly, the city's first Irish Catholic mayor, raised his glass in triumph. "God bless the two greatest organizations in the world, the Catholic Church and Tammany Hall!" After a short pause, one of Honest John's concelebrants asked, "What's the second one?" Whether or not this exchange actually occurred, the joke contains a truth that would have been self evident to any observer of American politics in the late-nineteenth century. In the Gilded Age cities of the industrial northeast and Midwest, the Democratic Party functioned as something like a de facto confessional party for Catholic immigrants. The largely Protestant reform movements dedicated to ridding city government of graft and corruption were also concerned with restraining what they saw as the unsavory and unconstitutional intrusion of the Catholic Church into American politics. Urban machine politics stood as simply the most glaring example of how immigrant Catholics promoted an "un-American" mixing of religion and politics. The properly American understanding of church state relations was itself unclear and in formation. Still, it is clear that in the process of this formation the Catholic Church bore the burden of guilt by association with the European tradition of established church—a tradition that had historically been embraced by all of the major confessional traditions of Protestantism that triumphed in the early modern wars of state formation.[1]

Changing attitudes toward church-state relations in the modern West are but one way in which the Roman Catholic Church both does and does not fit into the model of a confessional tradition in American Christianity. Nineteenth-century urban Catholics shared with the founders of the Episcopal, Lutheran, Presbyterian and Reformed churches an understanding of the public nature of faith that separates them all from a classically evangelical emphasis on private religious experience. That the mainline, confessional denominations quickly adopted a more evangelical, "prophetic" model of church-state relations in America suggests both the power of anti-Catholicism as a unifying force across confessional Protestant lines, and a certain tendency in the anti-authoritarian model of authority bequeathed by the Reformation in general. The confessional Protestant traditions affirmed specific religious truths, not general religious freedom; still, in America the shared principles of *sola fide* and *sola Scriptura* provided the basis for a pan-Protestant ecumenism that undermined the authoritative truths affirmed by the particular confessional traditions. Nineteenth-century

Protestant ecumenism came at the cost of ignoring doctrine and accepting differences. The Roman Catholic Church's refusal to participate in this style of
ecumenism appeared proof of its inherent authoritarianism.

Public polemics aside, there are substantive differences in the way that authority operates within the Roman Catholic and Protestant confessional traditions. At the most basic level, Roman Catholicism is a confessional tradition
without a confession. It has the creeds of the early Church, the decisions of various councils and the statements of various popes, but no single document that
serves as an authoritative reference point in the way that the *Augsburg Confession* has served the Lutheran church. The Roman Catholic Church locates authority not in particular documents *per se*, but in the broader tradition of the
Church, stretching back to the founding of the Church by Christ in the first century. The bishops as successors to the apostles, and the pope as successor to St.
Peter, function as the living, authoritative interpreters of this tradition. Though
Lutherans and Anglicans retained the office of bishop, in general confessional
statements were the classic Reformation substitute for the continuity of tradition.
These statements, and the writings of key theologians such as Martin Luther and
John Calvin, function as a kind of second revelation—though one that presents
itself as simply making clear the plain sense of Scripture distorted by Roman
tradition. In practice, the confessional Protestant traditions function in ways
quite similar to the Roman Catholic Church: the Bible, the confessions, and the
writings of Luther and Calvin all require interpretation. In theory, the Reformation assault on Rome severed authority from person and institution and fostered
a new ideal of the Bible as a kind of objective or self-interpreting text. Transformed by Enlightenment political philosophy, this understanding of authority
eventually issued the ideal of a government by laws, not men, which triumphed
in the American and French revolutions. Confessional Protestants with no historic ties to this novel political idea nonetheless came to see it as consistent with
their earlier revolt against Rome.

The attack on Catholic authoritarianism hampered the efforts of confessional Protestant churches to affirm their own authoritative traditions. Most of
these churches had pietistic or evangelical wings that chafed against the authority of the founding confessional documents. Early efforts to contain these energies within the various mainline orthodoxies eventually gave way to a theological liberalism reluctant to force compliance to confessional strictures.

Roman Catholicism, by contrast, managed to sustain institutional vitality
without having to compromise the defining theological positions outlined at the
Council of Trent (1545-1563), the Church's official response to the Reformation. It may be only slightly overstating the case to say that the Church did not
really begin to implement Trent on any kind of mass scale until the nineteenth
century, the same moment at which many of the mainline Protestant churches
were pulling back from their strong sixteenth-century positions. To be fair, the
Church in America lacked the vigorous intellectual life often the pre-requisite
for doctrinal deviation. At the same time, the Church continued to employ a
time-honored technique for channeling potentially deviant spiritual energy: Give
would-be rebels the option of starting their own religious orders organized

around a unique charism rather than a heretical doctrine. These circumstances and strategies for the most part helped to spare Catholic Church leaders in America any major theological battles. Significantly, the one major exception to this consensus on doctrine came at the point of intersection between theology and politics: What is the relation between the Church and modern democracy? American Protestants condemned the Roman Catholic Church as inherently un-democratic, and thus un-American. The Vatican seemed to confirm this assessment by repeatedly calling for a return to the hierarchical social order of the *ancien regime*. American Catholics insisted they could have it both ways: hierarchical authority in their faith and egalitarian democracy in their politics.

Against all logic, American Catholics largely succeeded in having it both ways up to the middle of the twentieth century. Beginning in the mid-nineteenth century, urban Catholics developed a political model that sought neither to re-turn to European forms of Church establishment nor follow American disestab-lishment on its secular trajectory toward the ideal of an absolute separation of Church and state. This urban Catholic political ideal flowed less from any deeply reflective consideration of constitutional principles than from the practi-cal realities of everyday political practice. Urban Catholics enthusiastically em-braced the political tradition of Jacksonian Democracy, whose idealistic celebra-tion of the common man carried with it the remarkably practical operational principle of "to the victors go the spoils." For Catholics, politics was a matter of patronage—or more broadly, jobs and concrete material benefits received in return for the honest (and sometimes dishonest) work of voting. The circle of patronage extended out from party operatives to their families, friends—and their church. Catholics never questioned the constitutional principle of disestab-lishment, but instead interpreted it in light of a traditional Catholic understand-ing of the mixing of spiritual and temporal power, an understanding confessional Protestants once shared but gradually abandoned as they aligned themselves with evangelical groups in a united Protestant assault on the "Great Whore of Babylon" in America.

Philip Hamburger has recently shown the nineteenth-century battles be-tween Catholics and Protestants were central to the development of our contem-porary understanding of the separation of church and state.[2] The American Revolution received support from a sufficient range of Protestant ministers to take the deist or anti-clerical edge off of the Enlightenment principles that unde-niably shaped the Declaration of Independence and the Constitution. The dises-tablishment clause of the first amendment itself spoke as much to the concerns of "Low-Church" Baptists and Methodists as to the prejudices of the French *philosophes*; just as importantly, it left open the option of establishment at the state level, thus ensuring no radical break from the pre-Revolutionary institu-tional arrangements of many of the former colonies. A transition smoothed was, for a time, also a battle deferred.

Before long, however, the federal precedent would come to shape debate at the state level. Thomas Jefferson's infamous phrase describing "a wall of sepa-ration between church and State" comes from a letter he wrote to the Danbury Baptist Association in response to a request for support in their battle against the established Congregational church in Connecticut. In 1801, the Danbury Baptists wrote to then-President Jefferson in the hopes that some public show of support on his part would influence local opinion in their upcoming fight with the state legislature. Significantly, though Jefferson expressed his full support in a letter fully intended for public purposes, the Danbury Baptists refused to exploit the office of the president, insisting "the President of the united [*sic*] States, is not the national Legislator, & . . . the national government cannot destroy the Laws of each State."[3] The Baptists' reluctance to invoke Jefferson's authority stemmed as much from tactical prudence as absolute principle. Still, the Baptists realized that it would be difficult to reconcile the noble end of freedom from state tyranny with the dubious means of what many would perceive as federal tyranny in a matter the federal constitution had left a concern of individual states. The Connecticut Baptists would eventually win their fight, but the victory would come through a combination of local political activism and the general ideological trajectory established by the First Amendment, not by federal fiat.

The early decades of the nineteenth century saw the gradual disestablishment of state churches. The Congregationalists in Massachusetts were the last holdout, but finally conceded defeat in 1833. Most Americans accepted the principle of disestablishment as normative, yet few outside of a small circle of freethinkers would have understood the institutional separation between church and state to imply any broader separation of religion and society. Following the norms of early modern Europe, High and Low-Church Protestants alike could agree that certain areas of social life, particularly education and social welfare, were the special responsibility of the churches.

The political and economic circumstances of the times placed new strains on the churches' ability to perform their traditional social functions. Representative government required an educated citizenry. By the 1830s, this belief had issued in the effort to establish universal public education as the norm for all children, an ambitious goal that far outstripped the churches' comparatively narrow traditional focus on catechesis and the training of clerical and professional elites. Urban churches found their resources additionally strained by the social welfare needs of a growing population of urban poor drawn to the commercial and industrial centers created by the market revolution of Jacksonian America.[4] All those involved agreed that the situation called for something more than purely private initiative, yet how they were to channel public initiative—particularly public funding—became a major political battle of the day.

The various denominations fought alternatively for control of certain public education and welfare initiatives or freedom from control by other denominations. Denominational lines were still strong and threatened to be yet another source of social division in a country still seeking to fill the political shell of the constitution with some more substantive, positive national identity. America was a nation of Protestants, but not yet a Protestant nation. It would only become such through its encounter with a common enemy: the Roman Catholic Church. When Catholics entered the battle for control of education and welfare funds, Protestants began to see talk of church-state cooperation as a symptom of creeping Romanism. Protestants of all denominational persuasions slowly began to

rally around an essentially Low-Church, evangelical ideal of church-state separation.

On the Catholic side, the towering figure in the pre-Civil War phase of this
battle is "Dagger John"—Archbishop John Hughes of New York. Born in 1797
in County Tyrone, Ireland, Hughes arrived in America some three decades before the Great Famine; still, he was every bit a model for the kind of Irish and
Irish-American prelate associated with Paul Cullen and the "devotional revolution" that transformed Irish Catholicism from a peasant faith to a modern church
in the decades following the Famine.[5] Hughes arrived in America in 1817, determined to make something of himself. He set his sights on the highest aspiration available to an Irish male of his time: the priesthood. John Dubois, rector of
Mount Saint Mary's seminary in Emmitsburg, Maryland turned Hughes away
due to his lack of education; Hughes offered to stay on and work as a gardener
provided he could pursue the primary and secondary education necessary for
admission to the seminary course of study.

For all of Hughes' commitment to hard work and education, he hardly fit
the Benjamin Franklin model of bootstraps individualism. Like most American
Catholics through the nineteenth century, Hughes rejected the emerging American model of education as liberation from the benighted past. Much closer to the
modern Roman discipline of a Cullen than to the folk Catholicism of his own
peasant background, Hughes still never forgot his roots. The experience of
Catholic oppression under British Protestant rule profoundly shaped his understanding of the role of Catholicism in American public life. He grew up in the
heavily Protestant province of Ulster and at one point was almost killed by a
Protestant mob. He never forgot the humiliation added to the family grief following of the death of his younger sister Mary: Forbidden by British law to enter
the cemetery grounds, the Catholic priest presiding at the funeral could only
bless a handful of dirt for the family to throw on the grave while he watched the
burial from outside the cemetery gates. Many years later, Hughes summed up
the status of Catholics under British rule in Ireland as follows: "They told me
when I was a boy that for five days I was on social and civil equality with the
most favored subjects of the British Empire. These five days would be the inter-
val between my birth and my baptism."[6]

Hughes saw Catholic-Protestant relations in Ireland as nothing short of a
degrading caste system. From an early age, he dreamed of "a country in which
no stigma of inferiority would be impressed on my brow simply because I pro-
fessed one creed or another."[7] Hughes' affirmation of religious freedom was in a
sense very American, yet the rhetoric and tone with which he defended Catholic
rights owed much to Old World resentments. To Protestant ears, Hughes' tone
would trump his message. As Archbishop of New York, Hughes would appear
the leader of a united Catholic attempt to impose Catholicism on Protestants
through control of American political institutions. Increasing tensions between
Catholics and Protestants would come to a point on an issue that had already
proven divisive within Protestant circles: control of the public schools.

The Philadelphia Bible Riots of 1844 stand as the most dramatic moment
in this ongoing battle for control of the schools, yet Hughes' handling of the

battle in New York proved more significant for the development of Church-State relations in the nineteenth century. Hughes was in fact ordained in Philadelphia and had experienced the early stages of the battle that would turn bloody in 1844. When he arrived in New York as co-adjutor bishop (to none other than his old nemesis John Dubois), he was well prepared to direct the fight for Catholic rights in education. New York was in many ways a much more dangerous place to be a Catholic: It may not have had a Massachusetts-style established church, but neither did it have the traditions of religious tolerance bequeathed to Pennsylvania by its Quaker founders. New York had a long history of hostility to Catholics and Catholicism.[8] Only with the Revolution did the New York legislature finally abolish a 1700 statute subjecting any priest found within the borders of the colony to perpetual imprisonment.[9] At the beginning of the nineteenth century, New York still effectively barred Catholics from public office by requiring an oath renouncing any and all allegiances to foreign powers, both civil and religious (i.e., the pope). No sooner did a new understanding of justice and a desire for Catholic votes bring about the abolition of these restrictions than a new battlefront developed in the area of public education.

At first glance, the peculiarities of New York history would seem to have worked in favor of Catholic participation in the emerging public school system. The Dutch who originally settled the colony that would become New York were firmly committed to sectarian education and were less likely than their English contemporaries to see education as merely a responsibility of the family.[10] As early as 1801, the state of New York established four public lotteries to support public education. During this early period, most of the state followed the Dutch model of sectarian control over schools; still, attendance was voluntary and fairly low, so there was little felt need to revise the curriculum in a more ecumenical direction. Battles among Protestant educators in New York City eventually called this upstate system into question. At first, New York City schools were operated by private religious groups; many of these groups were sectarian, but one organization, the Free School Society, explicitly conceived of itself in non-sectarian terms. By 1822, non-sectarianism had become a fighting faith. The Free School Society challenged the right of the Bethel Baptist Church to receive state funds for its school. By 1824, the New York City Common Council voted to end the practice of funding church schools, leaving the private Free School Society—now renamed the Public School Society—with a virtual monopoly on "public" education. Of course, the non-sectarian ideal was Protestant, not secular. It included classroom reading from the King James Bible and recitation of the Lord's Prayer. So long as New York City remained predominantly Protestant, this non-sectarian ideal kept the peace in the education wars.[11]

The dramatic rise in the Catholic population of New York City in the 1830s broke this Protestant truce. For Catholic leaders, non-sectarianism meant Protestantism. They demanded the right to send their children to schools under Catholic control. In 1840, the trustees of several Catholic schools in the city petitioned the Common Council for public assistance. The Council rejected the petition on the general principle that education should be non-sectarian—a rationale that ignored the Catholic critique of Protestant bias, yet also refrained from singling out Catholics as a threat to public education.[12] The language of the Council's rebuke reflected not simply high principle, but also a concern not to alienate Catholic voters who had already become a formidable bloc within the Democratic Party that controlled the Council. Protestant Democratic leaders worried about alienating Protestant voters by appearing to give Catholics special privileges, while Catholic politicians tended to bow to the decisions of party leaders. On the issue of education, one Catholic leader refused to defer to political prudence: John Hughes.

By the early 1840s, Hughes found himself struggling to minister to a rapidly growing flock of mostly poor immigrants. To the traditional financial burdens of building churches and caring for the poor, the new democratic age had added the requirement of something near to a full grammar school education for every Catholic youth. Hughes clearly saw the existing public school system as a threat to the faith of his flock. He asked not for abolition of public schools, but for sectarian alternatives within the existing system: "[G]ive us our just proportion of the common school fund and if we do not give as good an education apart from religious instruction as given in public schools, to one third a larger number of children for the same money, we are willing to renounce our just claim."[13]

This statement shows an early example of the kind of patriotic separatism that would shape American Catholicism for much of the next hundred years. Defiantly demanding both funding and control for his schools, Hughes nevertheless insists that in areas of instruction outside of religion Catholic schools will provide the general education necessary for all citizens in a republic, regardless of their faith or church affiliation. At first, Hughes' reasonable, moderate position met with, well, reason and moderation. The Public School Society opposed Hughes' alternative to the present system, but seemed to be willing to consider some alternative compromise. Nativist elements within the Society, however, soon jumped on the issue as yet another example of the Catholic attempt to subvert republican institutions.

The battle quickly shifted from debate over first principles to considerations of practical politics. Late in 1840, the Whig governor William Seward had won re-election on the coattails of William Henry Harrison's presidential victory; nevertheless, his attempt to woo immigrant voters through openness on the education issue had severely cut into the margin of victory he had enjoyed in the previous election. Democrats, in turn, feared the splitting of their party along religious lines and thought it best to keep with the status quo. In 1841, sensing that Catholic Democratic leaders were soft on the education issue, Hughes himself called a meeting to propose a slate of candidates for the upcoming state elections. This slate included many candidates already on the Democratic ticket, but five new candidates for positions in the assembly and senate. The "Carroll Hall ticket," named for the meeting place of Hughes' movement, appeared to many to be the opening salvo in a new religious war. James Gordon Bennett (a Catholic, but first of all a journalist who loved controversy) of the New York *Herald* attacked Hughes as a "foolish prelate," an "abbot of unreason" who has single-handedly brought about "a complete disorganization of all the old parties in New York, and probably the formation of the Protestant and Catholic factions with all the madness of the last century."[14] Despite these dire predictions, the Democrats were victorious in the November elections with candidates endorsed at the Carroll Hall meeting. Catholics had proven themselves a powerful force within the Democratic Party and Hughes had proven that, on political matters directly affecting the Church, the Democrats must take into consideration the concerns of Church leaders.

Despite his victory, Hughes was troubled by the whole episode. He confided to a lawyer friend from Baltimore, "If I did not go beyond my Episcopal sphere I went at least to the farthest edge of it."[15] Hughes realized that his public leadership was undermining the cause he still felt to be just, and by 1842 stepped back from direct involvement in party politics. Lay Catholic Democrats took control of the school issue; they succeeded in passing legislation that transferred control over public education from the (private) Public School Society to a democratically elected school board. Nativists interpreted this move to democracy as yet another instance of a Catholic subversion of democracy; only the intervention of police and local militia prevented a nativist mob from burning down Hughes' residence. The battle raged on in New York and other cities with substantial Catholic populations throughout the 1840s. Hughes refused to be intimidated by nativists. Following the Philadelphia riots of 1844, he posted armed guards at Catholic churches and threatened to turn New York "into a second Moscow" should nativists try the same in his diocese; there were no riots in New York.[16] Hughes won yet another battle, but was beginning to accept that he was losing the war. Protestant Bible reading continued in public schools and Protestants refused to endorse the general principle of proportional funding for a separate Catholic public school system. Hughes eventually abandoned the effort to secure public funds for Catholic schools and devoted his energies toward building a separate parochial school system, funded directly by the immigrant parishioners it served.

Catholics fared much better on the second major front in Church-State relations, that of social welfare. The ideology of the Revolution provided even less of a guide on this issue than on education. The Founding Fathers may not have agreed on the role of the government in public education, but all would have understood an educated citizenry to be essential to the proper functioning of a republic. Poverty, in contrast, had no place in the new society. According to the Enlightenment social theory that informed the Founders' social vision, poverty would simply disappear with the elimination of its source, the arbitrary, despotic authority of kings and priests. According to the market meritocracy of classical political economy, the development of natural talents through hard work would bring general prosperity to all who were willing to apply themselves to the pursuit of wealth. Responsibility for any poverty that might persist could, within this framework, be laid directly on the poor themselves. These Enlightenment views on poverty grew out of certain shifts in early modern Christianity. Catholics and Protestants alike tended to emphasize personal responsibility for poverty more than in the medieval period, but between these two major Christian traditions, Catholics retained a stronger sense of the older Christian notion that the poor will always be with us. The religious orders, moreover, kept alive the notion of poverty as a virtue. These cultural differences, combined with the reality of disproportionate poverty among Catholics in northern cities, made poverty seem almost the natural province of Catholics. Protestants were at the very least much more willing to refrain from demands for monopoly in the care, as opposed to the education, of the poor.

Public funding for poor relief in New York City at first followed a pattern similar to the early education systems. Early nineteenth-century poor houses were holdovers from the colonial period—multipurpose facilities that sheltered the poor, the unemployed, widows, orphans and the sick indiscriminately. Charity workers soon began to perceive a need for more specialization, particularly with respect to separating children from adults. With their vulnerability and distance from moral responsibility for their condition, children became the focus of early public poor relief; orphanages thus became the battleground for much of the early debates over the distribution of public funds to private charity groups.[17] Like the schools, early orphanages were officially "non-sectarian," but in reality Protestant, institutions. Founded in 1806, the New York Orphan Asylum had by 1811 begun to receive a modest state grant of five hundred dollars per year. In 1817, the Roman Catholic Benevolent Society (later the Roman Catholic Orphan Asylum, RCOA) formed to address the needs of the urban poor, particularly children. By 1833 it had begun to share in some state revenue with Protestant groups; by 1846, the New York City Common Council leased (at a nominal fee) property on Fifth Avenue to the RCOA for the purposes of constructing a major new asylum. Through the middle decades of the nineteenth century, the RCOA received thousands of dollars of public funding from state sources and, eventually, the local Board of Education.[18]

Protestant willingness to support Catholic charities with public funds stemmed more from practical necessity than from any new-found ecumenism. There simply were not enough Protestant charitable organizations to deal with the growing problem of urban poverty. Catholics had a much longer tradition of organized charitable work, particularly through the religious orders. The nineteenth century saw an enormous growth in both vocations to established orders and the creation of new ones. In the United States, Elizabeth Ann Seton, a convert from Episcopalianism, founded a new order, the Sisters of Charity, in 1813; this order would go on to found and operate the largest orphan asylum in New York City. The religious orders provided Catholic institutions with a cheap labor force that no Protestant organization could match. When battles arose over the distribution of public funds, defenders of Catholic charities could argue, much as John Hughes had done in education, that Catholic organizations give the government more "bang for its buck," providing care for more of the needy at a lower cost than any competing institution.[19] Often, even the bitterest opponents of the Catholic Church had no choice but to concede the truth of the argument. Despite the ever-present danger of sectarian strife, what Dorothy Brown and Elizabeth McKeown have called the "New York system" of using private agencies to administer public poor support continued to expand through the middle decades of the nineteenth century.[20] The nature of charity work simply did not lend itself to old-style, nativist attacks on Catholic authoritarianism and the subversion of republican freedom.

Protestant critics concerned to limit the access of Catholic charities to public funds would make their case on the new battleground of reform: graft and corruption in city politics. In the decades following Hughes' Carroll Hall Ticket, the political "boss" and his city "machine" came to rival priest and Church as threats to republican self-government. City Catholics were overwhelmingly Democratic, but they were more likely to identify their politics by club than by party: Catholics were, by and large, loyal sons of Tammany Hall. Though founded by nativists, the Society of St. Tammany quickly realized that it had more to gain from welcoming immigrants than from shunning them.

As the Democratic Party shifted its character from Jeffersonian idealism to Jacksonian populism, Tammany drew the slurs that minority elites have always directed at the practitioners of mass politics: Whigs styled themselves the party of disinterested public service and painted the Democrats as the party of demagoguery and corruption. To the old Jacksonian ideal of patronage— "to the victor goes the spoils"—the explosive growth of New York City added innumerable opportunities for public officials to enrich themselves through various building contracts and real estate transactions that helped the city to grow. Political bosses shared the wealth in return for support at the polls while the line between favoritism and outright graft often lay in the eyes of the beholder. As Catholic Charities seemed to benefit disproportionately from Tammany's largesse, Protestant reformers began to impute guilt by association and see the New York system as yet another instance of the Catholic Church crossing the line that separated church and state in America.

By the mid-1860s, Protestant groups took favoritism toward Catholic organizations as a rationale for prohibiting all disbursement of public funds to sectarian private charities. The favoritism itself was at one level undeniable. With Catholics still a minority within New York State as a whole, nearly half of the orphan asylums that received state funding between 1847 and 1866 were Roman Catholic. One review of state funding revealed that in the year 1866 alone, of the $129,029.49 disbursed to private charitable organizations, Protestant and Jewish groups received only a paltry $3,855.35. Such cold hard facts led the Presbyterian *New York Observer* to publish an editorial entitled: "Our State Religion: Is It Roman Catholic?" At the same time, as with the earlier issue of schools, Protestant groups refused to recognize the sectarian nature of so many of their officially non-sectarian charitable organizations. Catholics could not hide behind neutrality since canonical religious orders performed most of their charity work. *De facto* Protestant organizations, in many cases run by lay people, could claim non-sectarian status by virtue of a lack of official church ties.[21]

This double standard was nowhere more galling to Catholics than in the care of orphans. Non-sectarian organizations such as Charles Loring Brace's Children's Aid Society (CAS) sought to "save" children by taking orphans away from the corrupting environment of the city and placing them with rural farm families where they could learn the virtues of clean country living; in practice, this often meant taking Catholic children and placing them in Protestant homes to be raised as Protestants. As with Bible reading in the public schools, Catholics understood non-sectarian charity to be yet another way to lure poor and otherwise vulnerable Catholics away from their faith.

Education was, to be sure, still a live and contested issue. Though the period of Bible riots had passed, the rise of the parochial school system in no way ended the debate over public support for Catholic education. The cozy relationship between Tammany Hall and Catholic charities spilled over into Catholic schools as well. Public support for Catholic schools was in fact one of the pet projects of the most notorious machine boss of the nineteenth century, William Marcy Tweed. Himself of Presbyterian stock, Tweed nonetheless employed Irish Catholics—with names like Peter "Brains" Sweeny and Richard "Slippery Dick" Connolly—as his first lieutenants. More importantly, he had a vast Irish Catholic constituency. Poor Catholics had suffered financially under the burden of in effect a dual taxation system, having to pay taxes to support public schools while also paying the Church to support parochial schools. Any and all relief was welcome; Tweed was willing to provide it. Unlike other bosses, Tweed ran his machine while holding several high-profile elected offices. Serving in the State Senate in 1869, Tweed introduced a budget line in a larger budget proposal drafted by his Committee on Municipal Affairs that would give state aid to schools that were not public or charity schools—a rather ambiguous category of school that in effect applied only to Catholic schools. Before long, suspicious Protestants exposed the loophole as part of a broader "Papal conspiracy."[22]

Tweed responded as a true urban politician: "I believe in supporting all deserving charities. . . ."[23] To be fair, this stands as one of the few completely honest public statements Tweed ever made. He assisted Protestant charities and in at least one notable case helped to fund the building repairs for a Baptist church.[24] Protestant accusations of favoritism reflected less sour grapes than a fundamental misreading of Tweed's politics. Catholics may have benefited disproportionately from Tweed's reign in terms of their percentage in the population, but they benefited directly in proportion to their support for Tweed's machine. If Protestant groups got less, it was because they gave less in terms of political support. This fundamental rule of politics continued to be lost on Protestant reformers. The New York system of charity was contentious enough; when Tweed crossed the line into education, he summoned up all the old nativist nightmares of the 1840s and 50s.

The Tweed Ring finally fell in 1871. Funding of parochial schools with public money was hardly its most serious offense to political propriety. Despite Tweed's own ethno-religious background, urban Irish Catholics absorbed the brunt of the negative fallout from the scandal: once presented as advocates of a principled, if un-American, stand on Constitutional issues, Catholics now came to represent the lowest common denominator in graft and political corruption. Irish Catholic Democrats would indeed rule New York for the next sixty years, but the political style forever linked with this particular ethno-religious group would consistently cross party and ethnic lines throughout this period. The WASP Republican George B. Cox exerted Tammany-like control over Cincinnati; New York Democrat Franklin Roosevelt engineered the fall of his old Irish rivals at Tammany Hall by channeling New Deal patronage funds through the Italian American Republican "reform" mayor, Fiorella LaGuardia.[25] Even as ethnic and party lines blurred, the period saw the formation of what the historian Richard Hofstadter long ago identified as two clear and distinct political cultures, each defined by a clear set of political ideals:

> One, founded upon the indigenous Yankee-Protestant political traditions, and upon middle-class life, assumed and demanded the constant, disinterested activity of the citizen in public affairs, argued that political life ought to be run . . . in accordance with general principles and abstract laws apart from . . . personal needs, and expressed a common feeling that government should be in good part an effort to moralize the lives of individuals while economic life should be intimately related to the stimulation and development of individual character. The other system, founded upon the European backgrounds of the immigrants, upon their unfamiliarity with independent political action, their familiarity with hierarchy and authority, and upon the urgent needs that so often grew out of their migration, took for granted that the political life of the individual would arise out of family needs, interpreted political civic relations chiefly in terms of personal obligations, and placed strong personal loyalties above allegiance to abstract codes of law or morals. It was chiefly upon this system of values that the political life of the immigrant, the boss, and the urban machine was based.[26]

Coded religiously, these ideal types reduce American politics to a battle between Protestant reformers and Catholic bosses. At least since Edwin O'Connor's *The Last Hurrah*, assimilated, middle-class Irish Catholics have looked back on their bad-boy past with some nostalgia and more than a little envy.[27] Those in the trenches of the nineteenth-century culture wars could not afford the luxury of interpreting criminality as local color. Irish Catholics took association with the corruption of the Tweed Ring as a serious blow to their on-going efforts to achieve respectability in a country where anti-Catholicism remained a dominant popular sentiment. Still, as a writer for the *Irish American* stated soon after the fall of Tweed: "One no more goes outside the party to purify it than one goes outside the Church."[28] Irish Catholics took the fall of Tweed as an opportunity to gain full control of Tammany Hall: "Honest" John Kelly succeeded Tweed and became the first true Irish Catholic political boss in New York Kelly's marriage to the niece of John Cardinal McCloskey, Archbishop of New York, did little to allay Protestant fears concerning Tammany's record on church-state relations; his self-bestowed nickname failed to convince reformers he was serious about cleaning up corruption. The "honest graft" publicly extolled by Tammany men such as George Washington Plunkitt fell far short of the reformers' ideal of good government, but Kelly and his Irish Catholic successors did turn away from the more blatant forms of corruption practiced by the Tweed ring.[29] In the end, it was simply bad for business.[30]

At the same time, it was equally bad for a politician to ignore his obligations. As Protestant reformers continued to attack the New York system of charity on the grounds of church-state separation, Kelly continued to defend it as a way of serving his constituents. Catholic politicians created their own reform style to deal with corruption, yet refused to see sharing the legitimate privileges of political power with their Church as a form of graft. Developed in earnest by Charles Francis Murphy, Tammany boss from the 1890s through the 1920s, this synthesis of disinterested reform and partisan loyalty reached its peak in the political career of Al Smith. Under Murphy's tutelage, Smith pursued a progressive reform agenda, particularly on labor issues, through several terms in the New York State assembly. He never publicly denied his debt to Tammany and certainly never tried to hide his Catholicism, yet he had a broad enough appeal to earn several terms as governor of the state.

His downfall came when he tried to take his own New York system, if you will, to the nation. The 1928 presidential election, which pitted Smith against the Midwestern Protestant Herbert Hoover, showed the political battles of the last half-century to encompass more than issues of honesty and commitment to reform. With the exception of the issue of Prohibition, opposition to Smith stemmed less from any political position than from his culture and his faith: the very fact of an Irish Catholic presidential candidate was enough to call forth a nativist, anti-Catholic hysteria the likes of which had not been seen since the heyday of the American Party in the 1850s. Smith asserted his patriotism but refused to deny his roots. According to a recent Smith biographer, "as a result he got drowned in a sea of hate, facing the dirtiest campaign in American presidential history."[31] Opponents accused Smith of being an agent of the Vatican bent on establishing papal rule over America. Smith denied that his faith required him to take orders from the pope in matters of politics. Perhaps in the end Smith's New York accent said more than any reasoned defense of his position could. It did not help matters that he refused to shy away from public acts of religious submission, such as kissing the ring of his bishop.

The 1928 election proved that despite the claims of reformers, reform was not enough. Over the course of the twentieth century, the call for separation of church and state revealed itself to be a mask for a more thoroughgoing separation of culture and politics—or more precisely, for the objective necessity of substituting one political culture for another. By the time of John F. Kennedy, Catholic politicians had learned their lesson. Two generations of grooming had transformed the Kennedy family from Boston Irish Catholics to air brushed, Ivy League WASPS in everything but denominational affiliation. On matters of church and state, Kennedy had to be more Protestant than his Protestant critics. The national political aspirations of Catholics in the second half of the twentieth century actually pushed them to the forefront of the separation issue. Legal abortion challenged Catholic political loyalties as no previous single issue in American history. Every major Catholic leader in the Democratic Party chose their party over their Church. By the 1980s, New York governor Mario Cuomo had formulated the official position for Catholics who chose to have any serious standing in the Democratic Party: Cuomo asserted that while as a Catholic he personally opposed abortion, the principle of separation of church and state prohibited him from imposing his personal religious morality on non-Catholics.[32] In the name of advancing a secular liberal social agenda, Catholic Democrats began to adopt an evangelical position on church-state relations.

By the 2004 election, the debate had come full circle, with American evangelicals adopting what had traditionally been the Roman Catholic position. The Democratic candidate John Kerry, a Cuomo Catholic, accused the incumbent Republican president George Bush, a self-proclaimed born-again Christian, of violating the separation of church and state by opposing abortion and supporting the government funding of faith-based charitable organizations. Conservative Republicans rightly saw Kerry's pro-choice position on abortion much as nineteenth-century Catholics saw Bible reading in the public schools: a supposedly neutral position that advances a very particular cultural agenda. Liberal Democrats rightly saw Bush's support for charitable choice as yet another step in the privatization of social services in the name of limited government. Still, today's battles are not simply a replay of the nineteenth century, with party labels reversed. Both Kerry Democrats and Bush Republicans spoke the language of the reform tradition in American politics; though they seemed to disagree on principles, both claimed to place principle above party. Closer examination reveals a deeper consensus on a common principle: utilitarian, instrumental individualism. Democratic secular humanists emphasize libertarian freedom in cultural and sexual matters; they advocate government regulation of the economy in order to secure the democratic distribution of material resources necessary for the free exercise of this freedom. Republican free-market capitalists emphasize libertarian freedom in the economic realm; government regulation of cultural life helps to instill the moral discipline necessary for economic achievement and provides some measure of cultural stability to offset the social dislocation brought by economic change. In their own particular ways, each party holds up risk against stability, opportunity against security—with party allegiance at best a means to these ends. At a time when the word partisan has become a synonym for self-interest, the American Catholic political tradition at its best reminds us that it once meant loyalty—to party, friends, family, community and church. These personal loyalties were the principles Catholics brought to politics. As Catholics refused to separate the personal and the political, so they refused to separate church and state.

Notes

1. My characterization of these wars owes much to William T. Cavanaugh, *Theopolitical Imagination: Discovering the Liturgy as a Political Act in an Age of Global Consumerism* (London: T & T Clark, 2002). See especially ch. 1, "The Myth of the State as Saviour."

2. Philip Hamburger, *Separation of Church and State* (Cambridge, Mass.: Harvard University Press, 2002).

3. Hamburger, *Separation,* 163.

4. See in general, Charles Sellers, *The Market Revolution: Jacksonian America, 1815-1846* (New York: Oxford University Press, 1994).

5. See Emmet Larkin, "The Devotional Revolution in Ireland, 1850-75," *American Historical Review* 77 (June 1972): 625-652.

6. Quoted in Richard Shaw, *Dagger John: The Unquiet Life and Times of Archbishop John Hughes of New York* (New York: Paulist Press, 1977), 14.

7. Shaw, 15.

8. See in general Jason Duncan, "'A Most Democratic Class': New York Catholics and the Early American Republic" (Ph.D. diss., University of Iowa, 2000).

9. Shaw, 6.

10. John Webb Pratt, *Religion, Politics, and Diversity: The Church-State Theme in New York History* (Ithaca: Cornell University Press, 1967), 162.

11. Pratt, *Religion*, 162-167.

12. Pratt, *Religion*, 176.

13. Quoted in Shaw, *Dagger John*, 144.

14. Quoted in Shaw, *Dagger John*, 167.

15. Quoted in Shaw, *Dagger John*, 170.

16. Quoted in Charles R. Morris, *American Catholic: The Saints and Sinners Who Built America's Most Powerful Church* (New York: Vintage Books, 1998), 5.

17. Pratt, *Religion*, 205.

18. Pratt, *Religion*, 206. Dorothy M. Brown and Elizabeth McKeown, *The Poor Belong to Us: Catholic Charities and American Welfare* (Cambridge, Mass.: Harvard University Press, 1997), 19-20.

19. Brown and McKeown, *The Poor Belong*, 23.

20. Brown and McKeown, *The Poor Belong*, 15.

21. Pratt, *Religion*, 210-212.

22. Alexander B. Callow, Jr., *The Tweed Ring* (New York: Oxford University Press, 1965), 154.

23. Pratt, *Religion*, 216.

24. Ibid.

25. See in general Zane L. Miller, *Boss Cox's Cincinnati: Urban Politics in the Progressive Era* (New York: Oxford University Press, 1968). On LaGuardia, see George J. Marlin, *The American Catholic Voter: 200 Years of Political Impact* (South Bend: St. Augustine's Press, 2004), 204.

26. Richard Hofstadter, *The Age of Reform: From Bryan to F.D.R.* (New York: Vintage, 1955), 9.

27. Edwin O'Connor, *The Last Hurrah* (Boston: Little, Brown, 1956).

28. Quoted in Seymour J. Mandelbaum, *Boss Tweed's New York* (Chicago: Ivan R. Dee, 1990 [1965]), 84.

29. For the classic statement of honest graft, see William L. Riordan, *Plunkitt of Tammany Hall: A Series of Very Plain Talks on Very Practical Politics* (New York: Signet Classics, 1995 [1905]), 3.

30. See in general, *Charles Francis Murphy, 1858-1924: Respectability and Responsibility in Tammany Politics* (Northampton, Mass.: Smith College, 1968).

31. Robert A. Slayton, *Empire Statesman: The Rise and Redemption of Al Smith* (New York: The Free Press, 2001), ix.

32. On this issue, see Morris, *American Catholic*, 424-427.

The Eastern Orthodox Christian Church in North America: Continuity and Change in the Twenty-First Century

Frances Kostarelos
Governors State University

When we look to the Bible and church history seeking insight about permanency and change in the Church, we see that the Church has a "human form" just as Christ does. The human form of the Church consists in all of its human expressions, such as Scripture, liturgy, and so forth, and has been constantly changing throughout the ages.[1]

At the start of the twenty-first century, Eastern Orthodox Christians living in North America are influenced by world historical forces giving way to challenges and opportunities to engage other church families, share their faith, and develop institutions in ways that were unimaginable throughout most of the 1900s. Worldwide, the Eastern Church claims approximately two hundred to three hundred million adherents, living in Europe, the Middle East, Africa, Asia, and North America. Within North America, there are reported estimates of three and half million Eastern Christians, originating from an array of geographical, cultural, linguistic, and historical contexts. The Orthodox Church in North American is decentralized and administered by several jurisdictions with varying ties to original homelands.

The Greek Orthodox Church is the largest jurisdiction, claiming one and a half million adherents, a number this group has been reporting for several years. The Antiochian Orthodox Church and the Orthodox Church of America each report about one million adherents, with recent growth in both jurisdictions. The remaining number of Eastern Christians in North America is distributed among Serbian, Romanian, Bulgarian, Ukrainian, Russian, and Albanian groups. Each of these groups are from homelands where they witnessed the breakdown of the empires that gave way to the rise of nations and nationalism. The expansion of the nation-state system that organized personal and collective identity along ethnic lines had significant implications for the development of the Orthodox Church in North America and the Orthodox experience.

The Eastern Church lacks statistical strength when the number of adherents and institutions are compared to other Christian bodies that flowered on American soil during the 1900s.[2] There are about fifteen hundred Eastern Orthodox parishes in North America, a legacy of the waves of immigrant Orthodox Christians who planted churches within American borders throughout the 1900s. A contention of this chapter is that Eastern Orthodox parishes constitute a dynamic and vital infrastructure that is national in its scope (see Figure 1) and embodies a material and expressive culture carried to America by Orthodox Christians. These institutions harbor potential to minister to American-born adherents and to the steady stream of newcomers originating from non-Orthodox backgrounds.

Eastern Orthodox Christians embody a coherent worldview founded on shared beliefs and practices. While Orthodox Christians are geographically dispersed, multiethnic, linguistically diverse, and separated by administrative jurisdictions rooted in the long-standing world history of Orthodox people (see Figures 1 and 2), they are united by a shared understanding of the primacy of Scripture, Patristic authority, and Tradition. Eastern Christians in North America trace their doctrines, spiritual identity, ecclesiastical structures, and moral teachings to the apostolic period. These sources constitute theological principles and Orthodox narratives that frame a coherent moral identity and guided church development in North America in the 1900s. In an account of the Orthodox Church written from a Western perspective, Daniel Clendenin writes:

> Orthodoxy is so steeped in the traditions of the early church that it proudly identifies itself as the Church of the Seven Councils. In fact, like evangelicalism, it is sometimes criticized for being stuck in a static, backward-looking posture that is out of step with contemporary society. In some way the criticism is just. But for Orthodox intent on maintaining a direct link with its apostolic, patristic heritage, that criticism is a badge of pride, not of embarrassment. All good Orthodox Christians cherish the works of the great Eastern theologian John of Damascus that "we not change the everlasting boundaries which our fathers have set, but we keep them just as we received them."[3]

The coherent worldview combined with the infrastructure of parishes and emergent Orthodox institutions point the way to continuity in the face of social change unfolding in the twenty-first century. The Orthodox, unlike other confessional bodies in America, have not restructured or modified their churches and practices to accommodate the changing American socio-political landscape. In this respect the Orthodox have much in common with Protestant evangelical bodies standing firm in their belief that the Bible is the Word of God and the guiding light for the development of individual and collective moral identity and behavior.

Doctrinal unity and clarity of the Orthodox is augmented by the widespread range of Orthodox institutions evident in the location and concentration of Orthodox parishes (see Figure 1). Orthodox parishes are concentrated in large cities and regions with dense populations. Many of these churches are located in the inner city in locations that are recovering from the economic and social dislocations of the late 1900s. There is a concentration of parishes near established transportation systems. A rapidly emergent development that has not been assessed by scholars is the extensive use of the Web as the means by which Orthodox Christians are sharing their faith and growing their ministries. Orthodox parishes and Orthodox institutions are increasingly posting sites on the Internet with links that allow Orthodox Christians to share iconography, sacred texts, calendars, sacred music, and events with visitors to these sites. The Orthodox Christian Fellowship, a ministry for college students across the United States, is one example of dynamic use of the Internet. These students are among the first campus-based sociological cohorts engaging new technologies to share and grow their faith. These are just some of the infrastructural features that make contacts with the wider society possible.

There are significant sociological developments in the Orthodox experience in contemporary American society that await interpretation in the light of empirical research. There is a prolific body of scholarly literature on Orthodox Church history and theology. This scholarship is published in English and thus lifts the language gap that partly prevented Orthodox Christians from sharing their faith and scholarship in the North American context. The presses at Saint Vladimir's Seminary and Holy Cross Greek Orthodox School of Theology are moving at a steady clip to turn out texts that offer a discourse on church history, theology, and practice. The Orthodox are now in a position to share their faith with large numbers of individuals in the nation and in the world by way of changes in Orthodox culture and institutions made possible by the dialectical relationship between the qualities inherent in the body of Orthodox believers and the host society.

In sum, there are demographic, sociological, and technological forces converging to pave the way for pan-Orthodox unity and collaboration with other religious bodies that would have been difficult for earlier generations of Eastern Christians—who embodied a legacy of nationalism and race discrimination—to imagine and institute. Below we examine the legacy of race and ethnic division found on American soil and its impact on the Orthodox experience, as well as developments that are lifting barriers that historically militated against Orthodox unity and outreach. The strength and appeal of the Eastern Church stem from a vision of an unbroken past, an unrelenting commitment to the fundamentals of the faith, a conservative voice and vision challenging secular authority and chaos.

This account draws on ethnographic research I have conducted among Eastern Christians and institutions in Chicago, Berrien County, Michigan, and the campus of Holy Cross School of Theology and Hellenic College in Boston. In 2003-2004, I conducted site visits to Orthodox parishes in Boston, Chicago, Minneapolis, Baltimore, and rural Michigan. The account that follows is informed by participant observation in Chicago's Orthodox churches that I have conducted since the mid 1990s. I have collected oral histories among Eastern Christians who self-identified as "cradle," "convert," "foreign" and "American born." I gathered material in the field including parish histories and church bulletins. I also draw on information posted on the Web by Orthodox parishes, administrative bodies, and ministries. The argument in this account also relies on surveys of physical characteristics surrounding church buildings that may impinge on parish growth and development.[4]

My findings suggest that currents shaping the Eastern Church in North America include: a legacy of nationalism and ethnic conflict instituted in the body of churches during the first one hundred years of the Orthodox American landing; Protestant hegemony; the principles of religious freedom and individualism; pluralism; secular authority; a market economy that privileges a consumer culture promoted by powerful media outlets; social mobility; fragmentation; and rapid communication on the World Wide Web. Studies of social processes related to the development of Eastern institutions and experience in North America are limited. Published studies informed by social scientific concepts and methods are scant.[5] Notable exceptions are the publication of a collection edited by Anton Vrame, *The Orthodox Parish in America,* and the quantitative studies conducted by Alexey Krindatch as part of the Hartford Seminary Fact Initiative.[6] These scholars address empirical gaps and provide a framework for refined analysis of conceptual themes and social developments described in this chapter.

NATIONALISM, ETHNICITY, AND IDENTITY

During the period of migration and settlement in the 1900s, Eastern Christians planted several hundred churches on American soil that now constitute an institutional infrastructure that embodies a system of meaning and purpose encoded in sacred texts, iconography, and the enactment of liturgies and sacraments as understood and practiced by Orthodox Christians. The initial landing of Orthodox Christians occurred in Alaska in the late 1700s, while the territory was under Russian rule. A small group of missionaries from the Valaam Monastery of Lake Ladoga near the Finnish border spread Orthodox Christianity among Alaskan indigenous people. Support for this mission came to an end with the Russian Revolution. There is a concentration of parishes in Alaska and along the Northwest Pacific coast that are linked to this historical development (see Figure 1). The emphasis in this account is on the Orthodox landing on the Atlantic Coast that spread from East to West in the 1900s. These settlers carried ethnic and national hegemonic claims that undermined unity and contact with other Christian groups.

Cradle Orthodox living in North America embody ascribed status by their birth into the Orthodox Church. As a group, they have not been motivated to examine the tenets of their faith or to engage in meaningful interfaith dialogue. The present contact with other faith traditions in the North American context is challenging Orthodox Christians to examine their assumed primacy within the Orthodox Church based on their ethnic identity. The biographical narratives of individuals who have made the journey to the Orthodox Church reveal a story of difficulties encountered in the face of unexpected ethnocentrism and nationalism found in dispositions of cradle Orthodox Christians and institutions. Individuals who have joined the Orthodox Church from various streams of the American religious landscape speak to the enduring and cohesive qualities they find in Orthodoxy in the face of religious options that for them have strayed from the truth.

While barriers are lifting in the Orthodox experience today, there remains an unrelenting and divisive ethnic identity. Nationalism and ethnic hegemonic impulses divide Orthodox Christians. Moreover, while asserting the primacy of their ethnic identity and heritage, Orthodox Christians limit their capacity to engage other Christian bodies and non-Christians. Orthodox sacred texts, worship and sacramental life encode a vision of mission and outreach for all people. In North America, ethnic hegemony and race discrimination overpowered the evangelical message inherent in Orthodox theological discourse. Within the Orthodox experience today there is a counter-hegemonic impulse challenging barriers that prevented contact with Catholic and Protestant Christians. There are signs that cultural barriers are lifting that prevented Orthodox Christians from participating in Christian outreach, a prominent feature of the American religious history and experience.

The tenacity of ethnic assertions found in the Orthodox experience must be examined in the light of social histories of Orthodox Christians. The analytic framework must trace conditions in homelands that pushed Orthodox Christians out as well as conditions prevailing in the host country. Eastern Christians in North America originate from the Middle East, Eastern Europe, the Balkans, and Russia. These settlers were fleeing from various forms of foreign occupation, civil war, genocide, and economic destitution in their homelands. The collective sentiments of these settlers were shaped during a period of immense human suffering as dynasties crumbled, only to be supplanted by nation-state systems that oppressed local people. During the period of massive human suffering and social dislocation the Orthodox Church would prove resilient in its ability to assert its claims and authority. The mechanisms that allowed for Church survival and the position of the church towards ethnic cleansing and forced migration are not clear. Between the first and second World Wars the Orthodox Church adapted to a nation-state system and outlook informed by nationalism and territorial boundaries carved on the earth's surface along ethnic lines. Detailed case studies of Orthodox groups examining the particulars that led to migrations and the conditions that surrounded settlement in North America would add to our understanding of the Orthodox experience.

Most Orthodox settlers originated from rural villages and small towns sustained by small-scale agriculture and animal husbandry. Within their homelands Orthodox churches provided a system of moral and social solidarity. The collective consciousness of Orthodox Christian settlers who founded several hundred churches during the period of migration and settlement was shaped in the aftermath of declining empires that gave way to struggles for national independence and development of the modern nation-state system.[7] For these settlers the Orthodox Church and their nation provided a system of symbols to frame personal and collective identity. For Orthodox Christians during the period of immense devastation and dislocation in their national territories, the Orthodox Church did not have the moral or institutional authority to stop the civil wars and fratricide among Orthodox Christians. Historical accounts reveal long-standing issues of nationalism and ethnic hatred that led to incredible acts of cruelty and death.[8] The following account provides insight into the entrenched and pervasive nature of local contact with terror, fear, hate, and violence in rural and small town Greece.

The first systematic campaign of civilian assassinations in the Argolid began in November 1943 and was organized by the Communist-controlled National Liberation Front—or *EAM*—not the occupying authorities. The first wholesale destruction of a village in the Argolid by the German occupation troops also took place in the first days of November 1943, following the (accidental) killing of three German soldiers by *ELAS* (as the guerrillas were known). As a reprisal, the village of Berbati was burned down, and four villagers were killed while trying to flee. However, no mass reprisals took place.

The *EAM* terror campaign of the winter of 1944 was hardly peculiar to the Argolid. A similar wave of killings swept the entire Peloponnese during the same time, and most probably the whole country as well. The campaign of assassinations was carried out by *EAM*'s newly formed *OPLA* squads—a combination of secret police and death squads. (*OPLA* is the Greek acronym for Organization for the Protection of the People's Struggle; the acronym also means "weapons.") These groups established very rapidly a reputation for ruthless violence that is still alive in the memories of many among my informants. In an interview he gave me, a former *OPLA* member described his job starkly: "I was not a regular guerrilla; I was the devil's guerrilla."[9]

While local histories and trajectories vary,[10] social disintegration, political instability, violence, and economic ruin were widespread in the Balkans, Eastern Europe, the Middle East and Russia. Within this devastating social climate were formed the collective sentiments of contempt and suspicion aimed at outsiders that were carried to the New World by these villagers. Hostility and suspicion informed intra-Orthodox relations, resulting in barriers among them that would define the development of Orthodox institutions in North America.

In America in the 1900s, Orthodox Christians mobilized resources among themselves to establish churches to serve their own people. Group identity in North America was based on shared language, ethnicity, shared expressive and material culture, and unsettling knowledge of local histories of the kind reported in the above historical account. Greek social history may illustrate patterns evident among other Orthodox settlers in North America. Oral history of Greek immigrants in Chicago tells a story of plans to stay in America for a brief period to earn a living and wait out difficult years unfolding in Greece and the Balkans. The majority of Greeks who settled in Chicago in the early 1900s came from impoverished Southern Greek villages. Among villagers the church defined the cosmos and humanity's place in the cosmos. The sacred texts and practices the villagers enacted in their churches defined a system of personal and collective identity and meaning.

As Greeks settled in North America, they immediately established churches by collecting resources among themselves to secure space for worship and a priest from Greece to lead them.[11] Orthodox churches were a significant source of spiritual, moral and social authority and solidarity. The hope of returning to Greece diminished in the 1930s and 1940s as Greece struggled against foreign occupations and was devastated by the civil war. While Greek settlers remained attached to the homeland, they accepted the bitter reality that they could not return to Greece and expect to earn a living. Early Greek settlers drew on symbolic resources encoded in the understanding of the Orthodox Church and nation to construct social and cultural institutions that made sense to them in a hostile social climate. The institutions they developed were shaped by white discrimination and hostility aimed at southern Europeans. While Greek settlers defined themselves as descendents of a great and enlightened civilization, their claims were rejected by white America. In the early 1900s, Greeks in Chicago structured their life in the ethnic enclave, living with the hope that they would return to Greece. Attached to the churches were schools to educate Greek youth in language, history, and civilization with a view to preparing for life in Greece.

This divisive impulse the immigrants brought with them only ripened in the North American context with its legacy of slavery, racism, legal and de facto segregation in the aftermath of the Civil War. The settlers had little by way of linguistic and cultural ability to understand or engage the forms of religious ideas and institutions that were unfolding around them. The conception among Orthodox Christians that other church bodies were schismatic and heretical also mediated their vision of the various forms of church bodies they witnessed in their settlements and only deepened the wedge between them and Catholic and Protestant Christians.

The religious life of Eastern Christians would also be impacted by a market economy that would on the one hand provide great individual and collective prosperity and resources for institutional growth, and on the other would add class stratification as a force that would further divide people and the Church. These settlers followed migration routes formed by people escaping political persecution and unrest, economic ruin, and civil strife to a region that was rapidly industrializing and in need of wage labor power.

The vast majority of the settlers left rural villages where their livelihoods depended on small-scale farming, animal husbandry, and to some extent, hunting and gathering, to an urban setting where they were uprooted from the natural order and social structure they knew. Most labored in factories and other low wage labor sectors. Throughout the 1900s they would take a part in upward social mobility by operating businesses. Within American factories and other economic sectors, ethnic divisions were used to control and exploit wage labor,[12] deepening the antipathy Orthodox settlers brought with them towards other groups. In sum, migration across the Atlantic in the twentieth century was vast and rapid, leading to demographic shifts and the diffusion of ideas and material culture. A critical mass of Orthodox Christians was a part of this migration.

The social barriers and structures that functioned to isolate Orthodox Christians throughout the 1900s no longer prevail in North America. A worldview that distanced the other, language barriers, the expectation that North America is a temporary home until economic and social conditions in the homelands improve, have faded. Eastern Christians speak English and have adopted the outlook and customs of the American mainstream. They largely work and live in urban and suburban neighborhoods where overt bigotry and discrimination are no longer acceptable. They are better educated than their ancestors, and seek post-secondary education and professional training in large numbers. They are acclimated in mainstream American society and positioned to take advantage of opportunities that lead to social mobility.

The local parish is the major institutional body in which Orthodox Christians live and practice their faith. There are approximately fifteen hundred Eastern Orthodox parishes in North America. The histories and characteristics of these churches and their members vary in ethnicity, size, historical distance from the period of migration, region, and social class position of its members. The characteristics of Orthodox parishes reflect local histories and regional characteristics that may have influenced contact with other Christian bodies. While detailed congregational studies are not available, we know that church development was the work of groups who mobilized their resources to create institutions that made sense to them. Early churches were founded by groups who lacked the linguistic skills to move in the wider American mainstream. My findings concur with John Erickson, who argues that immigrants planted churches according to a model of the village church they new before the migration. I would add to the analysis that religious consciousness and identity for the migrants was shaped on a territory during a period that sought to wipe out ethnic and religious minorities through violence and forced migration both in their motherlands and in their host society. The settlers arrived with a sense of ethnic supremacy that remained unchallenged in their institutional bodies during the migration and before the Civil Rights movement.

Missing from the extant literature on the Orthodox Church in North America is a consideration of the profound impact that race and race discrimination have had in church development. The Orthodox Christians were among the people classified as marginal in twentieth-century scientific thought.[13] In the racial typologies developed by scientists in Europe and the United States between the wars, Orthodox Christians originated from homelands that produced inferior human beings. A scholarly account of race discrimination as it shaped the Orthodox identity, experience, and capacity to develop institutions is unavailable. Reconstruction, racial inequality, and discrimination were not issues that Orthodox migrant settlers understood or engaged. They lived and created church institutions in a world where de facto segregation determined where people could rent or own homes, were educated, worked, sought recreation, and worshiped. Orthodox Christians did not mobilize their resources—spiritual or institutional—to challenge white supremacy, racial injustice and inequality. Orthodox Christians embraced and articulated the racist ideas used by powerful whites to oppress them.

By the mid 1960s, white ethnic city-dwellers were caught up in "white flight," an urban phenomenon motivated by disillusionment and resentment among whites as integration was forced on them by the policies of the national government. For Orthodox Christians this meant relocating to white neighborhoods, leaving behind stately edifices they had established to define their humanity and to pursue their spiritual life in an otherwise alien and harsh environment. The 1960s would prove to be an unsettling period during which racial hatred would deepen and become entrenched. Orthodox Christians moved from the inner city to escape race riots, growing poverty among blacks who had come to the city from the South during the Great Migration, and the decline of urban neighborhoods and institutions resulting from the out-migration of manufacturing with the concomitant loss of jobs on which inner city people, including Orthodox Christians, depended.

Chicago's Greek Orthodox parishes illustrate the impact of white flight, race discrimination, and urban decline. Within Chicago's limits, Orthodox parishes disappeared or languished in neighborhoods that turned black during the late 1960s. White flight for Orthodox Christians meant leaving their neighborhoods and institutions. Examples of churches that declined over twenty years include Saint George Greek Orthodox Church, Saint Basil Greek Orthodox Church, and Assumption Greek Orthodox Church in Austin—a predominately black and poverty-stricken community to this day. In the early 1980s, Saint Basil Greek Orthodox Church was reduced to about twenty active families worshipping in a structure that had the capacity to seat 350-400. The building was in a state of disrepair and still proves to be more than the congregation of about two hundred members can keep up. During the period of white flight and urban decay, the church bodies that remained lacked a vision and interest in reaching out to poor ethnic minorities who arrived to the neighborhood. The Orthodox Church did not have an interest in learning about their black Protestant neighbors worshipping by the hundreds in countless evangelical storefront churches.[14] As poverty, joblessness, and occupational despair spread in the inner city, Orthodox Christians left for the suburbs. In doing so, they were complicit with the ideology of blaming the poor for the conditions that limited their life chances while overlooking the structural conditions of subsisting on low wages and inadequate support for public programs that left individuals and families destitute in the inner city.

TOWARDS A PAN-ORTHODOX AND INCLUSIVE CHURCH
This account argues that discrimination aimed at impoverished minorities is entrenched in the Orthodox experience. Moreover, there is no historical record of sustained effort to challenge racial and economic inequality from the Eastern Orthodox world. We have seen that there was no vision in Orthodox institutional development in North America to welcome strangers and share the Gospel with people of other ethnic groups or poverty-stricken minorities. This is also changing in the current climate.

American born Orthodox Christians are marrying across cultures and races. The impact of these marriages has also been under assessed. Ethnographic research in Chicago suggests that inter-faith couples marry in the church to satisfy the demands of the parents and community. Many of these couples maintain a nominal tie to the church. There are also those that leave the Orthodox Church once they have children, as they refuse to raise their children in what appears to them a church body that is out of step with contemporary social developments. A key issue facing the Orthodox Church is the language barrier established during the period of migration and initial church development. American-born Orthodox Christians and their offspring do not have the language skills to follow or understand services conducted in the languages spoken by the immigrant settlers. Orthodox clergy and leaders have been reluctant to give up the use of native languages in the churches, while the capacity to speak and understand the native language has been vanishing in the pews.

There has been a loss of interest in the church on the part of cradle Orthodox Christians for several reasons. During the period of white flight and racial segregation, Orthodox Christians became alienated from the message of brotherly love and mission encoded in Scripture and in the lives of exemplary saints. Nominal participation in church life became the norm for many as they mostly contacted the church for baptism, marriage, and burials and the celebration of Easter and Christmas. Unlike their immigrant parents and grandparents, there is a strand among the American-born settling for nominal ties to the church. Some are exploring other church options. Many claim the identity of an Orthodox Christian without an anchor in the life of an Orthodox parish; these individuals know little about the tenets of the faith or church history. They participate in the sacraments but do not see the point of regular church attendance.

Another strand influencing the Orthodox experience is found among American-born cradle Orthodox with deep ties to their church. This group has a strong commitment to work in lay and professional roles to grow the church along pan-orthodox and inclusive lines. This group has received post-secondary education. They are mostly urban. They have come of age in an era of rapid information flows made possible by digital technologies and the Internet. Their social outlook and disposition is tempered by the global and transnational world-historical developments that are moving people, ideas, and commodities across the globe with unprecedented speed. They look to the tenets of the Orthodox faith and tradition to guide their life journey. They are skilled at using digital technology to communicate with Orthodox Christian peers across the nation and the world.

Another impulse re-orienting the Orthodox experience is the steady stream of newcomers who bring an awareness of the American story of racial justice and a vision for social justice ministries. These individuals prize the spiritual legacy and outlook of the Orthodox Church. They are also individuals who are acclimated to global developments. These are individuals who see a place for the Orthodox Church within the wider American mainstream that reclaims its evangelical and inclusive legacy embodied in the history and theology of the Orthodox Church. While some Orthodox churches continue to limit their range to a group of insiders, others are seeking to expand their membership. The following welcoming statement posted on the web by a parish in an urban location in the South is indicative of an inclusive vision: The Holy Greek Orthodox Church "welcomes you to our Church Web Site, and invites you to become a member of this growing, spiritually dynamic, and liturgically viable Greek Orthodox Parish. . . .Our goal is to help you come to know Christ and discover the treasures to the Orthodox faith. Because of who we are as a Church, and what takes place liturgically and through our programs, we feel this goal—by the grace of God—is very attainable. Our door is always open to you."

In addition to the web-based resources that provide information about the Orthodox Church, the site listed several parish outreach ministries. Within the Orthodox parish bodies we are now seeing a wider commitment to mission and outreach missing in the past. This church is not an isolated example. How widespread are inclusive efforts? Narratives from my data suggest varying trajectories and possibilities for redirecting barriers that historically prevented the development of an inclusive Orthodox church.

Growth and development of Orthodox parishes is presently in the hands of American-born individuals. There is a vast network of Orthodox parishes with potential to attract new members. Each parish is under the jurisdiction of a church hierarch who appoints parish priests. While each parish is self-ruled, church routines follow well-established guidelines. Leaders and laity view the parish as a place to serve the needs of its members and depend on church hierarchs to guide the church. Ethnographic evidence indicates that Orthodox Christians may disagree with an incumbent hierarch but are respectful and deferential to the authority established by the Orthodox understanding of church polity and official administrative roles. Orthodox Christians are slow to criticize church leaders. There is some room for negotiation with respect to framing local ministries as long as they do not deviate from what are viewed by insiders as established doctrines and tradition. However, very little is known about the lived transactions that obtain between the hierarchical units and local parishes. The emphasis on local control, religious freedom, and self-reliant parishes are structural characteristics that may yield further adaptation and change within Orthodox parishes in the United States.

Within North America, the Standing Conference of the Canonical Orthodox Bishops in the Americas (SCOBA) was founded in the 1960s with the purpose of uniting canonical Orthodox Churches. Since the 1960s, SCOBA has formally sanctioned ministries that are pan-Orthodox. Present transnational and global conditions point to the strong possibility for an increase of pan-Orthodox developments under SCOBA. The contention in this account is that the catalyst for change is dialectically related to the constraints and possibilities in the American social structure. In the current climate there is a great deal of interest in pan-orthodox initiatives. One such example is found in the renewed organization of the college-based Orthodox Christian Fellowship (OCF), a development unfolding in contemporary North American college and university settings worthy of sociological study.

Church leaders and laity have presently inherited a substantial number of churches that together amount to a significant Orthodox Christian body on American soil. These churches are in the hands of individuals who have survived the wars in the homelands, the hardships of migration, the chaos of racial strife and economic injustice of the twentieth century. These individuals find themselves in a society where the cultural norms of endogamy that guided Orthodox marriages are giving way to marriages across ethnic and racial lines. They are seeing the use of their national homeland language in the church vanish as they modify the enactment of liturgies and church routines to accommodate individuals who only speak English. The process that is presently unfolding is not without misunderstandings and conflict. Some churches continue to look inward. Some are preparing for future growth and development, seeking to deepen their understanding of Orthodoxy while preparing to welcome newcomers.

One example of a group that is looking outward is found in Berrien County, Michigan, the Annunciation and Agia Paraskevi Greek Orthodox Church. A small group of committed Orthodox believers have built a church that can seat two hundred. The church building has a fellowship room and a class-room. In the adjacent lot there is a second building that houses the Hellenic American Cultural Center used for parish festivals and fundraisers. Services formerly held on alternate Sundays are now offered every Sunday as the congre-gation secured an assistant priest with a keen interest in leading parishioners in Bible study and in the study of the patristic writings and the lives of saints. While small in number, this organization is moving forward with confidence and vitality. The group has recently raised a new dome, visible from Interstate 94, and they have paved the parking lot that can hold about one hundred and twenty cars. On a local scale this group can claim its share of the religious landscape in Berrien County. The size of this Orthodox building, the lot and parking spaces are comparable if not slightly greater than the nearby Catholic and Lutheran Missouri Synod churches.

This account suggests that barriers that have historically isolated Orthodox Christians in the first one hundred years are lifting. The account directs attention to a spatial and social structural perspective. It argues that Orthodox Christians are in a position to grow the Church in North America. While race discrimina-tion has not ended in American institutions, the overt forms of racial hostility and bigotry that impinged on Orthodox institutional development are no longer socially acceptable or legal. The impact of converts who in many cases have come from the evangelical churches with a keen interest in Scripture and a heart for mission are also transforming the Orthodox church in ways that have not been fully assessed.

In sum, this is a very dynamic moment in the history of the Orthodox Church, as it re-orients itself to a world that is tempered by socio-cultural struc-tures in which individuals are free to choose among several options in pursuit of a religious identity and meaning in America. At the very start of the twenty-first century, Orthodox Christians privilege a pan-Orthodox vision and are moving across boundaries that augment resources that could be used for church expan-sion. There are those who prefer nominal ties to the church, those who have lost patience with race and ethnic discrimination in the church and have left, and those who trust that the Church will find meaningful and constructive ways to engage wider groups of people. This chapter has raised several issues and points to significant developments in the Orthodox experience that have not been fully understood or assessed. The hope of this discussion is to inspire research that would bring important historical and sociological developments to light.

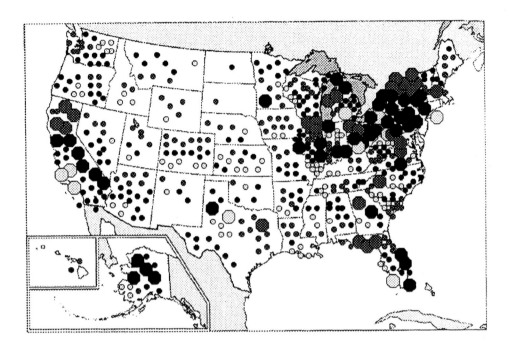

Figure 1 Distribution of the Eastern Orthodox Parishes

Large dots represent 10 parish units.

This map is based on parishes listed in the Directory of Orthodox Parishes and Institutions in North America 2004. It shows the diffusion and geographic reach of the Orthodox Church in the United States with concentrations of parishes in urban and suburban locations.

Table 1
Number of Eastern Churches by state based on figures reported in *The Directory of Orthodox Parishes in North America*, 2004.

	GOA	OCA	ANT	OTH		GOA	OCA	ANT	OTH
AL	6	2	1	2	AK	1	42	3	2
AR	3	1	2	3	AZ	6	5	3	6
CA	42	44	28	28	CO	8	6	6	1
CT	17	17	2	9	DE	2	2	1	1
FL	37	22	12	13	GA	9	9	2	4
HI	1	-	-	1	IA	6	-	2	-
ID	2	-	2	-	IL	35	15	5	26
IN	7	9	6	18	KS	2	2	6	2
KY	2	1	3	-	LA	4	1	4	-
MA	37	12	9	7	MD	8	5	3	8
ME	4	1	-	-	MI	22	17	9	15
MN	4	6	1	10	MO	4	1	-	4
MS	2	2	2	-	MT	2	3	-	2
NC	12	5	3	3	ND	-	-	-	1
NE	3	1	1	1	NH	11	3	-	1
NJ	25	23	4	27	NM	1	2	1	-
NV	4	3	1	4	NY	42	35	12	38
OH	21	36	9	30	OK	1	2	1	1
OR	3	5	2	5	PA	36	84	18	85
RI	3	1	1	2	SC	7	3	5	-
SD	1	-	-	-	TN	5	3	3	1
TX	18	12	14	6	UT	4	-	1	2
VA	9	9	1	4	VT	2	2	-	-
WA	8	7	5	2	WI	7	3	3	8
WV	6	2	3	3	WY	4	-	1	-
DC	2	3	1	3					

Table 2
Number of Eastern Churches by major American cities (Mega-Cities), based on figures
reported in *The Directory of Orthodox Parishes in North America,* 2004

	GOA	OCA	ANT	OTH	%	%	%	%
Atlanta	2	2	1	4	22	22	50	100
Boston	2	3	-	4	5	25	-	57
Chicago	9	6	1	10	26	40	5	38
Denver	1	1	2	1	12	16	33	100
Detroit	2	3	-	3	9	17	-	20
NY City	12	4	-	11	29	11	-	29
Pittsburgh	4	2	1	4	11	2	5	4
S. Francisco		4	1	3	4	9	3	10

Notes

1. Thomas Hopko, *Speaking the Truth in Love: Education, Mission, and Witness in Contemporary Orthodoxy* (Crestwood, N.Y.: Saint Vladimir's Press, 2004), 27.
2. Figures on the number of Eastern Christians in North America are based on published reports in the *Yearbook of American and Canadian Churches 2005.* These figures should be viewed with caution. Orthodox administrative bodies do not appear to collect numerical or statistical information on adherents and churches. Moreover, the Orthodox have not been active in studying their congregations or taking part in several important qualitative and quantitative studies conducted by sociologists of religion. Recent survey data collected by Alexey Krindatch as part of the Faith Communities Today project (FACT) offer a notable recent contribution towards developing a numerical profile of Orthodox churches in North America. Anton Vrame, *The Orthodox Parish in America, Faithfulness to the Past and Responsibility to the Future* (Brookline: Holy Cross Orthodox Press, 2003), is a very important collection outlining key themes to guide the sociological study of the Orthodox experience in North America.
3. Daniel Clendenin, *Eastern Orthodox Christianity: A Western Perspective* (Grand Rapids: Baker Books, 1994), 18.
4. I wish to thank the Institute for the Study of American Evangelicals for the invitation and support to explore themes articulated in this chapter. Support from the Office of Vocation and Ministry has provided recent site visits to Orthodox churches in connection with evaluation research conducted for the Theological Explorations of Vocation initiative underway at Hellenic College. I thank the OVM for this support and for conversation on the Orthodox experience. I also thank The Office of the Provost at Governors State University for supporting research on the religious landscape in Will County, Illinois and in Berrien County, Michigan. I would like to thank Professor Mark Noll—formerly at Wheaton College, and now at the University of Notre Dame—for encouraging a spatial perspective in rendering the American religious landscape. I would also like to thank Dr. Germana Peggion for her assistance in developing maps and tables rendered in this chapter.
5. Vrame, *The Orthodox Parish in America.*
6. See Alexey Krindatch, "Orthodox (Eastern Christian) Churches in the United States at the Beginning of the New Millennium: Questions of Nature, Identity, and Mission," *Journal for the Scientific Study of Religion* 41 (2002): 405-422.

7. Benedict Anderson, *Imagined Communities: Reflections on the Origins and Spread of Nationalism* (New York: Verso, 1983); and E. J. Hobsbaum, *Nations and Nationalism Since 1780* (New York: Cambridge University Press, 1992).

8. Mark Mazower, ed., *After the War was Over: Reconstructing the Family, Nation, and State in Greece, 1943-1960* (Princeton: Princeton University Press, 2000).

9. Stathis Kalyvas, "Red Terror: Leftist Violence during the Occupation," in Mazower, ed., *After the War Was Over*, 147.

10. Barbara Jelavich, *History of the Balkans: Twentieth Century* (New York: Cambridge University Press, 1983); George White, *Nationalism and Territory: Constructing Group Identity in Southeastern Europe* (New York: Rowman & Littlefield Publishers, 2000).

11. Thomas Burgess, *Greeks In America* (New York: Arno Press, 1970).

12. Patrick Manning, *Migration in World History* (New York: Routledge, 2005).

13. Elazar Barkan, *The Retreat of Scientific Racism: Changing Concepts of Race in Britain and the United States Between the World Wars* (Cambridge: Cambridge University Press, 1992).

14. Frances Kostarelos, *Feeling the Spirit: Faith and Hope in an Evangelical Black Storefront Church* (Columbia: The University of South Carolina Press, 1995).

Conclusion: Holding On to the Faith? The Complexity of American Confessionalism

Douglas A. Sweeney
Trinity Evangelical Divinity School

> If you confess with your lips that Jesus is Lord and believe in your heart that God raised him from the dead, you will be saved. For one believes with the heart and so is justified, and one confesses with the mouth and so is saved (Romans 10:9-10, NRSV).

Some readers will be surprised by the contents of this book. A few confessional partisans—we hope not many—will be disturbed. Finally, they will say, a scholarly book that focuses closely on confessional Christianity and its roles in American history and nary a word from those who champion such faith. None of the authors in this book belongs to the churches best known for strict confessional adherence: the Lutheran Church—Missouri Synod, the Orthodox Presbyterian Church, or any number of other proudly confessional bodies.[1] In fact, several emphasize their churches' unease and even repulsion regarding confessions and the people who promote them. The most confessional group discussed at any length within these pages comes under fire for the self-defeating fractiousness of its leaders, their manner of holding fast to the faith expressed in their confessions. The second-most confessional group here is the moderate Dutch Reformed, who hold to the Heidelberg Catechism, the kindest, gentlest doctrinal statement of the entire Reformation.

Indeed, this volume might confirm the worst fears of such critics, who feel that real, confessional Protestantism has long suffered neglect both from Christians in America's mainly evangelical, liberal and/or pietistic churches and from students of the history of religion in America, who spend the bulk of their time on "mainstream" Protestants. Darryl Hart, the most important recent writer on the subject, calls confessionalism "the lost soul of American Protestantism." It has been lost, he says, "not simply because of scholarly neglect but also because of pietism's role in the creation of a Protestant mainstream." Hart expounds this point with a view to making historiographical change, depicting confessionalism in *contradistinction* to pietism, revivalism, and evangelicalism. He calls for much greater attention to the staunchest Protestants, those who balk at assimilation into the mainstream of doctrinally insouciant America. "The recent efforts of religious historians . . . have laudably increased awareness of the diversity of faiths in the United States," writes Hart, "but, unfortunately, white Protestantism remains a religion with little variety beyond the evangelical and mainline labels. Introducing confessional Protestantism as a separate category, while also attending to differences among confessionalists, might actually reinvigorate the study of American Protestantism by moving it beyond the two-party paradigm" (i.e., the paradigm centered on the campaigns of evangelicals and liberals).[2]

Suggestions such as these rely on standard definitions of "confessional," "confessionalist," and "confessionalism." Like Hart, most observers use these terms most of the time in reference to doctrinal conservatives, those Christians most uneasy about adapting their confessions to the spirit of the age. The *Oxford English Dictionary*, which dates the origins of these terms to nineteenth-century church disputes, defines confessionalism accordingly as principled adherence to a formula of faith: "The principle of formulating a Confession of Faith; adherence to a formulated theological system."[3] Charles Porterfield Krauth, the archetypal representative of American confessionalism, defined this word similarly as doctrinal profession—made with attention to detail—above and beyond a formal commitment to the Bible and its authority (which sufficed for most of Krauth's American evangelical foils). In his now-classic book of essays on the "conservative Reformation," Krauth proclaimed,

> Faith makes men Christians; but Confession alone marks them as Christians. The Rule of Faith is God's voice to us; faith is the hearing of that voice, and the Confession, our reply of assent to it. By our faith, we are known to the Lord as his; by our Confession, we are known to each other as His children. Confession of faith, in some form, is imperative. To confess Christ, is to confess what is our faith in him. As the Creed is not, and cannot be the Rule of Faith, but is its Confession merely, so the Bible, because it is the Rule of Faith, is of necessity not its Confession. The Bible can no more be any man's Creed, than the stars can be any man's astronomy.[4]

Contemporary movements for "confessional renewal" within the Protestant mainline also use the word confessional in much the same way, thereby signaling concern about the threat of theological infidelity in their churches. The Fellowship of Confessional Lutherans, found in my own denomination (the Evangelical Lutheran Church in America), represents the fears of many. Its leaders articulate a concern in their movement's mission statement "that the prevailing mood within our Church not become one of cultural accommodation and theological relativization." They seek "to promote confessional integrity and biblical fidelity." They are committed "to the Scriptures and the Confessions of the Lutheran Church." In other words, groups like this define their purposes in overwhelmingly theological terms. Being confessional, for them, means confessing "with the mouth" in the manner of the epigraph above.[5]

From time to time this book's contributors assume such definitions, wielding them to measure the extent to which the subjects of their chapters proved "confessional." James Juhnke, for example, admits that "Anabaptists and Mennonites barely met the definition of a 'confessional tradition.'" They were "victims" of the magisterial Reformation confessions. And when compared to "Roman Catholics with their *Confession of Trent* (1556), Lutherans with their *Augsburg Confession* (1530), and other religious bodies with centrally defined and authoritatively enforced statements of faith," Mennonites do not appear confessional.

Indeed, when standard definitions of this word group are assumed, it is easy to see why many Mennonites would hesitate to embrace them; it is easy to understand why self-proclaimed confessional Protestants would feel misrepresented in the chapters of this book; and it is easy to comprehend why confessionalism is often said to stand at odds with the values of liberal, modern Western cultures. As Stephen Duffy suggests:

> In our own age, one given to non-creedal universalism, the authority of creeds and confessions has waned. Creeds do not sit well with such disparate elements as Enlightenment anti-dogmatic rationalism, liberal Protestantism, evangelical Christianity, nor with modern individualism and secular relativism, in its hard or soft variety. Scholarly and non- scholarly moderns have wanted to go back behind creeds and dogmas, even behind the gospels of creedal Christianity, to find the "real" Jesus, a humanistic teacher of a universal truth. For many, being a "nice person" is what religion is about and more important than correct beliefs, if indeed there are such. Some, wearied by religious wars, and others more fearful of disagreement than concerned about believing, contend that recognition   of normative creedal formulations and doctrinal differences only leads to bitter dissension and heresy hunts. . . . Antipathy to creeds and confessions outside and even inside the churches is in the mood of our time.[6]

As this volume seeks to show, however, confessionalism has always been more complicated than standard definitions have allowed. Despite the claims of *quia* subscriptionists,[7] there has long been more than one way to be confessional in America. As Mary Todd makes clear, even the *most* confessional groups have disagreed amongst themselves as to the best way to confess the faith within their national context. Further, many denominations commonly viewed as non-confessional have proven more confessional than most people assume.

Nowhere is this more evident, perhaps, than with the Mennonites. As Juhnke has shown above, their ardent pacifism and criticism of militaristic patriotism have functioned as powerful forms of Christian confession in America. Further, despite their reputation for holding doctrinal standards lightly, the Mennonites have always enjoyed a strong confessional heritage. *The Martyr's Mirror*, which stands at the center of the Mennonites' identity, contains the *Apostles' Creed* as well as three early modern Anabaptist doctrinal statements. And as several recent Anabaptist scholars have asserted, many other confessions have been published and put into practice during the history of their movement. In fact, as Karl Koop has noted, the Anabaptists "may have actually produced more confessions than any other Reformation tradition." According to Howard John Loewen, moreover, confessions have served to unify the Mennonites theologically: "there exists a common, consistent center in North American Mennonite confessions," he claims, "that revolves around the fourfold axis of one Lord, one church, one hope, and one God." Koop confirms this sentiment: "an identifiable and coherent Anabaptist-Mennonite theological tradition exists, and . . .

this tradition can play an important role for Anabaptist and Mennonite churches, who are seeking to more fully understand their identity, and who desire to express their beliefs in the context of the church and the world."[8]

Even at times and places where the most passionately confessional Protestant groups have gained momentum, the practice of confession has proved impressively diverse. Jaroslav Pelikan pointed out in his late work on creeds and confessions that while Lutherans have emphasized confession more than most, they have never held a monopoly on the practice. Roman Catholics, a wide range of Reformed church bodies, and the Anabaptists also have their own "confessionalisms."[9] And as Theodore Tappert limned in his well-known work on Lutheran confessionalism in nineteenth-century America (in the age of C. P. Krauth), even it was fueled by evangelical piety. Pace Hart, it was not a reaction to the forces of revivalism and evangelicalism, but a reaction to the rise of modern liberalism. It was shaped, as a matter of fact, by conservative pietism—and impelled by the awakenings of the early nineteenth century. Of "confessions" and "confessionalism," Tappert wrote the following:

> these locutions first came into use at the beginning of the nineteenth century, and then authority was thought to reside not only in historic confessions of faith but also in the distinctive theological formulations, liturgical customs, and types of piety that had grown up since the Reformation. Among other things, the scholasticism of the seventeenth century was reintroduced, but the consequent concentration on intellectual doctrine was generally accompanied by attention to religious experience, for the "confessionalism" that now emerged was as a rule woven out of a combination of orthodoxist and pietist strands.[10]

At times, confessional Protestants have pitted their doctrinal views against their pietistic foes. But at numerous other times they themselves have practiced pietism.[11] And since the 1930s, when the Confessing Church in Germany wrote the Barmen Declaration to denounce the Nazi sympathies of the so-called German Christians, confessions have tended to emphasize not only doctrinal matters but the importance of godly practices as well (their drafters defending the latter emphasis without a hint of irony on the basis of the sixteenth-century arguments concerning the obligation to confess during a time of persecution, a "situation of confession," or *status confessionis).*[12]

Especially in America, where the diversity of confessions reached unprecedented levels due to free-market forces, separation of church and state, denominationalism, pluralism, and multiculturalism, confessional Christianity has adopted multiple forms and confessionalists have had to contend with strange new tensions between their desires to maintain orthodoxy and gain respectability in the marketplace of religion. Indeed, American immigration has often led to a clash of values in confessional communities: between transnational ties that fortify one's sense of membership within a global Christian confession and the hope of securing a lasting place in American national culture; between confession as a means of boundary maintenance for one's group and confession as a way of reaching out in public witness; between the education of children in the ways of one's confession and the kind of education aimed at secular success; between a desire to be unique and the hope of fitting in.

Most confessional Americans want to have it both ways. They want uniqueness as confessionalists *and* clout in the mainstream. They want to continue *in* America, but not be *of* America.[13] They see themselves as players in an all-star game, sporting their own uniforms but playing on a team whose reach transcends their hometowns. The trouble comes when they begin to grow so fond of the national stage—and the privileges it brings—that they forget where they grew up and cease to honor their confessions. As the chapters in this volume testify repeatedly, it is difficult to persevere in the courage of one's confession when confronted with opportunities for greater power and influence beyond the narrow confines of one's own confessional group. Even the most confessional witness can be shaped by market forces. Even the most "prophetic" confessions often morph imperceptibly from countercultural stands against the secular powers that be (defined by the doctrines of one's group) to politically correct articulations of secular values (which could be parroted by anyone, regardless of confession). It has been all too easy on the American national stage to undermine one's confession for the sake of gaining adherents.

Of course, gaining market share is not the same as selling out—at least not necessarily. And many confessional groups have sought to acquire power and privilege in this land of opportunity in a highly selective manner, adapting to the ways and means of America's free markets without compromising the quality of their wares. Such selective adaptation, further, is not unique to America. Other confessional groups did the same thing in Europe, standing against the sins and structures of the Christian status quo without removing themselves completely from the market.

Still, American cultural history has magnified these tensions. It has complicated the practice of confession. At one level, in fact, the history of America's confessional traditions is a story of the struggle to redefine and renegotiate confessional identity in a world that has opened its arms, slowly but surely, to diversity—where the powers against which Christians feel the need to make confession have resided far less frequently in the government than in their own back yards.

If we are to make better sense of this confessional complexity, we need a broader view of what it means to be "confessional." This is *not* to say that older views are now passé. We need *more* work, rather, on the doctrinal component of confessional traditions if we want to understand those groups who choose to resolve the tensions in the paragraphs above in favor of doctrinal integrity. At present, this is work that most historians, even most historians of religion, stand ill-equipped to do. So Hart is right: historiographical revision is required. The new religious history, with its nearly exclusive emphasis on the methods of social history, needs to find a way to treat confessional thought with greater care if its practitioners intend to do justice to the millions willing to sacrifice leverage on American cultural power for the sake of orthodoxy.[14]

Yet confessional traditions have to do with more than doctrine and their members share a history of cultural adaptation that transcends any one set of theological norms. Denominational scholars need to come to terms with this fact—with the help of other thinkers—if they hope to make a difference in the way that outsiders treat the history of their groups. Historians of doctrine offer much that is needed. But until a greater number of them resolve their own tensions as participant-observers of confessional traditions in a manner that encourages sustained cooperation with others studying their movements, their work will be neglected on the national scholarly stage.

One way to advance *together* through the doctrinal terrain of confessional traditions is to track Christian confession as a form of human action. To confess is also to do. Doctrine can be dramatic. Human speech carries a strong perlocutionary force. For too long, religious historians have treated Christian doctrine as a static set of symbols, as second-order discourse aimed at regulating the meaning of more basic and material expressions of religion. But what if we analyzed confession as a way of *doing* religion, as a primal form of action giving rise to, shaping, even helping to explain a host of other Christian practices? The content of confessions would come to "mean" a lot more. The language of confessionalists would have to be studied carefully by those who seek to explain their contributions to America. Historians might come to see that they must work together with practitioners of religion, even Christian theologians, if they want to interpret accurately the relationship between their subjects' beliefs and other behaviors.[15]

All of this is simply to say that more remains to be done by those who would understand America's confessional traditions. This book is not the last word. Rather, we hope that you will read it as an invitation to join us as we study the myriad ways in which America has shaped the confessional churches dotting its landscape and those churches, in their turn, have shaped America.

Notes

1. At least one of our authors, Mary Todd, used to belong to such a church, the Lutheran Church—Missouri Synod, which she treats in greater detail in her book, *Authority Vested: A Story of Identity and Change in the Lutheran Church—Missouri Synod* (Grand Rapids: Eerdmans, 2000).

2. D. G. Hart, *The Lost Soul of American Protestantism*, American Intellectual Culture (Lanham, Md.: Rowman & Littlefield Publishers, Inc., 2002), xxiv-xxv, 182. Further analysis and critique of "the two-party paradigm" may be found in Douglas Jacobsen and William Vance Trollinger, Jr., "Historiography of American Protestantism: The Two-Party Paradigm, and Beyond," *Fides et Historia* 25 (Fall 1993): 4-15; and Douglas Jacobsen and William Vance Trollinger, Jr., eds., *Re-Forming the Center: American Protestantism, 1900 to the Present* (Grand Rapids: Eerdmans, 1998).

3. *The Oxford English Dictionary*, 2d ed., prepared by J. A. Simpson and E. S. C. Weiner, vol. 3 (Oxford: Clarendon Press, 1989), 704. The earliest instance of this word cited within the *OED* dates from 1876. However, "confessional" (1817) and "confessionalist" (1827) appeared much earlier. "Confessionalian" (1771), a term that quickly lost its currency, is defined in the *OED* as "one who advocates the principle that a church should have a formal Confession of Faith."

4. Charles P. Krauth, *The Conservative Reformation and Its Theology: As Represented in the Augsburg Confession, and in the History and Literature of the Evangelical Lutheran*

Church (Philadelphia: General Council Publication Board, 1899; orig. ed., 1871), 166. This quotation is taken from Krauth's famous article entitled "The Confessional Principle of the Conservative Reformation," in idem, 162-200.

5. The mission statement of the Fellowship of Confessional Lutherans may be found at www.foclnews.org.

6. Stephen J. Duffy, "Creeds and Confessions of Faith: From Ages of Belief to an Age of Creedal Malaise," *Religious Studies Review* 31 (January & April 2005): 43.

7. As distinguished in church history from *quatenus* subscriptionists, who adhere to their confessions only "insofar as" they reflect the doctrines of the Bible, *quia* subscriptionists subscribe "because" they believe their statements offer accurate reflections of the doctrines of the Bible.

8. Karl Koop, *Anabaptist-Mennonite Confessions of Faith: The Development of a Tradition*, Anabaptist and Mennonite Studies (Kitchener, Ontario: Pandora Press, 2004), 11, 13; and Howard John Loewen, *One Lord, One Church, One Hope, and One God: Mennonite Confessions of Faith in North America: An Introduction*, Text-Reader Series (Elkhart, Ind.: Institute of Mennonite Studies, 1985), 19. On the current contest over Mennonite confessionalism, see the September 2005 issue of *Mennonite Life*. Cf. John D. Roth, "Recent Currents in the Historiography of the Radical Reformation," *Church History* 71 (September 2002): 523-35.

9. Jaroslav Pelikan, *Credo: Historical and Theological Guide to Creeds and Confessions of Faith in the Christian Tradition* (New Haven: Yale University Press, 2003), 466-72.

10. Theodore G. Tappert, "Introduction," in *Lutheran Confessional Theology in America, 1840-1880*, ed. Theodore G. Tappert , A Library of Protestant Thought (New York: Oxford University Press, 1972), 8. For a brief, lucid, English language introduction to the confessional movement (*Bekenntniskirche*) in nineteenth-century Germany, see Claude Welch, *Protestant Thought in the Nineteenth Century, Volume I, 1799-1870* (New Haven: Yale University Press, 1972), 194-98. On the related Awakening (*Erweckung*) of nineteenth-century German Lutheranism, start with David Crowner and Gerald Christianson, eds., *The Spirituality of the German Awakening*, The Classics of Western Spirituality (New York: Paulist Press, 2003). Cf. Walter Conser, Jr., *Church and Confession: Conservative Theologians in Germany, England, and America, 1815-1866* (Macon, Ga.: Mercer University Press, 1984); Nicholas Hope, *German and Scandinavian Protestantism, 1700-1918*, Oxford History of the Christian Church (Oxford: Clarendon Press, 1995); and for expert commentary on the broader, nineteenth-century German intellectual context, Thomas Albert Howard, *Protestant Theology and the Making of the Modern German University* (Oxford: Oxford University Press, 2006).

11. Cf. F. D. Lueking, *Mission in the Making: The Missionary Enterprise among Missouri Synod Lutherans, 1846-1963* (St. Louis, 1964), 13-23.

12. On the history of debates regarding when and in what conditions Christians find themselves in *status confessionis* (or *in statu confessionis*, or *in casu confessionis*), see Article X of the *Formula of Concord* and its *Solid Declaration* (from which texts the debate has proceeded), in *The Book of Concord: The Confessions of the Evangelical Lutheran Church*, ed. Robert Kolb and Timothy J. Wengert (Minneapolis: Fortress Press, 2000), 515-16, 635-40. Then consult Eugene TeSelle, "How Do We Recognize a Status Confessionis?" *Theology Today* 45 (April 1988): 71-78; Martin Schloemann, "The Special Case for Confessing: Reflections on the *Casus Confessionis* (Dar es Salaam 1977) in the Light of History and Systematic Theology," *The Debate on Status Confessionis: Studies in Christian Political Theology*, ed. Eckhart Lorenz (Geneva: Lutheran World Federation, 1983), 47-94; Joachim Guhrt, "*Status Confessionis*: The Witness of a Confessing Church," *Reformed World* 37 (December 1983): 301-8; and D. J. Smit, "What Does *Status Confessionis* Mean?" in *A Moment of Truth: The Confession of the Dutch Re-*

formed Mission Church, ed. G. D. Cloete and D. J. Smit (Grand Rapids: Eerdmans, 1984), 7-32, esp. 8-16.

13. As Laurence Moore as shown, this kind of having it both ways has been quite common in our history, and has enriched the development of American civilization. See R. Laurence Moore, *Religious Outsiders and the Making of Americans* (New York: Oxford University Press, 1986).

14. On the new religious history (and its non-theological methods), see Philip R. VanderMeer and Robert P. Swierenga, "Introduction: Progress and Prospects in the New Religious History," in *Belief and Behavior: Essays in the New Religious History*, ed. Philip R. VanderMeer and Robert P. Swierenga (New Brunswick, N.J.: Rutgers University Press, 1991), 1-14; and Jay Dolan, "The New Religious History," *Reviews in American History* 15 (September 1987): 449-54. Among the recent collections of essays in the new religious history, see especially Harry S. Stout and D. G. Hart, eds., *New Directions in American Religious History* (New York: Oxford University Press, 1997); David D. Hall, ed., *Lived Religion in America: Toward a History of Practice* (Princeton: Princeton University Press, 1997); Thomas A. Tweed, ed., *Retelling U. S. Religious History* (Berkeley: University of California Press, 1997); and Laurie F. Maffly-Kipp, Leigh E. Schmidt, and Mark Valeri, eds., *Practicing Protestants: Histories of Christian Life in America, 1630-1965* (Baltimore: The Johns Hopkins University Press, 2006).

15. The understanding of Christian confession implicit in most historical work is shaped profoundly by the writings of Clifford Geertz and George Lindbeck, especially Geertz, "Religion as a Cultural System," in *The Interpretation of Cultures: Selected Essays* (New York: Basic Books, 1973); and Lindbeck, *The Nature of Doctrine: Religion and Theology in a Postliberal Age* (Philadelphia: Westminster Press, 1984). My own understanding of the dramatic, perlocutionary force of Christian doctrine is also shaped by Kevin J. Vanhoozer, *The Drama of Doctrine: A Canonical Linguistic Approach to Christian Theology* (Louisville, Ky.: Westminster John Knox Press, 2005).